THE

EVERYTHING®

ESSENTIAL BRAZILIAN PORTUGUESE BOOK

Dear Reader,

Ever since I started teaching Portuguese back in 1993, I dreamed of writing a concise, straightforward Portuguese book. This new book condenses the main topics while maintaining the essential concepts and grammatical structures. If you picked up this book, you are most likely a practical person who goes for what is important, carefully avoiding what is superfluous. Flipping through these pages, you will soon discover that you made the right decision: This book will give you the fundamentals of Portuguese, with a special focus on the Brazilian dialect. I am confident that you will have found precisely what you were looking for in an essential language book.

Fernanda Ferreira, PhD

D1021773

Welcome to the EVERYTHING® Series!

These handy, accessible books give you all you need to tackle a difficult project, gain a new hobby, or even brush up on something you learned back in school but have since forgotten. You can choose to read from cover to cover or just pick out information from our four useful boxes.

Alerts

Urgent warnings

Facts

Important snippets of information

Essentials

Quick handy tips

Questions

Answers to common questions

When you're done reading, you can finally say you know **EVERYTHING®**!

PUBLISHER Karen Cooper

MANAGING EDITOR, EVERYTHING® SERIES Lisa Laing

COPY CHIEF Casey Ebert

ASSOCIATE PRODUCTION EDITOR Mary Beth Dolan

ACQUISITIONS EDITOR Lisa Laing

SENIOR DEVELOPMENT EDITOR Brett Palana-Shanahan

EVERYTHING® SERIES COVER DESIGNER Erin Alexander

Visit the entire Everything® series at *www.everything.com*

THE EVERYTHING® ESSENTIAL BRAZILIAN PORTUGUESE BOOK

All you need to learn
Brazilian Portuguese in no time

Fernanda Ferreira, PhD

Adams Media
New York London Toronto Sydney New Delhi

To my mother, Iracema, who was essential in my life.

adamsmedia
Adams Media
An Imprint of Simon & Schuster, Inc.
57 Littlefield Street
Avon, Massachusetts 02322

Copyright © 2013 by Simon & Schuster, Inc.

All rights reserved, including the right to reproduce this book or portions thereof in any form whatsoever. For information address Adams Media Subsidiary Rights Department, 1230 Avenue of the Americas, New York, NY 10020.

An Everything® Series Book.

Everything® and everything.com® are registered trademarks of Simon & Schuster, Inc.

ADAMS MEDIA and colophon are trademarks of Simon and Schuster.

For information about special discounts for bulk purchases, please contact Simon & Schuster Special Sales at 1-866-506-1949 or business@simonandschuster.com.

The Simon & Schuster Speakers Bureau can bring authors to your live event. For more information or to book an event contact the Simon & Schuster Speakers Bureau at 1-866-248-3049 or visit our website at www.simonspeakers.com.

Manufactured in the United States of America

10

Library of Congress Cataloging-in-Publication Data has been applied for.

ISBN 978-1-4405-6754-4
ISBN 978-1-4405-6755-1 (ebook)

Many of the designations used by manufacturers and sellers to distinguish their products are claimed as trademarks. Where those designations appear in this book and Simon & Schuster, Inc., was aware of a trademark claim, the designations have been printed with initial capital letters.

Contains material adapted from the following title *The Everything® Learning Brazilian Portuguese Book* by Fernanda Ferreira, PhD, copyright © 2007 by Simon & Schuster, Inc., ISBN 978-1-59869-277-8.

Acknowledgments

Many thanks to Eileen Mullan, Lisa Laing, and the whole team at Adams Media for their continued support of my work. Their professionalism in the publishing business is above par. My dear friends Laura McAlinden, Anne Doyle, Marianne Toole, Frances Donovan, Wendy Miller, and Tanya Smith were always a source of inspiration and support. Thank you.

Contents

Introduction 11

1. Introducing the Portuguese Language 13
Why Learn Portuguese? 13
Similarities to Spanish 14
European Portuguese Versus Brazilian Portuguese 15
Tips on Learning Portuguese 17
Recognizing What You Already Know 20

2. The Sounds of Portuguese 25
The Portuguese Alphabet 25
Accent Marks 27
A Closer Look at the Portuguese Consonants 28
Stress Pattern in Portuguese 31
Oral and Nasal Vowels 32
Typing in Portuguese 35

3. Beginning Conversation 36
Greetings 36
Talking on the Phone 37
Quick Introductions 38
Saying Goodbye 40
Other Vocabulary You May Need 41

4. Nouns, Articles, and Contractions 44
Nouns: Persons, Places, and Things 44
From Nouns to Pronouns 48
Definite and Indefinite Articles 50
Demonstratives 52
Common Contractions 54

5. Who Are You? Introducing *Ser*. 58
Expressing Identity: *Ser* 58
Place of Origin 59
Characteristics. 61
Occupations 62
Personal Relationships 64
Numbers and *Ser* 65

6. How Are You? Introducing *Estar* 66
States of Being: *Estar* 66
Physical States. 67
Mental States 68
Location. 69
Estar in the Present Progressive Tense 70
Ser or *Estar*? 71
Agreement Rules 75
Plurals in Nouns and Adjectives 75

7. Describing People and Things in Portuguese. 78
From Nouns to Adjectives 78
The Order of Modifiers 80
Making Comparisons 82
Superlatives: The Best of the Best 85
Ownership and Possession 86

8. The Vocabulary of Numbers. 90
Cardinal Numbers 90
Ordinal Numbers 94
Days of the Week 96
Talking about Time. 97
The Months and Seasons. 98

9. First Conjugation Verbs 101
Regular –*AR* Verbs 101
Verbs with Prepositions 104
Vocabulary: Going Places 105
Vocabulary: Routine Activities 107

10. Second Conjugation and Beyond 109
Regular –*ER* and –*IR* Verbs 109
Special –*IR* Verbs 112
Exercise: Regular and Special Verbs 113
To Go and to Come: *Ir* and *Vir* 114
To Have: *Ter* 116
Vocabulary: Family Relations 119

11. Important Verbs to Know 122
To Be or to Exist: *Haver* 122
To Make or to Do: *Fazer* 123
Expressions with *Fazer* 124
To Know: *Saber* and *Conhecer* 126
More Special Verbs 128

12. Verb Tenses: An Overview 131
Present Tense 131
Preterite Tense 132
Imperfect Tense 134
The Preterite Versus the Imperfect 135
Future Tenses 137
Conditional Tense 139
Practice with the Future and Conditional Tenses 140

13. More Verbs 142
Using Two Verbs Together 142
Past Participles 146
Passive Voice 148

Reflexive and Reciprocal Verbs 149
Reflexive Verbs with Prepositions 150
Practice with Reflexive and Reciprocal Verbs 151

14. Negative Words and Constructions 153
How to Say No 153
Two Negatives Make a Negative 154
Common Negative Expressions 155
Positive Versus Negative 157

15. Questions and Exclamations 159
How to Ask Questions 159
Interrogative Words 160
Question Tags 163
Exclamations 163

16. The Future and Other Tenses 166
The Present Versus the Future or the Preterite 166
The Personal Infinitive 167
Impersonal Assertions 171
Discussing the Weather 172
The Vocabulary of Clothes 173

17. Imperative and Subjunctive Constructions 177
Imperative Constructions 177
Introducing the Subjunctive 180
Past Subjunctive 181
Future Subjunctive 182
Indicative or Subjunctive? 183
Practice with the Subjunctive Forms 184
Expressions with the Verb *Dar* 185

18. Means of Communication 187
In Person 187
Communication by Mail 192
Making Phone Calls 194
Vocabulary: *Ficar, Tornar-se, Fazer-se* (to Become) 197
More Vocabulary: Expressions with *Estar com* and *Ter* 198
Communication Practice 199

Appendix A.
English to Portuguese Glossary 201

Appendix B.
Portuguese to English Glossary 216

Appendix C.
Answer Key 233

Index 252

Introduction

You picked up this book because you might have already watched a Brazilian movie, listened to a *bossa nova* song, or learned what *capoeira* means. Perhaps you already know that Brazilians love soccer and that they have won the World Cup five times. But you might still struggle with the Portuguese language, even if the Brazilian dialect sounds fascinating to you. *Boas notícias!* (Good news!) This book will help you in your journey to become more fluent in this beautiful language.

The chapters in this book cover everything from the origins of the Portuguese language to accent marks, formal greetings, various verb forms, and conjugations. The chapters on more discrete grammatical points are replete with practical, easy-to-follow exercises. The Answer Key (Appendix C at the back of the book) is available so you can check your work and evaluate your progress as you move through the chapters. There is no particular order in which you should read this book, although grammar topics are introduced in an increasing level of difficulty. That said, the instructions are easy enough that any reader should be able to grasp the content without having to refer constantly to previous pages.

Learners face many challenges as they try to master a new language. The most important element to remember is motivation. Research into second language acquisition has shown time and again that motivation is a crucial part of learner success. And that the establishment of clear goals from the beginning will also contribute to your success. Once you have decided what you want to get from this experience, devise a clear game plan, and set out to get it! Don't forget that practice makes perfect, so study for shorter time periods but study often!

As the author of *The Everything® Essential Brazilian Portuguese Book*, I hope that after you finish reading it you will have a better grasp of the intricacies of the Portuguese language, its pitfalls for the English speaker, and its unexpected beauty. At the same time, I hope that you will have a better understanding of what makes Brazilians who they really are.

CHAPTER 1

Introducing the Portuguese Language

Not many people know that Portuguese is spoken in Brazil, one of the few Latin American countries where Spanish is not the official language. In fact, Portuguese is spoken in far-reaching parts of the globe, such as Goa (India), Macau (China), Guinea-Bissau, Angola, and Mozambique, among other countries. So what are the origins of this language? How is it similar to or different from Spanish? What makes Brazilian Portuguese different from European Portuguese? And why should you learn it?

Why Learn Portuguese?

Have you ever listened to a *bossa nova* love song and wondered what the lyrics mean? Perhaps you have always been intrigued by fascinating exotic places such as the Amazon jungle or Copacabana beach. Maybe your grandparents emigrated from the Azores, Madeira, or Portugal, and you always wanted to write to them in their language. Or you might be interested in learning Portuguese to communicate with your coworkers.

Many people in the world (close to 200 million) speak Portuguese. You might be interested to know that many African and Asian countries have Portuguese as their official language. In addition, there is a growing Portuguese-speaking population in the United States. Because it is an uncommonly taught language, being fluent in it will probably serve you well when you look for a job! Also, learning Portuguese will help you understand the lyrics of famous *bossa nova* songs, the lines in

Oscar-nominated Brazilian films, and the prose of an incredibly diverse body of literature.

Whatever the reason, be it reclaiming your heritage, learning more about the diversity of Latin America, or discovering new worlds of cuisine, literature, and history, learning Portuguese is a great step in your life. So put on your *samba* shoes and let's get started!

Similarities to Spanish

Portuguese and Spanish can be called "sister languages" due to their intrinsic similarities. After all, they both derive from spoken Latin. The following table shows the similarities in orthography between these languages.

▼ COMPARING PORTUGUESE TO SPANISH: PART I

Portuguese	Spanish	English
classe	*clase*	class
casa	*casa*	house
livro	*libro*	book
caderno	*cuaderno*	notebook

However, these similarities should not fool the serious Portuguese student. When using your knowledge of Spanish to help with your Portuguese, be mindful that these are different languages, and similarity in orthography does not always mean similarity in pronunciation. Always learn how to pronounce the "sounds" of Portuguese instead of relying on your Spanish. What about differences in words and meanings? The following list shows how these languages can vary significantly:

▼ COMPARING PORTUGUESE TO SPANISH: PART II

Portuguese	Spanish	English
cedo	*temprano*	early
desenvolvimento	*desarrollo*	development
envelope	*sobre*	envelope
irmã	*hermana*	sister

If that wasn't enough, there are some tricky words that are commonly referred to as "false cognates." These words sound similar to English or Spanish but mean something completely different in your target language, in this case, Portuguese. The novice student needs to watch out for these "false friends."

▼ **FALSE COGNATES**

Portuguese	Spanish
cuchilo (nap)	*cuchillo* (knife)
tirar (to take)	*tirar* (to throw away)
escritório (office)	*escritorio* (desk)
embaraçada (confused, ashamed)	*embarazada* (pregnant)

The trick here is to use a good Portuguese-English dictionary and always make sure you are saying the correct word, depending on the social situation. Some awkward moments may occur, but most of the time native speakers will understand and help you out.

European Portuguese Versus Brazilian Portuguese

When the Portuguese arrived in Brazil in the early sixteenth century, they found many speakers of different Native American languages already living there. It has been estimated that there were more than 1,000 indigenous languages spoken in Brazil at the time of the Portuguese arrival. With the advancement of white populations into the coastal areas of Brazil, these native populations were slowly decimated by disease or genocide, so that nowadays we are left with about 170 different Native Brazilian languages in Brazil.

The development of Brazilian Portuguese is a complex one, but one that is fascinating nonetheless. Portuguese colonization in Brazil really started in 1548 with the introduction of a system of *capitanias* or territories awarded to Portuguese officials on a hereditary basis. Most of these territories failed economically, except for São Vicente (today's São Paulo state) and Pernambuco. Later, there was a system of governorships that responded directly to the King of Portugal. With the invasion of Portugal by Napoleon, the Portuguese royal family was transferred to Rio de Janeiro. This transatlantic move had a significant impact on the Portuguese educational policy in Brazil, especially with regard to the development of language instruction.

The path followed by Brazil after it became independent in 1822 was very different from that followed by other Portuguese colonies, such as Angola and Mozambique. In these countries, the Portuguese-speaking community is a learned minority. In Brazil, Portuguese has been spoken by many generations of Brazilians, giving it a distinctly Brazilian flavor. Also, one has to account for linguistic contact with the Brazilian indigenous population, whose languages, including Tupi Guarani and others, contributed words to the Brazilian dialect.

Fact

In 2002, the city of São Gabriel da Cachoeira, a municipality in the state of Amazonas, passed a law making the indigenous languages Nheengatu, Tukano, and Boniwa official languages along with Portuguese.

In addition, one cannot forget the influence of millions of black Africans who were forcibly brought to Brazil to work in the sugar cane fields, gold mines, and the homes of Portuguese masters. These Bantu and Kwa speakers offered a unique twist to the way Portuguese is spoken in Brazil.

▼ WORDS OF INDIGENOUS ORIGIN IN BRAZILIAN PORTUGUESE

Brazilian Portuguese	English
plants	
abacaxi	pineapple
caju	cashew fruit
animals	
piranha	piranha
sucuri	anaconda
arara	macaw

place names	
Guanabara	
Jacarepaguá	
Tijuca	
personal names	
Araci	
Iracema	
supernatural beings	
Tupã	supreme being of the Tupi people
Curupira	human-like creature whose feet are backward; brings bad luck or death to those who see him

Not all scholars agree on the extent to which or even the very idea that African languages influenced Brazilian Portuguese. Some think that these languages simply added to the richness of vocabulary, while others think that the influence can be felt to the core of the language. For these scholars, Brazilian Portuguese might have changed so much, it could even be considered a semi-creole! The jury is still out on this issue, but the fact remains that Brazilian Portuguese has characteristics that clearly show that it evolved differently from European Portuguese in significant ways.

▼ WORDS OF AFRICAN ORIGIN IN BRAZILIAN PORTUGUESE

Brazilian Portuguese	English
senzala	slave quarters
caçula	youngest offspring
mucama	young slave girl who fetches things
quilombo	village of marooned slaves
tanga	very short bikini or loincloth
berimbau	one-stringed African instrument

Tips on Learning Portuguese

First remember that the longest journey starts with the first step. And, as you begin traveling down this road, you must come prepared. Remember that just as on any other journey, there are incremental steps, and that you cannot expect to get to the end of it without following a well-traveled path. The following are helpful tips in the incredible linguistic expedition of acquiring Portuguese.

Relax!

Studies have shown that students do better with a language when they are less stressed about learning. Give yourself a break and don't expect to know and blurt out everything perfectly after you have heard it only once. Language learning takes time and effort, but it can be incredibly rewarding.

Use What You Learn

When learning Portuguese, concentrate on the variations of phrases or expressions instead of individual words. Don't just translate each word from/to English. Concentrating on the target language rather than on the translation will also boost your learning. Instead of lists and lists of words, try to place expressions in subcategories, according to their situation, such as "greetings," "introductions," or "ordering food."

Essential

Consider buying a good Portuguese-English dictionary. There are several excellent options on the market that can help you; you can choose according to your learning style. Learn how to "decode" the various symbols in the dictionary ("n" for noun, "a" for adjective, etc.) and always double-check the English-Portuguese side of the dictionary to make sure you have the correct idiom.

Once you have learned a new word or phrase, you should use it immediately and often, preferably in a real situation. But don't worry about saying it as a native speaker from the start. The message, or what you say, is more important than the native-sounding pronunciation, at least at first. Remember that we all have accents, even the so-called native speaker; it's just a question of degree.

Picture It

Many successful language learners use pictures to remember words in the target language. Instead of long translated lists, try creating a set of flashcards with stick-figure drawings or pictures of common vocabulary items cut out of magazines. You don't have to be an artist; just draw clearly enough for you to get the message.

Another nice idea is to simply "label" every appliance and piece of furniture in your home with adhesive labels. After a while, you will notice that you won't need the labels anymore, and the word will come to you immediately.

Study Often and in Short Bursts

Learning a new language can be tiring. It is a known fact that students who study for shorter periods of time (fifteen to twenty minutes per day, five days a week) acquire more language than those who cram their studies into one day, and only do this once in a blue moon. If you feel that you can study for a longer period of time, don't forget to take short breaks.

Use the Web

The wealth of information easily available to you at your fingertips is just incredible. There are millions of sites written in Portuguese, with information on the culture, cuisine, entertainment, sports, and famous celebrities of Portuguese-speaking countries. Also consider joining newsgroups or checking out blogs in Portuguese or about Brazil. You will learn a lot by exchanging information with Portuguese speakers electronically.

Concentrate on Your Interests

Combine what you like about sports, cuisine, and music with your desire to learn Portuguese. Learn the vocabulary of your favorite pastimes in this newfound mode of communication. The same goes for your profession. Whether you are an architect, artist, photographer, musician, or lawyer, there are specific words in Portuguese that relate to your area of expertise. Learning those will not only make you more marketable, but will also give you a sense of connection to colleagues in the global arena.

Immerse Yourself

Try out your own version of an immersion program. If available in your area, taste a *churrasco* at a Brazilian restaurant, take *samba* or *lambada* dancing lessons, learn how to play *capoeira*, and listen to Brazilian music CDs. In some American markets, there are cable channels in Portuguese, such as *Globo*. Any good bookstore or local library will have travel books about Portuguese-speaking countries. Take one home and become inspired by the sites and images of exotic places. Your local big-box store should have at least a couple of more recent Oscar-nominated Brazilian movies. Watch with the subtitles and be amazed at how much you already know in Portuguese. Movies are also an incredible window into the culture of a country; try to find the similarities to, not just the differences from, your own. If you are a religious person or are curious about religious culture, try to go to a Catholic church in an area with a large Brazilian population. Because of the increase in the Brazilian population in the United States, more and more American dioceses have masses celebrated in Portuguese.

Recognizing What You Already Know

Because both Portuguese and English are Indo-European languages, some words in Portuguese have a similar spelling to English, and thus it is easy to identify them and guess their meaning. Look at the following list and see how many words you are already familiar with.

- *acidente*
- *adorável*
- *animal*
- *ator*
- *automóvel*
- *bagagem*
- *catedral*
- *central*
- *ciclista*
- *condutor*
- *conversível*
- *criatura*
- *crime*
- *cruel*
- *elefante*
- *famoso*
- *favor*
- *físico*
- *futebol*
- *hospital*
- *hotel*
- *humor*
- *idéia*
- *importante*
- *inevitável*
- *informação*
- *inventar*
- *local*
- *motor*
- *música*
- *natural*
- *plano*
- *popular*
- *potente*
- *presidente*
- *rádio*
- *respeitável*
- *sinistro*
- *táxi*
- *telefone*

Aside from the interesting ways in which some of these words end, each can be easily associated with a similar word in English. You can figure out their meanings as you read them because they are *cognates*. Later, you will learn how to pronounce them in Portuguese.

You must have noticed that a few words have the exact same spelling as in English, such as *favor*, *hotel*, *local*, and *motor*. These are true pure cognates because they are orthographically identical and have the same meaning in both languages. Others on the list have close to the same spelling, and also have the same meaning, such as *adorável* (adorable), *bagagem* (baggage), *rádio* (radio), and *telefone* (telephone). These are called true cognates, meaning that they have similar but not identical spelling.

The way languages evolve led to orthographic as well as semantic (i.e., meaning-related) changes throughout the ages. These changes inadvertently created pairs of words that have similar spelling but different or closely related meanings in both languages. Don't be misled by these "false" cognates. Here is a short list, which you can add to as you learn Portuguese.

▼ **FALSE COGNATES**

Portuguese	English
assistir	to attend or to watch, not to assist
constipado	congested, when suffering from a cold, not constipated
delito	crime, not delight
futebol	soccer, not American football
pretender	to intend to, not to pretend
recordar	to remember, not to record

Common Suffixes

As you learn to decipher words in Portuguese, some "clues" may help you along the way. Pay attention to the endings of words and relate them to corresponding endings in English. This technique makes your life easier when learning new words, and it will help you guess the meaning of words, as well as their grammatical class.

▼ **COMMON SUFFIXES AND THEIR MEANINGS**

Suffix	Meaning
–al (pertaining or related to; an extension of; a place)	
fenomenal	phenomenal, pertaining to a phenomenon
bambuzal	plantation of bamboo trees
usual	usual, or an extension of use
–ável/–ível (having the ability or aptitude to, or the capacity of)	
adorável	adorable, capable of being adored
conversível	convertible, capable of being converted
–or (agents that are or do; abstractions)	
inventor	inventor, one who invents
amor	love, abstract noun

These endings are referred to as suffixes. These suffixes often enlighten you as to the meanings of words. A complete list of examples would be too long, but here are a few:

▼ **PORTUGUESE COGNATES WITH SUFFIXES *–ÁVEL/–ÍVEL*, *–AL*, AND *–OR***

–ável/–ível	*–al*	*–or*
acessível	*abdominal*	*ardor*
biodegradável	*cordial*	*destruidor*
compreensível	*emocional*	*fervor*
durável	*federal*	*instrutor*
evitável	*fundamental*	*mentor*
falsificável	*ilegal*	*pastor*
incomparável	*nacional*	*professor*
lamentável	*normal*	*protetor*
miserável	*oficial*	*refletor*
negociável	*original*	*rumor*

There are also other types of cognates that are similar to English, though not identical:

▼ SUFFIXES SIMILAR TO ENGLISH

Portuguese Example	English Translation
–agem (pertaining to, particularly broadened to a collection; similar to English "–age")	
bagagem	baggage, luggage
–ano/–ana (pertaining to origin, location; relating to beliefs and affiliations; similar to English "–an")	
americano	American
republicano	Republican
–ante/–ente (related to an event, the nature of, or an agent; similar to "–ant" and "–ing" in English)	
acidente	accident, an unexpected event
importante	important, something of great effect
potente	potent, of powerful nature
presidente	president, one who presides
–ção/–são (abstraction of an act or state of being; similar to the English "–tion" and "–sion")	
atenção	attention
informação	information
–ico/–ica (relating to; being similar to; similar to the English "–ic" and "–al")	
físico	physical, physicist
idêntico	identical
–ista (pertaining to one who does; similar to English "–ist")	
artista	artist, one who creates art
ciclista	cyclist, one who rides a bicycle
–oso/–osa (relating to possession or characteristic; similar to English "–ous," "–ful," and "–y")	
curioso	curious
famoso	famous
–ura (abstraction of an act or state of being; similar to English "–ture," "–ure," and "–ness")	
criatura	creature
cultura	culture
–ário/–ária (pertaining to the subject; relating to an act or thing; similar to English "–ary")	
milionário	millionaire
voluntário	voluntary, volunteer

Portuguese Example	English Translation
–ncia (relating to an act or state; result of an action; abstraction; similar to English "–nce" and "–ncy")	
abstinência	abstinence
elegância	elegance
insistência	insistence
–dade (relating to an abstraction or a state of being; similar to English "–ty," "–ness," and "–hood")	
brevidade	brevity
claridade	clarity
felicidade	happiness
–ismo (pertaining to an action or practice; state or condition; principles similar to "–ism")	
atletismo	athleticism
idealismo	idealism
–mente (pertaining to the manner, the timing, and the place of an action; similar to "–ly")	
felizmente	fortunately
claramente	clearly

Congratulations! You were just able to read a great number of words in Portuguese, and you probably understood most of them. Try to see the patterns of similar words as you encounter them in the language. Go back to these words often and try to incorporate them into your active Portuguese vocabulary. If you feel that some of them are too obvious, then you know you don't have to look them up again in the dictionary.

Exercise: Suffixes

Now, try your best to complete this short suffix challenge! Write down the Portuguese translations of the following English words. Check your answers in Appendix C.

1. incident: incidente
2. mechanical: mecanico
3. identity: identidade
4. unfortunately: ~~unfortunamente~~
5. resistance: ~~resistência~~ resistência

infelizmente

CHAPTER 2

The Sounds of Portuguese

It's now time to learn about the Portuguese alphabet and all the different sounds in the language. How do you pronounce the vowels? What about the nasal sounds? What are nasal diphthongs? How do you pronounce consonant combinations such as *–nh–* and *–lh–*? What is the typical stress pattern in Portuguese? In this chapter you will learn all of this plus how to write electronic documents in Portuguese using all the accent marks.

The Portuguese Alphabet

Like almost all Romance languages, Portuguese follows the Latin alphabet and incorporates six diacritics, or special characters. There are the three accents (acute: *ó*; circumflex: *ê*; and grave: *à*), plus the cedilla *ç*, the tilde *ã*, and the dieresis *ü*. The written system also has three letters (*k*, *w*, and *y*) that are part of the official alphabet but are very rarely used, mostly appearing in foreign words (windsurf, kitsch) and some personal names (Wagner, Darcy, Yaracilda). The following are the Portuguese letters and the way they are pronounced.

▼ **THE PORTUGUESE LETTERS**

Letter	Portuguese Name	Pronunciation	Example	Approximate English Sound
a	*a*	*AH*	*casa*	**f**ather
b	*bê*	*BEH*	*berço*	**b**asement

Letter	Portuguese Name	Pronunciation	Example	Approximate English Sound
c	*cê*	*SEH*	*centro*	**c**ent
			com	**c**omb
d	*dê*	*DEH*	*dado*	**d**ance
e	*é or ê*	*EH*	*ele*	**c**ake
f	*efe*	*E-fee*	*fala*	**f**act
g	*gê*	*JHEH*	*gente*	meas**u**re
h	*agá*	*a-GAH*	*hóspede*	[silent]
i	*i*	*EE*	*cinco*	s**ee**k
j	*jota*	*JOH-tah*	*já*	pleas**u**re
k	*ká*	*KAH*	*kiwi*	**k**itchen
l	*ele*	*EH-lee*	*lavar*	**l**oud
m	*eme*	*EH-mee*	*mesa*	**m**ouse
n	*ene*	*EH-nee*	*não*	**n**ever
o	*ó or ô*	*AW or OH*	*óbvio*	**awe**
p	*pê*	*PEH*	*pão*	**p**aint
q	*quê*	*KEH*	*quinze*	**k**ey
r	*erre*	*EH-hee*	*Rio*	**h**eap
			carrego	un**h**appy
			caro	bu**tt**er
s	*esse*	*EH-see*	*santo*	**s**imple
t	*tê*	*TEH*	*tempo*	**st**eak
u	*u*	*OOH*	*caju*	**j**uice
v	*vê*	*VEH*	*veja*	**v**ery
x	*xis*	*SHEES*	*roxo*	**sh**oe
w	*dáblio*	*DAH-blee-oo*	*watt*	**w**ater
y	*ípsilon*	*EEP-see-laun*	*Yara*	**y**ear
z	*zê*	*ZEH*	*zinco*	**z**ebra

There are also special letters and combinations of letters that make up unexpected sounds in Portuguese:

▼ **SPECIAL LETTERS AND COMBINATIONS OF LETTERS**

Letter(s)	Portuguese Example	English Translation	Pronunciation
–ç–	*caça*	hunt	like English *s*
–nh–	*tamanho*	size	a little softer than the Spanish *ñ*
	façanha	feat	
–lh–	*filho*	son	like the middle sound in "medallion"
	trabalho	work	
–ch–	*chá*	tea	pronounce as in "shovel"

Accent Marks

The accent marks in Portuguese help with the correct pronunciation of words. They indicate to the reader where to put the emphasis on the word, or even if a vowel is more "open" or "closed." Become familiar with these special diacritic marks of the language.

▼ **ACCENT MARKS**

Marks	Name in English	Name in Portuguese
á, é, í, ó, ú	acute	*acento agudo*
ê, ô	circumflex	*acento circunflexo*
à	grave	*acento grave*
ã, õ	tilde	*til*
ü	dieresis	*trema*

Essential

It is important to remember that accent marks are not immediately intuitive to the second-language learner. When learning Portuguese, give yourself a while to learn where to include these accents. However, as you read more and more materials in Portuguese, keep track of the accents and where they usually go on the word. Familiarity with the written word will boost your confidence and spelling accuracy in Portuguese!

A Closer Look at the Portuguese Consonants

Sometimes the same sound in a language can be expressed by different letters. This is the case in English, as with the [f] sound that is pronounced using the upper teeth and the bottom lip and can happen at the beginning of a word like *fact* or at the end of a word like *enough*. The same happens in Portuguese. The same [s] sound can be heard in words such as ***simples*** (simple), *cartaz* (poster), ***c**inema* (movie), or even in ***excelente*** (excellent). Similarly, the same letter can refer to very different sounds. In the following paragraphs, we will cover the major pitfalls of spelling and pronunciation in Portuguese, letter by letter.

The Letter C

Before vowels *e* or *i*, this letter has a "soft" [s] sound as in the English word "for**c**e." Examples are *centro* (center) and *cinco* (five). However, before vowels *a*, *o*, *u*, and most consonants, the letter has a "hard" [k] sound as in the English word "**c**oat." Some examples are *casa* (house), *comida* (food), *cuidado* (care), *crédito* (credit), or *clínica* (clinic).

The Letter G

This letter often stands in for a sound that does not appear at the beginning of English words, but can be found in the middle of the word "mea**s**ure." In Portuguese it appears at the beginning of words when the vowels *e* or *i* follow it, such as in *gente* (people) and *ginásio* (gym). It has a "hard" sound when it appears before vowels *a*, *o*, *u*, and other consonants, as in the English word "**g**ame." Examples are *gato* (cat), *gota* (drop), *guri* (young boy), and *grande* (big).

The Letter S

This letter can stand in for two different but closely related sounds. The first sound is very similar to the sound in English words "**s**ink" and "ca**s**t." The Portuguese examples are *sopa* (soup), *esse* (this one), and *lápis* (pencil). The second is a raspier [z] sound as in the English words "tho**s**e," "wi**s**dom," and "tran**s**it." The counterpart examples in Portuguese are *casada* (married), *desde* (since), and *trânsito* (traffic).

The Letter Z

This letter is very similar to the English letter, especially in the start of words. As with the English word "**z**ebra," the same sound is found in Portuguese with *zero* (zero) and *prazer* (pleasure). However, this letter has a sound similar to the English word "cook**s**" at the end of segments, such as in the Portuguese example *cartaz* (poster).

The Letter T

In some dialects of Brazilian Portuguese, such as the *carioca* (the name of the dialect of Rio de Janeiro), this letter can have a very unexpected sound. Before the vowels *i* and sometimes *e* if unstressed and at the end of a word, it will sound as in the English word "***ch**eer*!" So Portuguese words such as *tipo* (type) and *elefante* (elephant) will sound like CHEE-poh and eh-leh-FAHN-chee. This does not happen in all contexts. In the case of the letter appearing before other vowels and consonants, it sounds as in the English word "**t**ime" (without the added aspiration). Portuguese examples are *terra* (earth) and *trem* (train).

The Letter D

As with the previous letter, a similarly unexpected sound appears when in close contact with the letter *i*. So, much like the sound in the English word "**j**eans," the Portuguese word *dia* (day) might be pronounced like JEE-ah. In all other contexts, the letter behaves like the English word "**d**en," yielding Portuguese examples such as *dar* (to give) and *droga* (drug).

Essential

Because these curious sounds with the letters *t* and *d* before *i* are pronounced by speakers of Rio de Janeiro, a more economically developed area, they are seen as more prestigious pronunciations. However, for most of the north, northeast, and south of Brazil, they are mostly ignored, and speakers communicate successfully pronouncing the *t* and the *d* similarly to the English letters.

The Letter R

This letter has two basic sounds, which are very different from the English *r*. First, it is pronounced like the [h] sound as in the English word "**h**eat." Portuguese examples are *rua* (street), *dor* (pain), *guardanapo* (napkin), *carro* (car), and *genro* (son-in-law). Second, this letter in Portuguese is pronounced similarly to the *r* at the end of English words "letter" or "later." It can be found in Portuguese words such as *caro* (expensive) and *branco* (white).

Essential

You will notice that Brazilians will leave out the [r] sound at the ends of words, such as *amor* (love) or *chamar* (to call). This is not seen as a reflection of uneducated speech or laziness, but rather an evolution of the language. The same happened with French, whose final consonants are never pronounced. So, to sound more native, make sure to drop the end-word *r* in Portuguese!

The Letter L

The one thing to remember about this letter is that at the end of words, the *l* sounds like a *w* as in the English word "now." So the Portuguese word *Brasil* sounds like BRAH-zeew. The letter behaves like the English letter *l* at the beginning of words.

The Letters M and N

As you might have noticed, Portuguese has a good many nasal sounds. The letters *m* and *n*, when appearing at the end of a word or syllable, are an indication that the previous vowel is nasalized. Thus, the combination of vowel plus *m* or *n* should not be perceived as two different sounds (vowel plus consonant) but actually a nasal-sounding vowel. Portuguese words such as *sim* (yes) and *bom* (good) are pronounced by making more air come out of your nostrils and avoiding putting your lips together at the end. The letters behave like English letters when they come at the beginning of a word such as *mesa* (table) and *nome* (name).

The Letter X

Amazingly, there are four different sounds that could be uttered when this letter appears in Portuguese words. The first is similar to the English word "**sh**eep." Portuguese examples are *xadrez* (chess) and *lixo* (trash). The second sound is similar to the English word "fi**x**," as in the Portuguese *complexo* (complex). Thirdly, this letter can sound like a normal [s] sound, as with the English word "fea**s**t." Portuguese examples are *excluir* (to exclude) and *excepcional* (exceptional). Finally, it is very common to hear a [z] sound as in the English word "ama**z**ing." Portuguese examples are *exótico* (exotic) and *roxo* (purple).

Stress Pattern in Portuguese

The study of the vowels and the stress pattern in a language are intimately connected. That is because the "stress," or the emphasis that one puts on a word, normally happens on the vowel. In order to sound native in Portuguese, the student should learn how to put the correct amount of force or stress on the center of the correct vowel, that is, on the right syllable.

In Portuguese, words are usually stressed on the next-to-last syllable, though there are also words that are stressed on the last syllable or the third-to-last syllable. Here are some examples:

▼ **WORD STRESS**

Next-to-Last Syllable	Last Syllable	Third-to-Last Syllable
piloto (pilot)	*café* (coffee)	*capítulo* (chapter)
imagem (image)	*baú* (chest)	*código* (code)
contente (happy)	*caquí* (kind of fruit)	*árvore* (tree)
fácil (easy)	*dominó* (domino)	*fósforo* (match)

All verbs in infinitives ending in *–r*, such as *amar* (to love), have the stress on the next-to-last syllable. When a nasal diphthong ends a word, such as *irmão* (brother), the stress is on the last syllable.

Oral and Nasal Vowels

The vowel system of Portuguese is a little more complex than that of Italian or Spanish, which could be considered "phonetic" languages (what you see is what you get). There are twelve distinct vowel sounds in Portuguese, including oral and nasal vowels. Oral vowels are what English speakers are normally familiar with, and nasal vowels are partially produced with the nasal tract. The difference between a vowel and a consonant is that vowels are produced without obstructions from the vocal tract, with air flowing freely and some minor constriction of the lips or opening of the mouth. Consonants, on the other hand, are produced by the interplay of air flow and obstructions produced by the lips, the teeth, or the back of the throat, as well as other parts of the vocal and nasal tract. The following is a detailed account of the vowels in Portuguese.

▼ THE VOWEL A

Type	English Word	Portuguese Examples
Stressed	father, cot	*garfo* (fork), *caro* (expensive)
Unstressed	tuba	*porta* (door), *filha* (daughter)
Nasal	before nasal consonants or with tilde	*banho* (bath), *irmã* (sister)

▼ THE VOWEL E

Type	English Word	Context	Portuguese Examples
Open	net	written with the acute é	*café* (coffee)
Closed		written with a circumflex ê	*pêssego* (peach)
Longer	me	at the end of a word	*filme* (movie)
		at end of one-syllable word	*de* (of), *e* (and)
Nasal		before nasal consonants	*senha* (code), *bem* (well)

▼ THE VOWEL I

Type	English Word	Context	Portuguese Examples
Longer	**see**	at the end of syllable	*saí* (I left), *país* (country), *raiz* (root)
Shorter	**say**	at the end of the word	*pai* (father), *leite* (milk)
Nasal		before nasal consonants	*tinha* (he had), *sim* (yes)

▼ THE VOWEL O

Type	English Word	Context	Portuguese Examples
Open	**saw**	written with the acute ó	*dominó* (domino)
Closed		written with a circumflex ô	*complô* (scheme)
Longer	**glue**	at the end of a word	*pato* (duck)
		at the end of one-syllable word	*do* (of the), *o* (the)
Nasal		before nasal consonants	*sonho* (dream), *com* (with)

▼ THE VOWEL U

Type	English Word	Context	Portuguese Examples
Longer	**tooth**	at the end of syllable/ word	*caju* (cashew fruit), *tu* (you), *grúa* (forklift)
Shorter	**bow**	at the end of the word	*pau* (wood, stick), *nau* (boat)
		in the combinations qua and gua	*quadro* (board), *guarda* (policeman)
Nasal		before nasal consonants	*punha* (he would put), *um* (one)

Alert

The vowel u is silent when used in the combinations *que, qui, gue,* and *gui.* In these cases only pronounce the "hard" consonants, as in *queijo* (cheese), *quinze* (fifteen), *guerra* (war), and *guitarra* (electric guitar).

Diphthongs

Diphthongs are combinations of two vowels pronounced together in one syllable. There can be oral or nasal diphthongs in Portuguese. Some of them do not have a corresponding English sound, but you will be able to say them in no time.

▼ ORAL DIPHTHONGS

Approximate English Sound	Portuguese Examples
my	*pai* (father)
cow	*autor* (author)
	papéis (papers)
hay	*rei* (king)
	deus (god)
	céu (sky)
	oi (hi)
coy	*dói* (it hurts)
	viu (she saw)
	cuidado (careful)

▼ NASAL DIPHTHONGS

Portuguese	English
mãe	mother
cão	dog
põe	she puts

Alert

There are some nasal diphthongs that are not expressed orthographically with the ~ (tilde) but rather with nasal consonants. This is the case with words ending with *–em* or *–en* as in *porém* (but) and *podem* (they can). In addition, there is one special nasal diphthong that starts with a nasal consonant: *muito* (many, very).

Hiatus

A hiatus is a combination of vowels that are in separate syllables. While diphthongs are two graphic vowels together, one pronounced longer and slower than the other, the hiatus expresses two strong vowels said very clearly. Here are some examples:

- *tia* (aunt)
- *rua* (street)
- *caos* (chaos)
- *rio* (river)

Typing in Portuguese

When writing electronically, it is important to add the accent symbols and diacritics that are part of the Portuguese language. There is a big difference between an accented vowel *é* (is) and one without an accent, *e* (and). The following table shows how to add these accents into your electronic documents.

Windows Keys	Result
Control + ' [apostrophe], then any vowel	á, é, í, ó, ú
Control + ` [grave], then a	à
Control + Shift + ~ [tilde], then vowel	ã, õ
Control + , [comma], then c	ç
Apple Keys	**Result**
Option + e, then any vowel	á, é, í, ó, ú
Option + ` [grave], then a	à
Option + n, then vowel	ã, õ
Option + c	ç

Now practice writing the following words in your computer: *maçã* (apple), *sofá* (sofa), *às quatro* (at four), and *corações* (hearts).

CHAPTER 3

Beginning Conversation

Traveling abroad can be stressful, but you'll probably find it a lot easier if you know some basic survival phrases. In this chapter you will learn how to say hello, introduce yourself, bid goodbye, and greet people over the phone. You will also learn some important emergency words that may come in handy when visiting a foreign country. You will make a great first impression with your Portuguese after reading this chapter.

Greetings

This might be the easiest communication strategy you will learn in a second language. Go ahead and start by greeting people in Portuguese when traveling to Brazil. Brazilians will appreciate your efforts in trying to speak their language, and help you along. Start by greeting the doorman at the hotel, salespeople, and taxi drivers. Use this list of common greetings:

▼ **GREETINGS IN PORTUGUESE**

Portuguese	English
Olá!	Hello!
Oi!	Hi!
Alô!	Hello! (when answering the phone)
Bom dia!	Good morning!
Boa tarde!	Good afternoon!
Boa noite!	Good evening!/Good night!

Portuguese	English
Como vai?	How are you?
Bem, obrigada (for women).	Fine, thanks.
Bem, obrigado (for men).	Fine, thanks.
Tudo bem?/Tudo bom?	How is it going?
Tudo bom!/Tudo bem!	Everything's great!

There are many colloquial ways of saying "How are you?" in Brazilian Portuguese, from *tudo jóia* (literally "everything's a jewel") to *tudo legal*, meaning exactly what it appears to mean, that everything is "legal," so nothing bad at all. Also, when answering the question *tudo bem?* you can reply with *tudo bom* or vice versa.

Talking on the Phone

You might have guessed that talking on the phone in your second language is actually harder than it appears. Since you cannot rely on visual cues, such as hand gestures, facial expressions, or lip movements, it is a lot more complicated to decode what people are saying on the other line. So don't be discouraged; just keep on trying and ask for a lot of repetition. A common telephone dialogue would go as follows:

Q: José: *Alô?* (Hello?)
A: Luci: *Alô, posso falar com Fernando?* (Hello, may I speak to Fernando?)
Q: José: *Quem quer falar com ele?* (Who wishes to talk to him?)
A: Luci: *Aqui é a Luci, ele está em casa?* (This is Luci, is he at home?)
Q: José: *Não, ele não se encontra, quer deixar recado?* (No, he's not in, do you want to leave a message?)
A: Luci: *Sim, por favor, diga para ele que a Luci ligou.* (Yes, please tell him that Luci called.)
Q: José: *Tá certo.* (Okay.)
A: Luci: *Obrigada, tchau!* (Thanks, bye!)
Q: José: *Tchau.* (Bye.)

Most people who live in big cities in Brazil have a traditional landline, but the sale of cell phones has increased tremendously in Brazil and

Latin America as a whole. Part of the reason is that telephone lines are very expensive, and it takes a long time (sometimes months) to have a line bought through the official channels. Some people buy landlines from other people who have them and advertise their sale in the newspaper. After they buy the line privately, they have their names transferred and installation happens rather quickly. However, the advantages and ease of buying a cell phone, especially a prepaid one, have generated a virtual boom in wireless telephony in Brazil.

Alert

When taking your cell phone with you to Brazil, make sure it is compatible. Some popular U.S. carriers do not carry telephones that are usable in Latin America. Always check with your wireless service to verify if your cell phone will work in Brazil or, if possible, add international service to your plan before traveling.

Even though using a telephone is a convenient way to talk, most Brazilians still prefer face-to-face communication. So don't be surprised if people say very little on the phone and arrange to meet with you right away. It's just another cultural difference that underscores Brazilians' love of the *bate-papo* or a friendly chat!

Quick Introductions

Once you have learned how to greet someone, the next best thing to do is to introduce yourself. Here are some common ways to do that in Portuguese:

▼ **COMMON INTRODUCTIONS**

Portuguese	English
Eu me chamo Laura.	My name is Laura.
Meu nome é Fabíola.	My name is Fabíola.
Muito prazer.	Nice to meet you.
Igualmente.	Same here.

Portuguese	English
Esse é o meu marido, João.	This is my husband, João.
Essa é a minha esposa, Clara.	This is my wife, Clara.
Como é (o) seu nome?	What is your name?
Como o senhor se chama?	What is your name (sir)? [formal]
Como a senhora se chama?	What is your name (ma'am)? [formal]
De onde você é?	Where are you from?
O que você faz?	What do you do?
O que você estuda?	What do you study?

Notice that there are formal ways of addressing people in Portuguese. This is more common in the European rather than in the Brazilian Portuguese dialect, but nevertheless it is part of Latin American courtesy. When Brazilians are speaking to someone who is older or of a higher social class, or to someone whom they simply are not acquainted with, Brazilians will normally use the phrases *o senhor* for a man and *a senhora* for a woman. Social distance can be measured in many different ways—age, social class, level of education, and familiarity, among other social cues. After getting to know someone, you may switch to the more colloquial pronoun *você* (you).

Essential

A good general rule is to use *o senhor* and *a senhora* until they give you permission to call them by *você*. Since Brazilians are normally pretty informal, that might happen right away! As far as how Brazilians address their parents, not very long ago children were required to use *o senhor* and *a senhora*. But nowadays, this has become obsolete.

What about hugs and kisses? And what do you when you are introduced for the first time? In the south of Brazil (in big cities like São Paulo), it is common for women to kiss on one cheek once. In Rio de Janeiro and in other parts of Brazil, such as the northeastern cities of Recife and Salvador, women normally give each other two kisses, one on each cheek. This may happen every time you see each other, if you are friendly acquaintances.

For closer relationships, such as cousins, sisters, or close friends, this is not common. Men and women will do the same, one or two kisses, while men will pat each other on the back and shake hands warmly.

Exercise: What to Say?

Fill in the blanks with the best words in the following dialogues. Check your answers in Appendix C.

1. Marcos: *Olá, meu* nome *é Marcos.*
2. Fabíola: *Eu me* chama *Fabíola. Muito* prazer.
3. Marcos: *Igualmente. De* onde *você é?*
4. Fabíola: Eu *sou do Rio de Janeiro.*

Saying Goodbye

You've learned the most common ways of greeting people and introducing yourself. But what about when you have to say goodbye? Instead of just leaving the room without being noticed, try and use these words to bid farewell to your newfound Brazilian friends. It will earn you positive points on the social scale, which will help you out next time you see them.

▼ SAYING GOODBYE

Portuguese	English
Tchau!	Bye!
Até logo./Até breve.	See you soon.
Até mais.	See you later.
Até amanhã!	See you tomorrow!
Tudo de bom.	All the best.
Boa viagem.	Have a good trip.
Vou nessa.	I'm leaving./I have to go. [very informal]
Volte sempre.	Come back always./Come again.
Amanhã a gente se fala.	We'll talk tomorrow.
Me diverti muito!	I had a lot of fun!
Boa noite!	Good night!

As far as saying goodbye, the same kissing rules apply: one or two kisses for women, warm handshakes for men. Don't be surprised if a Brazilian will kiss you three times and say *três pra casar*, meaning "three times so you can get married." This is sort of a little play with the two-kiss rule, and one that can lead to closer friendships.

Exercise: Goodbye!

Now test what you've learned about saying goodbye in Portuguese. Fill in the blanks in the dialogue below, according to the context. Check your answers in Appendix C.

1. Lúcia: *Olá, Seu Ivanildo,* _____ *vai o* _____*?*
2. Seu Ivanildo: *Vou bem,* _____*, Lúcia. E você?*
3. Lúcia: Tudo de bom _____ *bom. Tchau!*
4. Seu Ivanildo: *Até* mais _____.

Other Vocabulary You May Need

Unfortunately, you might find yourself in a situation where you'll need some emergency words. If you lose your checkbook, your car breaks down, or worse, you will need to know words that will help you communicate your predicament. You might also want to learn a list of helpful words and questions that will aid you in learning Portuguese. First, let's start with some helpful vocabulary items that may be essential in a sticky situation.

▼ EMERGENCY VOCABULARY

English	Portuguese
an accident	*um acidente*
arrest, to	*prender, pôr na cadeia*
attorney	*o advogado, a advogada*
bag	*a bolsa*
billfold	*a carteira*
consulate	*o consulado*
documents	*os documentos*

English	Portuguese
dollars	*os dólares*
help!	*socorro!*
judge	*o juiz*
key, keys	*a chave, as chaves*
money	*o dinheiro*
necklace	*a corrente, o colar*
police	*a polícia*
traveler's checks	*os cheques de viagem*

The following is a quick guide that might help you in getting important information in Portuguese. This list of questions and expressions can be a great reference.

▼ HELPFUL WORDS AND EXPRESSIONS IN PORTUGUESE

Portuguese	English
Por favor.	Please.
Com licença.	Excuse me. [before you do something]
Desculpe!/Perdão!	I'm sorry! [after you do something]
Desculpe, não entendi.	Sorry, I didn't get that./I didn't understand.
Poderia repetir, por favor?	Could you repeat that, please?
Você fala inglês?	Do you speak English?
Falo um pouquinho (de português).	I speak a little bit (of Portuguese).
Como se diz isso em português?	How do you say that in Portuguese? [as you point to it]

Although not exhaustive, this list of expressions can really be handy as you interact with Portuguese speakers in Brazil. Hopefully, this brief chapter helped you with an initial understanding of the Portuguese language and the way Brazilians talk and interact with each other. These helpful hints and vocabulary terms should be practiced often and consistently so that you may master them in a timely fashion.

Exercise: Chapter Review

Now let's review what you've learned! Write the word that you would say in Portuguese depending on the situation presented. Check your answers in Appendix C.

1. After you stepped on somebody's foot inside a crowded bus.
   Desculpe! / perdão
2. When you want to get through as you walk a busy street.
   com licença
3. You would like to thank someone.
   obrigada
4. Somebody said something, but you didn't quite catch it.
   Desculpe, não entendi
5. You want to tell someone that you speak a little Portuguese.
   Falo um pouquinho de português
6. You want to know the name of a fruit you see in a street market.
   Como se diz isso em português?

CHAPTER 4

Nouns, Articles, and Contractions

What makes a word feminine or masculine in Portuguese? How are plurals formed? How many ways can you say "the"? What is the difference between "definite" and "indefinite" articles? In this chapter you will find out all about singular and plural nouns, articles, demonstratives, and those common contractions in Portuguese.

Nouns: Persons, Places, and Things

One of the first things you learn while in grade school is that nouns refer to persons, places, and things. When learning a second language, you will find that copious lists of nouns make up most of the words you learn in the beginning. It is also easier to learn nouns because most of them refer to something concrete. However, they also refer to abstract elements, ideas, and qualities. You will notice that in Portuguese, nouns fall under two categories: masculine and feminine. So, the words *mesa* (table), *bolsa* (bag), and *chave* (key) belong to the feminine gender, while *caderno* (notebook), *livro* (book), and *pente* (comb) are masculine. Most of the time you can tell by the ending of the word which gender it belongs to. However, there are some tricky examples, as you might expect, as in the previous examples that end in *–e* (*chave* and *pente*), which can be either feminine or masculine. Here is a list of common nouns and their gender classification.

▼ PORTUGUESE NOUNS

Masculine	Feminine
livro (book)	*mochila* (backpack)
tio (uncle)	*tia* (aunt)
espelho (mirror)	*escola* (school)
quadro (blackboard)	*mesa* (table)
título (title)	*página* (page)
gesto (gesture)	*janela* (window)

What are the basic rules that you can follow in order to find out the gender of a noun? The first thing you should keep in mind is that nouns that end in *–o* are almost always masculine, as in the previous examples. Second, nouns that end in (unstressed) *–a* are normally feminine, as in the examples. What if a noun does not end in either of those vowels? Here are some general rules:

▼ NOUNS ENDING IN THE CONSONANTS *–L*, *–R*, AND *–Z*, THE VOWEL *–U*, AND THE LETTERS *–UME* ARE MASCULINE

Portuguese	English	Portuguese	English
hotel	hotel	*cartaz*	poster
casal	married couple	*peru*	turkey
mar	sea	*tatu*	armadillo
professor	teacher, professor	*ciúme*	jealousy
rapaz	young man	*legume*	vegetable

Aside from the most common unstressed *–a* ending for feminine nouns, there are other nouns with suffixes that are typically feminine. The following table outlines those endings with some examples.

▼ NOUNS ENDING IN THE SUFFIXES *–DADE*, *–AGEM*, AND *–ÇÃO* ARE NORMALLY FEMININE

Portuguese	English	Portuguese	English
identidade	identity, ID card	*viagem*	trip
liberdade	liberty	*comunicação*	communication
garagem	garage	*atenção*	attention

You will have noticed that nouns that end in *–dade* usually translate to a word in English that ends in "–ty," while a Portuguese word that ends in *–agem* most of the time compares to English words ending in "–age." Finally, Portuguese words ending in *–ção* are often translated into words that end in "–tion" in English, and are mostly feminine in Portuguese. But be careful! Some very common words that end in *–(ç)ão* are masculine. These are *coração* (heart) and many words related to transportation, such as *avião* (airplane) and *caminhão* (truck).

Alert

Most nouns that end in a stressed *–á* are masculine. For example, *chá* (tea) and *sofá* (sofa), as well as the names of countries such as *Canadá* and *Panamá*. The best way to learn the gender of these words is to write them down with the article, as in *o chá* (the tea). As you learn more words, continue adding them to your list.

Another very tricky set of words are the ones that end in an unstressed vowel *–a*, but are unexpectedly masculine. This happens because these words are originally from Greek, so they are not Latin-based. Here is a list of common examples:

▼ **MASCULINE WORDS OF GREEK ORIGIN ENDING IN *–A***

Portuguese	English
o cinema	movie theater
o mapa	map
o planeta	planet
o problema	problem
o programa	program
o telefonema	phone call

You will notice that most of them end in the combination of *–ma*. If you can identify that combination as you read or hear the word, then you can guess that it is masculine. Finally, there are some words that have the same ending for the masculine and feminine forms. You can say that

Maria é uma ótima pianista (Maria is a great pianist) while *Mário é um grande jornalista* (Mario is a great reporter). These words generally refer to professions, so they are easy to spot. The following is a list of examples.

▼ NOUNS THAT END IN *–ISTA* (BOTH MASCULINE AND FEMININE FORMS)

Portuguese	English
artista	artist
dentista	dentist
especialista	expert
jornalista	journalist
pianista	pianist
tenista	tennis player

Exercise: Practice with Gender

In the next set of words, write the article "the" in Portuguese before each one: Use *o* for masculine and *a* for feminine. If the word has the same spelling for masculine or feminine, write *o/a*. Check your answers in Appendix C.

1. o *caderno* (notebook)
2. a *contagem* (act of counting)
3. o *caminhão* (truck)
4. o *armazém* (storage facility)
5. o *amor* (love)
6. a *ação* (action)
7. a/o *socialista* (socialist)
8. o *avental* (apron)
9. o *crachá* (identification tag)
10. a *alfândega* (customs)
11. o *esquema* (scheme, plan)
12. a *liberdade* (liberty)

Although gender is an important part of Portuguese grammar, it is not immediately mastered by speakers whose native language does not include these categories. In English, some gender is still reflected when objects such as ships or boats are referred to as "she" (i.e., "Before the *Titanic* sank, she was considered an unsinkable ship"). More to the point, grammatical gender can be seen in the English possessive pronouns "his" and "hers." Simply think of gender in Portuguese as that "gender quality" found in English pronouns, only extended to all nouns. Unfortunately, there is no hidden key to grammatical gender; there is no rhyme or reason for *garfo* (fork) to be masculine and *faca* (knife) to be feminine. You just have to learn its gender!

Essential

One tip for learning the gender of nouns is to write them together in categories. With any list of vocabulary that you learn, you should find ways in which words can be connected (be it "school objects," "home appliances," or "my favorite clothes"). Think of your brain as a "closet" that is organized in "drawers" or categories. If you put socks and shirts in their own designated places, it will be easier to retrieve them later. The same happens with Portuguese words!

From Nouns to Pronouns

Saying the same noun every time you had to refer to something in normal discourse could get really repetitive. It would sound somewhat like this: "I went to **the movies** with **Robert**, but **Robert** got to **the movies** late; then we watched **the movie**, and **Robert and I** liked **the movie**, but **Robert and I** did not like the popcorn at **the movies**." Notice that the words in bold are repeated at least twice, which makes the entire utterance sound too repetitive, almost silly. Normally, we would replace the words "Robert" for "he," "Robert and I" for "we," "the movie" for "it," and "the movies" for "there." The same happens in Portuguese, where we substitute nouns for pronouns, which are words that are used in place of nouns. The following is a list of personal pronouns in Portuguese.

▼ PERSONAL PRONOUNS IN PORTUGUESE

Singular	Plural
eu (I)	*nós/a gente* (we)
tu/você (you)	*vocês* (you, y'all, you guys)
ele (he)	*eles* (they)
ela (she)	*elas* (they)

You will notice that there are two basic ways of referring to "we" in Brazilian Portuguese: *nós*, which is a little less used and more formal; and *a gente*, which is more common and more colloquial. The important rule to follow when using these two personal pronouns is to conjugate the verb in the plural when using *nós* and in the singular when using *a gente*. It might seem counterintuitive, but *a gente* literally means "we the people," so it is grammatically singular, even though it refers to more than one person.

Alert

You might notice that more traditional Portuguese grammars include the plural form *vós* for "you" plural or "y'all." This form is archaic and never used in Brazilian Portuguese. You might hear the word *convosco* (with you [pl.]) in church (for example, *O Senhor esteja convosco* [May God be with you]), and the possessive forms *vosso* and *vossa* (yours) are uttered by many speakers from Portugal, but not in Brazil.

There are two forms for "you" in Portuguese. Here you just have to learn what the Brazilians are saying and follow along. Some of this variation is dialectal, based on the geographical regions. In the south of Brazil, in states such as Rio Grande do Sul and Santa Catarina, the *tu* form is regularly used, with its separate verb conjugation. In the big urban and cultural centers, such as Rio de Janeiro and São Paulo, and in the state of Minas Gerais, you might hear the form *você* as well as its reduced form *cê*. Finally, in many places in the northeast of Brazil, such as in the cities of Recife and Fortaleza, the familiar *tu* is used, albeit with similar verb conjugations belonging to the *você* form. Although this might be daunting at first, you cannot go wrong if you stick to using *você* for "you." They will all understand you and respond accordingly.

What about the levels of formality? Although this is not as grammatically ingrained as it is in Spanish, Brazilians will show a certain level of respect as they address different people. When first introduced to an older gentleman or woman, use *o senhor* and *a senhora* respectively. This form of address might be used always with such persons, unless they indicate that they do not mind being addressed with the *você* form. When referring to people in the third or second person, it might be common to hear *Seu José* for "Mr. José" and *Dona Maria* for "Mrs. Maria" as a form of respect. Here is a sample dialogue:

Q: Robert: *Olá, Seu José, como vai?* (Hello, Mr. José, how are you?)
A: José: *Bem, obrigado, Robert, e você?* (Fine, thanks, Robert, and you?)
Q: Robert: *Tudo bem, e como vai sua esposa, Dona Maria?* (Great, and how is your wife, Mrs. Maria?)
A: José: *Ela vai muito bem, obrigado.* (She's very well, thanks.)

Exercise: Addressing Others

Now it's time to see what you've learned! Write the word *você* next to the people that you should address in a more familiar tone, and the words *o senhor* or *a senhora* (for men and women, respectively) if they require a higher level of formality. Check your answers in Appendix C.

1. your cousin: você
2. the local shopkeeper (male): o senhor
3. your grandfather: o senhor
4. your best friend: você
5. your classmate: você
6. the librarian (female): a senhora

Definite and Indefinite Articles

How many ways are there to say "the" in Portuguese? What about using "a/an" or "some"? The answer to these two questions has to do with the agreement system of the language, that is, the fact that all nouns have masculine and feminine forms, as well as singular and plural variants.

First, let's talk about the definite articles. By "definite" we mean that the referent refers to a specific thing. So, use it when you mean specifically "the Portuguese book," not "the French book." In addition, you might want to say, for example, *o livro* to reference "the book," the one that you had mentioned before, not any old book. The following table presents the Portuguese definite articles:

▼ DEFINITE ARTICLES

Number	Masculine	Feminine
singular	*o livro* (the book)	*a mesa* (the table)
plural	*os livros* (the books)	*as mesas* (the tables)

As you can see, there are four ways of saying "the" in Portuguese, depending on the gender and number of the noun. In Portuguese, we use the definite article more often than in English. For example, when referring to general things, such as "friends and family," we say *os amigos* ([the] friends) and *a família* ([the] family), using these definite articles. The same goes for set expressions such as the English "love is blind," which would be translated in Portuguese as *o amor é cego*, again using the definite article to start the sentence. Definite articles are so often used that they are even common when referring to proper names. It is common to hear people address others in some parts of Brazil by adding a definite article in front of their first name, such as in *o José*, meaning "Joe," or literally "the Joe," to refer to someone. Finally, one of the most interesting features of Portuguese is the fact that we might opt to say *o meu livro*, literally "(the) my book," when using possessive pronouns. Possessives will be discussed in detail in Chapter 7.

What about indefinite pronouns? These are used when we refer to things that are nonspecific or that we mention for the first time in discourse. They also follow the agreement rule in Portuguese. Here they are:

▼ PORTUGUESE INDEFINITE ARTICLES

Number	Masculine	Feminine
singular	*um livro* (a book)	*uma mesa* (a table)
plural	*uns livros* (some books)	*umas mesas* (some tables)

The important thing to remember is that indefinite articles are used for nonspecific things, so you might say *Eu li um livro* for "I read a book," while you might say *Eu li o livro de português* for "I read the Portuguese book," which is more specific. As far as pronunciation goes, the nasal consonants are there to indicate that the vowels are nasalized, and are not really pronounced as the English *m* or *n*.

Exercise: Definite or Indefinite?

Now you give it a try. Fill in the blanks with a form of the definite article (*o, os, a, as*) or the indefinite article (*um, uns, uma, umas*), depending on the context. Check your answers in Appendix C.

1. *Eu tenho* um *lápis,* um *caderno, e* uma *caneta.*
2. *Cláudio tem* um *livro de português.*
3. *Essas são* as *suas canetas?*
4. *Os amigos chamaram* o *José para a festa.*
5. *Não coma muito, você pode ter* um *ataque cardíaco!*

Demonstratives

When speaking, it is often common for you to refer to things and people by including a demonstrative, such as "this" or "that," before it, depending on the relative or perceived distance involved. In Portuguese the same is true, although speakers also follow the familiar system of gender and number agreement. The following chart summarizes the demonstrative system.

▼ **DEMONSTRATIVES IN PORTUGUESE**

Number	Masculine	Feminine	English
singular	*este/esse*	*esta/essa*	this
plural	*estes/esses*	*estas/essas*	these
singular	*aquele*	*aquela*	that
plural	*aqueles*	*aquelas*	those

In some Portuguese textbooks, you will find that the *este* group is used for things that are closer to the speaker, while the *esse* group is used for referents that are closer to the listener. But what if something is located between the two speakers at the same relative distance? It is safe to say that Portuguese speakers do not follow those distinctions too closely, interchanging between *esse* and *este* quite frequently, regardless of the fact that some grammar and textbooks will translate them consistently—*este* (this) and *esse* (that)—without making allowances for variation. In fact, the *este* group is losing ground to the *esse* group in colloquial speech. So, a nonnative speaker of Portuguese will more frequently use the demonstrative *esse* (this) when referring to almost all things that are relatively closer. What is definitely clear in Portuguese grammar is that *aquele*, meaning "that" or "that over there," refers to things that are a bit far away or remote from everyone.

Essential

In written language, *este* and its variations are used when referring to things that follow in the text. So, in the sentence *Ele disse estas palavras* (He uttered these words), the comment will follow the sentence. By the same token, if the sentence is *Ele disse essas palavras* (he uttered these words), the comment would have been placed before it.

When you use demonstratives for the first time in discourse, they are followed by a noun, which of course determines the form of the demonstrative. So, you say *essas janelas* (these windows) and *esta porta* (this door). However, once the noun has been said, it can be omitted in subsequent interactions, such as in the dialogue that follows.

Q: Maria: *Ai, que frio! Fecha essa janela.* (Wow, it is cold! Close this window.)
A: Marcos: *Qual? Essa?* (Which one? This one?)
Q: Maria: *Sim, essa mesmo.* (Yes, this very one.)

There are also neutral forms that are used when the referent is unknown or not determined by gender. So, use the words *isto* and *isso* (this) and *aquilo* (that) by themselves when referring to unknown concepts. These are very handy words to know, especially when you want to know what things are in Portuguese. Look at the following dialogue.

Q: Vinícius: *O que é isso?* (What is that?)
A: Chico: *Isso é um sapo.* (That's a frog.)
Q: Vinícius: *E o que é aquilo que ele está comendo?* (And what is that thing that he's eating?)
A: Chico: *É uma mosca.* (It's a fly.)

Common Contractions

When using prepositions ("to" and "from") followed by determiners (the articles and demonstratives we have just learned), interesting things happen in Portuguese. Saying these groups of words together causes them to "contract" or combine in order to form a different, shorter word. Here are some common contractions in Portuguese:

▼ USING *DE* + DEFINITE ARTICLE IN PORTUGUESE

Preposition + Definite Article	Contraction	English
de + o	*do*	from the
de + a	*da*	from the
de + os	*dos*	from the
de + as	*das*	from the

When would you have to use these contractions? Frequently, as they are required and very common in everyday conversation, such as when you say sentences that refer to your origin, for example, *Eu sou **dos** Estados Unidos* (I am from the United States). Thus, when saying *Ele é **do** Brasil* you are literally saying "He is from 'the' Brazil." Some examples of common contractions are included in the following dialogue.

Q: Roberto: *Eu sou **do** Brasil, e você?* (I am from Brazil, how about you?)
A: Jennifer: *Eu sou **dos** Estados Unidos. E a Ana?* (I am from the United States. And Ana?)

Q: Roberto: *Ela é **da** França.* (She's from France.)
A: Jennifer: *É mesmo? E o Jacques? De onde ele é?* (Really? And Jacques? Where's he from?)
Q: Roberto: *Eu acho que ele é **do** Canadá.* (I think he's from Canada.)
A: Jacques: *Não, eu sou **das** Filipinas!* (No, I'm from the Philippines!)

Again, you will notice that even countries have gender and number, and thus must follow the same gender/number system spelled out in previous sections. You would have to know the "gender" of the country, and whether it takes a definite article, in order to say these sentences correctly.

Alert

Some countries do not require the use of the definite article (*o, a, os, as*), so there is no contraction, just the bare preposition. The most noted examples are *Ela é **de** Portugal* (She's from Portugal), *Ele é **de** Moçambique* (He's from Mozambique), and *Eles são **de** Cuba* (They are from Cuba).

Another common contraction is between the preposition *em* (in, on, at) and the definite articles. Here are the examples.

▼ USING *EM* + DEFINITE ARTICLE IN PORTUGUESE

Preposition + Definite Article	*Contraction*	*English*
em + o	*no*	in the
em + a	*na*	in the
em + os	*nos*	in the
em + as	*nas*	in the

When would you use these contractions? How about when talking about where you live? Here is a sample dialogue that includes some of these contractions.

Q: Anita: *Rogério, onde você mora?* (Rogério, where do you live?)

A: Rogério: *Eu moro **no** estado do Amazonas, no Brasil.* (I live in the state of Amazonas, in Brazil.)
Q: Anita: *Nossa, e você, Nilda?* (Wow, and you, Nilda?)
A: Nilda: *Eu moro **na** ilha da Madeira, Portugal.* (I live on the island of Madeira, Portugal.)
Q: Rogério: *Eu adoraria visitar vocês dois.* (I would love to visit both of you.)
A: Anita: *Você será sempre bem-vinda **na** nossa casa!* (You are always welcome in our house!)

What about indefinite articles? Do they contract? Sure! The common contraction involving the preposition *em* (in, on, at) and the indefinite articles *um, uma* (a/an) is summarized here.

▼ USING *EM* + INDEFINITE ARTICLE IN PORTUGUESE

Preposition + Indefinite Article	Contraction	English
em + um	*num*	in a
em + uma	*numa*	in a
em + uns	*nuns*	in some
em + umas	*numas*	in some

Again, in order to express indefinite ideas, a speaker could use those indefinite pronouns. For example, one could say *Eu vivo num bairro elegante* (I live in an elegant neighborhood), or *Eu estudo numa universidade muito cara* (I study in a very expensive university). Notice that in these two examples, the places were not specifically mentioned. In this chapter you learned some basic building blocks of Portuguese grammar. In the next chapter you will be able to use some of these words with some basic verbs.

Exercise: Contractions

Now let's test what you've learned about contractions. Write in the missing contractions in the following translated sentences. Check your answers in Appendix C.

1. I am **from the** United States.
   Eu sou dos *Estados Unidos.*
2. I live **in a** dorm.
   Eu moro na *residência estudantil.*
3. She is **from** Cuba.
   Ela é de *Cuba.*
4. They are **from the** Island of Madeira.
   Eles são da *Ilha da Madeira.*
5. I study **in a** big university.
   Eu estudo na *universidade grande.*

CHAPTER 5

Who Are You? Introducing *Ser*

First impressions count! As you learn Portuguese, you will notice that the verb *ser* (to be) is used a lot, especially as you talk about yourself, your physical characteristics, your personality, and your occupation. Finally, you will see that *ser* is used for counting and telling time. Read on and you will see how important *ser* really is.

Expressing Identity: *Ser*

If someone were to ask you about yourself, how would you answer? Look at the following examples and notice how Mário Rodrigues describes himself.

Meu nome é Mário Rodrigues. (My name is Mário Rodrigues.)
Sou médico. (I am a medical doctor.)
Sou simpático, de estatura mediana. (I am friendly, of average height.)
Sou de Campinas. (I am from Campinas.)

You will notice that Mário Rodrigues has indicated his name, his profession, his physical characteristics, his personality, and his place of origin. All of these traits are part of his identity, and are not likely to change. These somewhat permanent characteristics are expressed using the verb *ser* (to be) in Portuguese.

▼ THE VERB *SER* IN THE PRESENT TENSE

Portuguese	*English*
eu sou	I am
você é	you are
ele/ela é	he/she/it is
nós somos	we are
vocês são	you (plural) are
eles/elas são	they are

Remember that there is also the *tu* form that is used in some parts of Brazil, and is conjugated as *tu és* for "you are." Also remember that often Brazilians will use the phrase *a gente* for the first person plural or "we," so you would say *a gente é* for "we are." If you want to be more formal, use the second person *o senhor* and *a senhora* with the conjugated form *é* for "you sir/ma'am are."

Place of Origin

As mentioned previously, use the verb *ser* to talk about place of origin, such as your nationality. Here is a sample dialogue.

Q: *De onde você é?* (Where are you from?)
A: *Sou dos Estados Unidos.* (I am from the United States.)
Q: *Então, você é americana?* (So, you are American?)
A: *Sim, sou americana!* (Yes, I'm American!)
Q: *Muito prazer!* (Nice to meet you!)

What follows is a list of some nationalities in Portuguese. The first form is the masculine, followed by the feminine form. If only one form is listed, the adjective can be used for both masculine and feminine referents.

▼ COUNTRIES AND NATIONALITIES

Country	Nationality
Alemanha	*alemão, alemã*
Angola	*angolano, angolana*
Argentina	*argentino, argentina*

Country	Nationality
Austrália	*australiano, australiana*
Áustria	*austríaco, austríaca*
Bélgica	*belga*
Brasil	*brasileiro, brasileira*
Canadá	*canadense*
Chile	*chileno, chilena*
China	*chinês, chinesa*
Colombia	*colombiano, colombiana*
Costa Rica	*costa-ricense*
Ecuador	*equatoriano, equatoriana*
Egito	*egípcio, egípcia*
França	*francês, francesa*
Grã-bretanha	*britânico, britânica*
Grécia	*grego, grega*
Haiti	*haitiano, haitiana*
Holanda	*holandês, holandesa*
India	*indiano, indiana*
Inglaterra	*inglês, inglesa*
Irã	*iraniano, iraniana*
Iraque	*iraquiano, iraquiana*
Irlanda	*irlandês, irlandesa*
Israel	*israelense*
Itália	*italiano, italiana*
Jamaica	*jamaicano, jamaicana*
Japão	*japonês, japonesa*
México	*mexicano, mexicana*
Nicarágua	*nicaragüense*
Panamá	*panamenho, panamenha*
Polônia	*polonês, polonesa*
República Checa	*checo, checa*
Suécia	*sueco, sueca*
Suíça	*suíço, suíça*
Tailandia	*tailandês, tailandesa*
Venezuela	*venezuelano, venezuelana*

You can use these forms as an adjective; for example, *Ele é um médico japonês* (He is a Japanese doctor); or as a noun, as in *Ele é japonês* (He is Japanese). As far as the plural of these forms goes, most of the time you will use the masculine and add an *–s* at the end, so *americano* > *americanos*, and *canadense* > *canadenses*. Feminine plural forms do exist, but only with the adjectives that end in *–o* in the masculine singular, which changes to *–as*, as in *americano* > *americanas*.

Exercise: Name the Nationalities

Now let's practice with an exercise. Indicate the nationalities of the following people. Check your answers in Appendix C.

1. *Stefi Graff é de Berlim. Ela é* _____.
2. *Pelé é de São Paulo, Brasil. Ele é* _____.
3. *O senhor e a senhora Petrov são de Moscou. Eles são* _____.
4. *Sofia Loren e Marcelo Mastroianni são de Roma. Eles são* _____.
5. *O senhor Yamamoto é de Tóquio. Ele é* _____.

Characteristics

What do you look like? What are your major, unchangeable characteristics? The adjectives that reflect this part of your identity are expressed also using the verb *ser* (to be). The following is a list of adjectives that go with this verb.

▼ **COMMON CHARACTERISTICS**

Portuguese	*English*	*Portuguese*	*English*
alto, alta	tall	*forte*	strong, stocky
baixo, baixa	short	*gordo, gorda*	fat
barato, barata	cheap	*idoso, idosa*	elderly
bonito, bonita	pretty	*inteligente*	intelligent
burro, burra	stupid	*jovem*	young
careca	bald	*louro, loura*	blond

Portuguese	English	Portuguese	English
doce	sweet	*magro, magra*	thin
elegante	elegant	*moreno, morena*	dark-skinned
engraçado, engraçada	funny	*pobre*	poor
estudioso, estudiosa	studious	*ruivo, ruiva*	redheaded
famoso, famosa	famous	*sério, séria*	serious
feio, feia	ugly	*velho, velha*	old

If only one word is given in this list, the same form can be used for both masculine and feminine, as in *inteligente* (intelligent). Otherwise, the masculine is written first, followed by the feminine form.

Occupations

Your occupation can hardly be considered a permanent characteristic; however, it immediately identifies you to others. For example, if you want to say that you are a doctor, you should use the verb *ser* (to be). By the same token, if you want to say that you are a student, you should also use *ser*, even if your status as a student is not a permanent condition!

Following are a few examples:

Qual é sua profissão? (What is your profession?)
O que você faz? (What do you do?)
Eu sou médica. (I'm a doctor.)
Eu sou engenheiro. (I'm an engineer.)

Notice that in Portuguese there is no need to add the indefinite article "a" or "an" before the profession, as we do in English. So you are saying, literally, "I am doctor." If you say *Eu sou um médico* (I am a doctor), you are actually saying that you are "one doctor," as opposed to two! The only time when you might have to say *um* or *uma* before a profession or a noun, is when you give a description afterward. In other words, you should say *Eu sou um estudante inteligente* (I am an intelligent student).

Here is a list of some well-known professions in Portuguese:

▼ ***PROFISSÕES E OCUPAÇÕES* (PROFESSIONS AND OCCUPATIONS)**

Portuguese	English
advogado, advogada	lawyer
ator, atriz	actor, actress
analista	psychotherapist
analista de sistemas	systems analyst
arquiteto, arquiteta	architect
bancário, bancária	bank teller
cantor, cantora	singer
consultor, consultora	consultant
contador, contadora	accountant
costureiro, costureira	clothes designer, dressmaker
diretor, diretora	director
empregado, empregada	employee, maid
engenheiro, engenheira	engineer
estudante	student
farmacêutico, farmacêutica	pharmacist
fotógrafo, fotógrafa	photographer
garçom, garçonete	waiter, waitress
gerente	manager
jornalista	reporter, journalist
juiz, juíza	judge
operário, operária	factory worker
músico, música	musician
pianista	pianist
professor, professora	teacher, professor
vendedor, vendedora	salesperson
vendedor ambulante, vendedora ambulante	street vendor

If it is not specifically listed, the feminine form is the same as the masculine form, such as in *gerente* (manager) and *pianista* (pianist).

Exercise: Name That Profession!

Now give the following exercise a try. Fill in the blanks with a word that describes the person's profession or occupation. Check your answers in Appendix C.

1. He plays the piano beautifully.
   Ele é _____.
2. She teaches at a high school.
   Ela é _____.
3. He works in a bank, as a teller.
   Ele é _____.
4. She makes decisions in court.
   Ela é _____.
5. She helps customers with their purchases.
   Ela é _____.

Personal Relationships

As you can see, the verb *ser* is not only used for permanent characteristics and occupations, but also for describing relationships between people! It would be hard to try to fit all types of relationships into a category defined as "permanent." That is why the best description for the uses of this verb is "identification." As you say *Eu sou o irmão dela* (I am her brother), you are identifying yourself and describing your relationship to someone. Here are some other examples:

Carolina é amiga de Raul. (Carolina is Raul's friend.)
As duas alunas são companheiras. (The two students are friends/partners.)
Marcos e José são sócios. (Marcos and José are business partners.)
José e João são concorrentes. (José and João are competitors.)
Helena é filha de Orlando. (Helena is Orlando's daughter.)
Eu sou filha de Iracema. (I am Iracema's daughter.)
Minha irmã e eu somos filhas de Eraldo. (My sister and I are Eraldo's daughters.)

Note that not all personal relationships have to do with family. Many relationships are of close friendships, competitors, or even business associations. They all have to be described using this verb. To learn more about the vocabulary of "family," check out upcoming chapters.

Numbers and *Ser*

The verb *ser* is very versatile; it is also used when dealing with numbers and counting. You could explain the usage of *ser* with numbers by associating it with truthful, immutable descriptions. Thus, two plus two is always four, so *dois e dois são quatro.* For a complete overview of numbers, refer to Chapter 8. What follows is a series of sentences that describe mathematical operations.

$3 \times 4 = 12$	*três vez quatro são doze*
$2 + 2 = 4$	*dois mais dois são quatro*
$9 - 1 = 8$	*nove menos um são oito*
$6 \div 2 = 3$	*seis dividido por dois são três*

Essential

If you would like to ask for the bill at a restaurant, simply say *Quanto foi a conta*? (How much was the bill?) Because it related to activities in the past, the verb *ser* is expressed in the past tense, *foi* (was). The answer to your question could be *São vinte reais* (It is twenty reais). Notice that when dealing with numbers, the verb is in the plural form in Portuguese.

When referring to cost of products and services, you can use *ser*, as in *Um quilo de arroz é dois reais* (One kilogram of rice is two reais). *Real* is the Brazilian currency, and *reais* is its plural form. More commonly, Portuguese speakers will use the verb *custar* (to cost) to deal with prices and costs. An example of a typical sentence would be *Quanto custa a pedicure?* (How much is the pedicure?); in other words, how much does it cost?

CHAPTER 6

How Are You? Introducing *Estar*

Now that you have mastered the use of *ser* (to be), we will move on to another "to be" verb: *estar.* While we associate *ser* with physical characteristics and identity, *estar* is associated with physical states, mental conditions, and location in space. Now let's see where you are in your progress.

States of Being: *Estar*

Use *estar* to help you communicate how you are at a certain point in time. This verb is also used to express the location of someone or something, and the (frequently temporary) states of being. Here are some examples:

A senhora está bem? (How are you, ma'am?)
Estou bem, obrigada. (I am well, thanks.)
Onde você está? (Where are you?)
Estou na escola. (I am at school.)

For the other forms of *estar,* refer to the following table.

▼ **THE VERB *ESTAR* IN THE PRESENT TENSE**

Portuguese	English
eu estou	I am
você está	you are
ele/ela está	he/she/it is

Portuguese	English
nós estamos	we are
vocês estão	you (plural) are
eles/elas estão	they are

It is important to pronounce the forms *estou* (*eu* form) and *estão* (*vocês/eles* form) very clearly, since they might sound similar at the beginning. Practice these two forms out loud, especially the first person singular, which you might have to use more frequently.

When Brazilians are talking, they will very often cut off the first syllable, *es–*, of these verb forms. Be prepared to hear *tou*, *tá*, *tamo(s)*, and *tão* in spoken conversation. You might even start saying them too!

Alert

Many grammars of Portuguese use the distinction "temporary" states for *estar* versus "permanent" aspects for *ser*. This is a good general rule, but it does not tell the whole story. For example, you should say *Eu sou estudante* (I am a student) even though this is (hopefully!) not a permanent condition. Rather it is just a way of identifying yourself. You also say *O gato está morto* (The cat is dead), even though being dead is not a temporary condition. Rather it is a change in physical state.

As clearly put by the well-known Portuguese linguist Mário Perini, *ser* introduces qualities that are seen as inherent to the subject, while *estar* captures qualities that are seen as transitory or otherwise nonessential. More information about other uses of *estar*—specifically, its use with physical states—is presented in the next section.

Physical States

Use a form of the verb *estar* with the adjectives and adverbs in the following table to express how people feel, look, or seem. Don't forget that some adjectives and adverbs need to "match" their respective subjects, especially if the masculine form ends in *–o*. For example: *Ele está cansado* (He is/looks tired); *Ela está cansada* (She is/seems tired). As you can see, sometimes we can translate the verb *estar* (to be) for the verbs "to seem," "to appear," or "to feel" in English, because they reflect not an immutable physical characteristic, but rather a condition or state. The following are some common physical states that are used with the verb *estar.*

▼ VOCABULARY: DESCRIBING HOW YOU FEEL

Portuguese	English	Portuguese	English
acordado	awake	*enjoado*	sick, boring
bêbado	drunk	*fraco*	weak
bem	well	*limpo*	clean
cansado	tired	*mais ou menos*	so-so
descansado	rested	*ocupado*	busy
doente	sick	*pálido*	pale
dormindo	asleep	*sóbrio*	sober

Here is a sample dialogue where a lot of these words may be used:

Q: *Oi, Roberto, como estás?* (Hi, Roberto, how are you?)
A: *Estou bem, mas um pouco cansado.* (I'm fine, but a little tired.)
Q: *Estás bêbado ainda?* (Are you still drunk?)
A: *Não, estou sóbrio, mas de ressaca!* (No, I'm sober, but I'm hung over!)
Q: *Eu sei, e hoje eu vou estar super ocupado.* (I know, and today I will be very busy.)
A: *Eu também, e só agora estou acordado.* (Me too, and only now am I awake.)
Q: *E a casa, 'tá limpa?* (And the house, is it clean?)
A: *Eh . . . mais ou menos!* (Hmm . . . sort of!)

Mental States

Besides physical conditions, there are also mental states that should be expressed with *estar.* Look at some sample vocabulary to aid you in communicating how you feel mentally or emotionally.

▼ VOCABULARY: DESCRIBING HOW YOU FEEL

Portuguese	English	Portuguese	English
amedrontado	scared	*impressionado*	impressed
animado	excited	*irritado*	irritated
ansioso	anxious	*louco*	crazy
apaixonado	in love	*nervoso*	nervous
contente	happy	*preocupado*	worried
envergonhado	embarassed	*satisfeito*	satisfied
estupefato	stunned	*tranqüilo*	calm
excitado	aroused	*triste*	sad
feliz	happy		

Take a look at the following dialogue, which includes many of the adjectives you just reviewed.

Q: *E então, Maria, foi ver o Roberto Carlos?* (So, Maria, did you go see Roberto Carlos?)
A: *Sim, ele é lindo e maravilhoso!* (Yes, he is so handsome and wonderful!)
Q: *Nossa, você está apaixonada, não?* (Wow, you are really in love, huh?)
A: *Claro, eu estou louca de amor por ele.* (You bet, I am crazy in love with him.)
Q: *Você está mesmo animada. Eu estou estupefata!* (Yes, you look really excited. I am stunned!)
A: *Assim é o amor!* (That's how love is!)

Location

The verb *estar* can express where something is in a particular place at a particular time. So, if you ask *Onde você está?* (Where are you?) you can answer *Estou em casa* (I'm at home). Physical location usually refers to something or someone that is only temporarily located in a place, such as a book on a table, or a person at a bank, for example.

Essential

In order to describe where places (buildings, cities, etc.) are located, Portuguese speakers use the verb *ficar* (to be located). For example, *Onde fica o supermercado?* (Where is the supermarket?); *Fica na esquina da Rua Quinze* (It's at the corner of Fifteenth Street).

Here are some words that help locate things or persons when using the verb *estar* with physical location.

▼ **EXPRESSING LOCATION WITH PREPOSITIONAL PHRASES**

Portuguese	English	Portuguese	English
embaixo de	under	*debaixo de*	under
em cima de	on top	*sobre*	over, on top
dentro de	inside	*atrás*	behind
fora de	outside	*em frente de*	in front of
perto de	close to	*detrás de*	behind
longe de	far from	*defronte de*	facing, in front of

You can also use the verb *estar* to indicate a location that is not necessarily associated with space, but rather time. You can say *Estou no meu segundo dia de prova* (I am on my second day of exams), meaning that you are in a certain place in a process of being tested.

Estar in the Present Progressive Tense

The present progressive is the verb tense you use when you want to express actions or feelings that are continuous or ongoing. This tense is comparable to the English progressive, which is done by using the verb "to be" plus an "–ing" ending, as in "I am writing." By comparison, in Brazilian Portuguese we use the verb *estar* plus the *–ndo* ending, as in *Estou falando* (I am talking). Here is how this verb tense is constructed.

▼ PRESENT PROGRESSIVE TENSE

Type of Verb	*estar + –ndo*	English
–ar verbs	*estou estudando*	I am studying
–er verbs	*estou escrevendo*	I am writing
–ir verbs	*estou assistindo*	I am watching

As far as the use of progressive tenses, English speakers use "–ing" structures more often. For example, you use the "present" progressive in the sentence "I'm flying tomorrow" even though it is about the future. This particular usage is not permitted in Portuguese. We would instead use the regular present tense, as in *Eu viajo amanhã* (I fly tomorrow). Most commonly, the present progressive tense in Portuguese is used to reflect ongoing actions or to reflect situations at the moment of speech. As with many other structures in the language, it does not have to be describing an action; it could denote a nonaction, as in *Eu estou pensando* (I'm thinking). Here are some other examples of action and nonaction present progressive sentences:

Eu estou falando português. (I am speaking Portuguese.)
Ela está comendo feijão com arroz. (She is eating rice and beans.)
Ele está comendo arroz. (He is eating rice.)
Nós estamos assistindo à televisão. (We are watching television.)
Eles estão andando no parque. (They are walking in the park.)
Elas estão refletindo sobre a proposta. (They are reflecting on the proposal.)

Ser or *Estar*?

It might be tricky to decide whether to use *ser* or *estar* in Portuguese, since it is all the same in English—that is, you use the verb "to be" for most instances. But there are some very clear distinctions, as can be seen in the following chart.

▼ **GUIDELINES FOR USING *SER* AND *ESTAR***

Uses of *Ser*	Uses of *Estar*
Identification	**Physical States**
Eu sou estudante. (I'm a student.)	*Eu estou doente.* (I am/feel sick.)
Place of Origin/Nationality	**Mental States**
Você é do Brasil. (You are from Brazil.)	*Você está contente.* (You are/feel happy.)
Você é canadense. (You are Canadian.)	
Physical Traits	**Point of Location**
Ele é alto. (He is tall.)	*Ele está em casa.* (He is at home.)
Profession/Occupation	**Present Progressive**
Ela é médica. (She is a doctor.)	*Ela está trabalhando.* (She is working.)
Ela é estudante. (She is a student.)	
Personal Relationships	
Nós somos irmãs. (We are sisters.)	
Nós somos sócios. (We are business partners.)	
General Statements	
O amor é cego. (Love is blind.)	
Numbers and Time	
Dois mais dois são quarto. (Two plus two is four.)	
São doze horas. (It is twelve o'clock.)	

Peculiar Uses

When talking about geographical location, there are at least three possibilities in Portuguese, all grammatically acceptable: (a) *São Paulo é no Brasil*; (b) *São Paulo está no Brasil*; and (c) *São Paulo fica no Brasil*, all of which are translated as "São Paulo is (located) in Brazil." Although *ser* would be the logical choice here, since the fact that a city is located in a particular country is inherent to it, both *estar* and *ficar* seem to be gaining ground in such cases.

There are some adjectives that are used with both *ser* and *estar* resulting in different interpretations of meaning, and thus different translations in English. If we say *Ele é gordo* (He is fat), we mean that being fat is this person's intrinsic quality. Another example of this is in the sentence *Os elefantes são grandes* (Elephants are big); it is clear that being big is part and parcel of being an elephant. On the other hand, if we say *Ele está gordo!* (He is fat!), we mean that he looks or appears to be fat, because perhaps he has gained a lot of weight recently, and in demonstrating this recent change of state, we use *estar* to express surprise. The following are a series of examples with *ser* and *estar* and their translations.

▼ USING BOTH *SER* AND *ESTAR*

Portuguese	English
Ele é louco.	He's crazy. (He should be committed.)
Ele está louco.	He's crazy. (He did something crazy, at that moment.)
A professora é chata.	The teacher is boring. (She is always boring.)
O filme está chato.	The film is boring. (The statement is the speaker's impression; it is not necessarily true.)
Eles são magros.	They are skinny. (That's their intrinsic quality.)
Eles estão magros.	They are skinny. (They lost a lot of weight.)
Eu sou feliz.	I am happy. (That's how I am in general, a happy person.)
Eu estou feliz.	I am happy. (Something happened that made me happy; I am happy at the moment.)
Isso é difícil.	This is difficult. (It's an intrinsically difficult subject.)
Isso está difícil.	This is difficult. (It's more difficult than expected.)

Think you've got a handle on all this? Give it a try with the following exercises.

Exercise: Choosing *Ser* or *Estar*

Decide whether *ser* or *estar* belongs in the following sentences. Check your answers in Appendix C.

1. *Clarice é/está no hospital.* (Clarice is in the hospital.)
2. *Ela é/está médica pediatra.* (She is a pediatrician.)
3. *Ela é/está uma pessoa contente por natureza.* (She is a happy person by nature.)
4. *Clarice e Kadu são/estão brasileiros.* (Clarice and Kadu are Brazilian.)

5. *Agora eles são/estão no Rio de Janeiro.* (Now they are in Rio de Janeiro.)
6. *Kadu é/está estudante de medicina.* (Kadu is a medical student.)
7. *Ele é/está nervosa com os exames.* (He is nervous about exams.)

Exercise: Now You Conjugate!

Write in the correct verb form, using either *ser* or *estar.* Check your answers in Appendix C.

1. *Meus pais* _____ *na Europa.* (My parents are in Europe.)
2. *O vermelho* _____ *uma cor linda.* (Red is a beautiful color.)
3. *Meu amigo Jonas* _____ *engenheiro civil.* (My friend Jonas is a civil engineer.)
4. *O livro de português* _____ *em cima da mesa.* (The Portuguese book is on top of the table.)
5. *Fortaleza* _____ *no Nordeste do Brasil.* (Fortaleza is located in the northeast of Brazil.)
6. _____ *sete horas da noite.* (It's seven o'clock at night.)
7. *Nós* _____ *muito contentes com os nossos filhos.* (We are very happy with our children.)

Exercise: Time to Translate

Translate the following sentences into Portuguese. Check your answers in Appendix C.

1. She looks thin. _____
2. They are teachers. _____
3. He is furious. _____
4. We are Cuban. _____
5. You are in the city. _____

Agreement Rules

One important concept that students of Portuguese must learn is the fact that all the elements of the noun phrase need to "agree with" or be in the same gender and number as the noun. So, Portuguese speakers say *um cantor famoso* for "a famous singer" who is male and *uma cantora famosa* for "a famous singer" who is female. By the same token, if there is more than one element, the nouns and adjectives also have to "agree" in terms of number. Speakers say *uns cantores famosos* for famous singers like the Beach Boys and *umas cantoras famosas* for the Dixie Chicks. Here are some more examples of noun phrases in Portuguese where the agreement rule is clearly at play.

um cartaz bonito (a pretty poster)
uns livros interessantes (some interesting books)
uma janela aberta (an open window)
umas alunas engraçadas (some funny [female] students)

You'll find out more details about gender and plural agreement in the next few sections.

Plurals in Nouns and Adjectives

In formal written Portuguese and very formal speech, number agreement is followed pretty strictly. This does not happen in colloquial or less careful speech. Some words are easy to guess the plural, and others either follow a predetermined rule or are exceptions and must be learned by heart. Here are the rules for forming plural nouns in Portuguese.

First, as a general rule: add an *–s* to the singular form.

gato (cat)	*gatos* (cats)
mesa (table)	*mesas* (tables)
chave (key)	*chaves* (keys)
mão (hand)	*mãos* (hands)

All plural words in Portuguese end in *–s*. However, there might be changes to the previous vowels or consonants that come before. The plural formation depends on the stress of the words and whether diphthongs are found at the end.

If the word ends in *–l*, drop *–l* and add *–is*. If the result is *–iis*, drop one *i*.

jornal (newspaper)	*jornais* (newspapers)
papel (paper)	*papéis* (papers)
fuzil (rifle)	*fuzis* (rifles)

If the word ends in *–l* but the last syllable is not stressed, drop *–l* and add *–eis*.

fóssil (fossil)	*fósseis* (fossils)
réptil (reptile)	*répteis* (reptiles)

If the word ends in *–s* or *–x*, and the last syllable is not stressed, the plural is identical.

lápis (pencil)	*lápis* (pencils)
clímax (climax)	*clímax* (climaxes)

If the word ends in *–m*, drop *–m* and add *–ns*.

jovem (youngster)	*jovens* (youngsters)
bombom (bonbon)	*bombons* (bonbons)

If the word ends in a consonant, add *–es*.

amor (love)	*amores* (loves)
cartaz (poster)	*cartazes* (posters)

The words in the next group end in *–ão* in the singular and have three different possibilities in the plural. Here is how this works:

If the word ends in *–ão*, and the last syllable is not stressed, add *–s*.

órgão (organ)	*órgãos* (organs)

If the word ends in *–ão* and the last syllable is stressed, add *–s*, or *–ões*, or *–ães*:

irmão (brother)	*irmãos* (brothers)
melão (melon)	*melões* (melons)
capitão (captain)	*capitães* (captains)

The first example (*irmãos*) shows the simple "add an *–s*" rule. However, this is not the most common plural for words ending in *–ão*. The second example (*melões*) is actually the most common result for the singular words that end in *–ão*. If one had to guess the plural of a word ending in *–ão*, this would be the best guess. Finally, the last example (*capitães*) is the least common case. There are only a handful of words in Portuguese that have this plural ending, including *pães* (breads) and *alemães* (Germans). Even though it might seem daunting at first, plurals are manageable in Portuguese once you learn the general rules.

Exercise: What's the Plural Form?

Now let's see what you've learned about singular and plural forms of words in Portuguese. Write the plural forms of the following words in Portuguese. Check your answers in Appendix C.

1. *coração* (heart): _____
2. *canil* (kennel): _____
3. *pincel* (paintbrush): _____
4. *pão* (bread): _____
5. *órfão* (orphan): _____
6. *difícil* (difficult): _____
7. *cantor* (singer): _____
8. *tórax* (thorax): _____

CHAPTER 7

Describing People and Things in Portuguese

In the previous chapter, you learned that nouns and adjectives need to agree in gender and number in Portuguese. In this chapter you will learn how to arrive at the plural of nouns, how to determine the correct order of elements in a noun phrase, how to make comparisons, how to talk about the "best" and the "worst," and how to express ownership and possession.

From Nouns to Adjectives

What are adjectives? Adjectives modify the nouns that they are attached to. The masculine form is usually accepted as the "default" form, from which the feminine is somehow "derived." This is one reason why new words entering the language are generally masculine. Whichever gender, the fact remains that all elements in the noun phrase must match. How do you get from the masculine to the feminine form? If the masculine ends in *–o*, you should drop the *–o* and add *–a* to get the feminine form. If the masculine word ends in *–u* or *–ês*, simply add *–a* to the word to create the feminine counterpart. The following are some examples of masculine and feminine descriptive adjectives, which have to agree with the nouns they modify.

▼ **MASCULINE AND FEMININE ADJECTIVES**

Masculine	Feminine	English
amarelo	*amarela*	yellow
bonito	*bonita*	pretty

Masculine	Feminine	English
cru	*crua*	raw
vermelho	*vermelha*	red

Some adjectives have the same form for feminine and masculine. This happens often with adjectives that end in *–e*, such as *inteligente* (intelligent), *doente* (sick), and *contente* (happy). There are also a good number of adjectives that end in consonants that have the same form for both masculine and feminine, such as *azul* (blue), *capaz* (able), *familiar* (familiar), *internacional* (international), *marrom* (brown), and *virgem* (virgin). It is easy to see the changes in masculine and feminine adjectives by looking at a list of common nationalities. As you learn Portuguese, you might want to communicate your citizenship, or refer to people of various nationalities. Here is a short list of adjectives of nationality:

▼ MASCULINE AND FEMININE NATIONALITIES

Masculine	Feminine	English
americano	*americana*	American
brasileiro	*brasileira*	Brazilian
mexicano	*mexicana*	Mexican
inglês	*inglesa*	English
canadense	*canadense*	Canadian
alemão	*alemã*	German

You will notice that *canadense* ends in *–e* and therefore has the same form for both masculine and feminine. For masculine words that end in *–ão*, the feminine form is derived by removing the *–o* and leaving the nasalized vowel *–ã* at the end, as in the word *alemão*, *alemã* (German). There are some nationalities/religions that do not change in form, regardless of gender. These are *hindu* (Hindu) and *zulu* (Zulu), among others.

Additionally, words ending in *–eu* in the masculine change to *–éia* in the feminine, such as in the word *hebreu*, *hebréia* (Hebrew).

Nationalities are not written with capital letters in Portuguese, as they are in English. They follow the same rule as other adjectives and begin with lowercase letters.

Exercise: Transforming Adjectives

Now let's see what you've learned about transforming adjectives. Make the appropriate changes so that the masculine form becomes the feminine one. Check your answers in Appendix C.

1. *francês* (French): _____
2. *indiano* (Indian): _____
3. *nu* (naked): _____
4. *ateu* (atheist): _____
5. *jornaleiro* (newspaper seller): _____
6. *japonês* (Japanese): _____
7. *israelense* (Israeli): _____
8. *colombiano* (Colombian): _____

The Order of Modifiers

As with any language, Portuguese has a certain order that must be followed by the elements of the noun phrase. Modifiers are the parts of the phrase that influence and change the meaning of the noun. You can say "the book," "a book," or "good book," and all those phrases have different meanings. That is because those modifiers (the, a, good) modify or add to the noun "book." In Portuguese, some modifiers precede the noun, while others (usually descriptive adjectives) follow the noun. First, let's look at the list of common modifiers that precede the noun:

▼ ORDER OF MODIFIERS OCCURRING BEFORE THE NOUN

Group I	Group II	Group III
predeterminers	determiners	quantifiers/possessives/numerals
todos (all)	*o* (the)	*poucos* (few)
ambos (both)	*um* (a/an)	*muitos* (many)
	este/esse (this)	*vários* (several)
	aquele (that)	*tantos* (so many)
	algum (some)	*meus, seus, etc.* (my, your, etc.)
		dois, três, quatro (two, three, four)

Other possibilities, such as the words *qualquer* (any) and *tal* (such), are also part of group III, but are not mentioned here for the sake of simplicity. Suffice it to say that the examples in the previous table are very common in spoken as well as written language. The following are some examples of noun phrases that include a combination of modifiers:

Todos	*meus*	*amigos*	All (of) my friends
I	II	[noun]	
Ambas	*as*	*blusas*	Both (of) the blouses
I	II	[noun]	
As	*poucas*	*explicações*	The few explanations
II	III	[noun]	
Meus	*dois*	*amigos*	My two friends
III	III	[noun]	
Meus	*muitos*	*amigos*	My many friends
III	III	[noun]	

As you can see, it is common to have phrases that include elements from groups I and II, as well as combinations that include elements from groups II and III. And, as can be seen from the fourth and fifth examples in the previous table, it is possible to have at least two items from group III, most commonly when a possessive is followed by another modifier from the same group.

Descriptive Adjectives

Descriptive adjectives are modifiers that usually follow the noun in Portuguese. In Portuguese we say the noun first, and then we give it qualifications. So, unlike in English, you say *um carro vermelho*, literally "a car red." Imagine how hard it would be for simultaneous interpreters to translate a long description from English to Portuguese: They would have to wait until all the adjectives were said, keep them in mind, then translate the noun, and only then add all the adjectives in Portuguese!

Exercise: Put It All in Order

Read the jumbled words in each item and rewrite the noun phrase using the correct order of modifiers. Check your answers in Appendix C.

1. *vermelho um carro* (a red car): _____
2. *casas novas umas* (some new houses): _____
3. *amigos os todos meus* (all my friends): _____
4. *aluno o inteligente* (the intelligent student): _____
5. *laranja blusa uma* (an orange blouse): _____
6. *livros ambos os* (both of the books): _____
7. *a amiga minha* ([the] my friend): _____
8. *carro um novo* (a new car): _____

Making Comparisons

Sometimes it is not enough to simply describe something; you need to compare it with something else in order to give a clearer idea of what you are talking about. There are two main kinds of comparisons: ones in which unequal elements are being compared and ones in which equal elements are being compared.

Comparing Unequal Elements

Comparing unequal elements is simple. Whenever you say that one thing is bigger, better, stronger, heavier, and so forth, than another thing, you are saying that these two things are unequal. You probably make comparisons of inequality in English all the time; now let's see how to do it in Portuguese.

▼ **COMPARISON OF UNEQUAL ELEMENTS**

X	verb	*mais* (more)	ADJECTIVE	(*do*) que (*than*)	Y
Brad Pitt	*é*	*mais*	*bonito*	*que*	Will Ferrell.
Brad Pitt	is	more	handsome	than	Will Ferrell.

X	verb	*menos* (less)	ADJECTIVE	(*do*) *que* (than)	Y
A minha casa	*é*	*menos*	*confortável*	*que*	*a sua casa.*
My house	is	less	comfortable	than	your house.
X	**verb**	***mais* (more)**	**NOUN**	**(*do*) *que* (than)**	**Y**
José	*tem*	*mais*	*amigos*	*que*	*o irmão dele.*
José	has	more	friends	than	his brother.
X	**verb**	***menos* (less)**	**NOUN**	**(*do*) *que* (than)**	**Y**
João	*tem*	*menos*	*dinheiro*	*que*	*José.*
João	has	less	money	than	José.

In spoken language, the particle *do* is usually not heard. But it is possible to see it written, as in *João tem mais paciência* ***do*** *que José* (João has more patience than José). Although most comparisons follow the formulas you saw in the table, there are some irregular comparatives that should be noted. The adjective *bom* (good) has the comparative *melhor* (better), and the adjective *ruim* (bad) has the comparative *pior* (worse). Some examples are *Rita é melhor estudante que Pedro* (Rita is a better student than Pedro) and *Teresa é pior atleta que Jacinto* (Teresa is a worse athlete than Jacinto).

Exercise: Comparing Unequal Elements

Now you give it a try. Read the information below about the people and write a comparative sentence. Here's an example: Pedro, eighteen years old/Jacinto, seventeen years old. > *Pedro é mais velho que Jacinto.* (Pedro is older than Jacinto.) Check your answers in Appendix C.

1. Rita, IQ = 120/Teresa, IQ = 110.

   _____

2. Marta, forty-three years old/Rodrigo, forty-six years old.

   _____

3. Amaro, 1m 70c in height/Cláudio 1m 80c in height.

   _____

4. Jorge, 90 kilos in weight/Maria, 63 kilos in weight.

_____

5. Bill Gates, $$$$/Donald Trump, $$.

_____

Comparing Equal Elements

Just as you commonly need to compare things that are unequal, you also need to compare things that are equal in nature. The following table demonstrates how to do this in Portuguese.

▼ **COMPARISON OF EQUAL ELEMENTS**

X	verb	*tão*	ADJECTIVE	*quanto*	Y
Martha	*é*	*tão*	*famosa*	*quanto*	*Donald.*
Martha	is	as	famous	as	Donald.
Dave	*é*	*tão*	*engraçado*	*quanto*	*Jay.*
Dave	is	as	funny	as	Jay.
X	**verb**	***tanto*, os, a, as**	**NOUN**	***quanto***	**Y**
Jacinto	*tem*	*tanto*	*dinheiro*	*quanto*	*Pedro.*
Jacinto	has	as much	money	as	Pedro.
Eu	*tenho*	*tanta*	*paciência*	*quanto*	*a minha esposa.*
I	have	as much	patience	as	my wife.
Eu	*tenho*	*tantos*	*amigos*	*quanto*	*a minha irmã.*
I	have	as many	friends	as	my sister.
Rita	*tem*	*tantas*	*canetas*	*quanto*	*Teresa.*
Rita	has	as many	pens	as	Teresa.

As you can see from the examples in the previous table, the expression *tanto . . . quanto* (as much/many as) in Portuguese can have four different forms depending on the noun: *tanto*, *tantos*, *tanta*, *tantas*. Always keep in mind these four categories, which intersect: singular, plural, masculine, and feminine.

Exercise: Comparing Equal Elements

Now give it a try. Fill in the blanks with the correct words in these comparative sentences. Check your answers in Appendix C.

1. *Jorge é* _____ *feio* _____ *Vicente.* (Jorge is as ugly as Vincent.)
2. *Martha é* _____ *rica* _____ *Donald.* (Martha is as rich as Donald.)
3. *O Porsche tem* _____ *potência* _____ *o Ferrari.* (The Porsche has as much power as the Ferrari.)
4. *Meu computador tem* _____ *problemas* _____ o seu. (My computer has as many problems as yours.)
5. *Gilberto tem* _____ *talento* _____ *Chico.* (Gilberto has as much talent as Chico.)

Superlatives: The Best of the Best

Now that you know how to compare two individuals or things, we can talk about comparing individuals or things to a whole group to which they belong. Superlatives are a way to make this comparison. Imagine that you are Goldilocks and you have come into the bears' house. If you had to compare the three beds, you would make a decision about which is the best one of the three. And if Goldilocks spoke Portuguese, she would say *Esta é a cama mais confortável das três* (This is the most comfortable bed of the three). Here is a summary of how superlatives are expressed in Portuguese.

▼ **SUPERLATIVES IN PORTUGUESE**

[individual/ thing]	is	the [category]	*mais/menos de* [quality]	[group]
Guga	*é*	*o tenista*	*mais famoso*	*do Brasil.*
Guga is the most famous tennis player of Brazil.				

[individual/ thing]	is	the [category]	*mais/menos de* [quality]	[group]
São Paulo	*é*	*a cidade*	*mais populosa*	*da América do Sul.*
São Paulo is the most populated city in South America.				
Joaquim	*é*	*o aluno*	*menos aplicado*	*da classe.*
Joaquim is the least dedicated student of the class.				

Notice that the usage of the preposition *de* (of) + definite article results in a contraction such as *do* and *da* (of the) in Portuguese. Although most superlatives follow the previous structure, there are some irregular superlatives in Portuguese. These are *o melhor* (the best), *o pior* (the worst), *o maior* (the biggest), and *o menor* (the smallest).

Exercise: Fill in the Superlative

Fill in the blanks with the best answer in these superlative sentences. Check your answers in Appendix C.

1. *O futebol é o esporte* _____ *popular* _____ *Brasil.* (Soccer is the most popular sport in Brazil.)
2. *Brasília é a capital* _____ *moderna* _____ *América Latina.* (Brasília is the most modern capital of Latin America.)
3. *Amália Rodrigues é a* _____ *canora de Fado* _____ *Portugal.* (Amália Rodrigues is the best Fado singer of Portugal.)

Ownership and Possession

Possessives are words that explain who "owns" or "possesses" things. In English they are commonly used and also follow a gender and number system, at least for third person (notice the words "his," "her," and "their"). The Portuguese possessive system does the same, with some intricacies. First, let's present the possessives for first and second persons:

▼ FIRST AND SECOND PERSON POSSESSIVES IN PORTUGUESE

Person	Pronoun	Possessive Forms	English
First Singular	*eu*	(*o*) *meu* [noun], (*os*) *meus* [noun]	"my"
		(*a*) *minha* [noun], (*as*) *minhas* [noun]	
Second	*você*	(*o*) *seu* [noun], (*os*) *seus* [noun]	"your"
		(*a*) *sua* [noun], (*as*) *suas* [noun]	
Second	*tu*	(*o*) *teu* [noun], (*os*) *teus* [noun]	"your"
		(*a*) *tua* [noun], (*as*) *tuas* [noun]	
First Plural	*nós*	(*o*) *nosso* [noun], (*os*) *nossos* [noun]	"our"
		(*a*) *nossa* [noun], (*as*) *nossas* [noun]	

The definite articles in parentheses are optional in Brazilian Portuguese.

Although it might seem overwhelming at first, you will soon realize that it all depends on the thing "owned," not the person who "owns" it, and the whole system becomes much clearer. Since the form of the possessive depends on the noun that comes afterward, it makes sense that there would be four forms, masculine and feminine, singular and plural, as in *meu*, *meus*, *minha*, *minhas* for "my." Also notice that the table gives both the *tu* and the *você* forms, which refer to the second person singular pronoun "you." You might come across someone in Brazil asking you *Como é* ***teu*** *nome?* (What is your name?) and you can respond easily by starting with ***Meu*** *nome é* . . . !

Exercise: Who Owns It?

Now try your hand at an exercise. Translate the following noun phrases using the correct first and second person possessive pronouns. Check your answers in Appendix C.

1. my pen: _____
2. your book: _____
3. my friends: _____
4. our parents: _____
5. your backpack: _____
6. our house: _____
7. your notebooks: _____
8. my sisters: _____

More Possessive Pronouns

Now let's turn our attention to the remaining possessive pronouns. These are somewhat different because they refer to the third person (he, she, it, they) and follow more colloquial rules. Here is a summary:

▼ **THIRD PERSON POSSESSIVE PRONOUNS IN PORTUGUESE**

Pronoun	Possessive Forms	English
ele (he)	*o* [noun] *dele*	his [noun]
	a [noun] *dele*	his [noun]
	os [noun] *dele*	his [noun]
	as [noun] *dele*	his [noun]
ela (she)	*o* [noun] *dela*	her [noun]
	a [noun] *dela*	her [noun]
	os [noun] *dela*	her [noun]
	as [noun] *dela*	her [noun]
eles (they [men or mixed])	*o* [noun] *deles*	their [noun]
	a [noun] *deles*	their [noun]
	os [noun] *deles*	their [noun]
	as [noun] *deles*	their [noun]
elas (they [women])	*o* [noun] *delas*	their [noun]
	a [noun] *delas*	their [noun]
	os [noun] *delas*	their [noun]
	as [noun] *delas*	their [noun]

Notice that the position of the noun with respect to the possessive pronoun changes, as compared to the first and second person. When you talk about the third person (he, she, it, they), you are literally saying "the book of his" (e.g., *o livro dele*) and not "his book." Notice also that each "person" can own singular or plural things. Thus, we can say *os livros dele*, meaning "the books of his" or better yet "his books," as well as *o livro delas* (their book). With time you will be able to tackle this complex system and become a master at it! Let's see how much of it you have already understood.

Exercise: Translation

Translate the following noun phrases using the correct third person possessive pronouns. Check your answers in Appendix C.

1. Their (female) classes: _____
2. His computer: _____
3. Her pencil: _____
4. Their (male) house: _____
5. Her books: _____
6. Their (female) car: _____
7. His glasses: _____
8. Her purse: _____

CHAPTER 8

The Vocabulary of Numbers

Numbers are perhaps one of the first things you tackle when learning a new language. In this chapter you will become familiar with cardinal numbers (one, two, three, etc.) and ordinal numbers (first, second, third, etc.) in Portuguese. You will also see how these are important when you learn the days of the week and how to tell time. And don't forget the months and the seasons; these are all vocabulary of time.

Cardinal Numbers

These numbers are used for counting and expressing quantities. In Portuguese, the number one has two forms: *um* for masculine and *uma* for feminine. The same is true for the number two: *dois* and *duas*. The basic number sequence that you must learn is zero through fifteen. See the following table.

▼ **NUMBERS ZERO TO FIFTEEN**

zero	*zero*	ZEH-roh
one	*um, uma*	UHN, UHN-ah
two	*dois, duas*	DOY-sh, DOO-ahsh
three	*três*	TREYSH
four	*quatro*	KWA-troh
five	*cinco*	SIN-koo
six	*seis*	SEYSH
seven	*sete*	SEH-tchee, SHE-tee

eight	*oito*	OY-too
nine	*nove*	NOH-vee
ten	*dez*	DEH-ish
eleven	*onze*	OHN-zee
twelve	*doze*	DOH-zee
thirteen	*treze*	TREH-zee
fourteen	*catorze*	kah-TOHR-zee
fifteen	*quinze*	KEEN-zee

Notice that the number *sete* (seven) has variable pronunciation in different regions of Brazil. The speakers from the southeast, especially those from Rio de Janeiro, will have a more palatal variant (SEH-tchee), which is heard with the combinations *te* and *ti*, such as the word *tia* (aunt), pronounced TCHEE-ah. Now the next set of numbers is a combination of "ten" plus a unit number. See the following table:

▼ NUMBERS SIXTEEN TO NINETEEN

sixteen	*dezesseis*	deh-zeh-SEYSH
seventeen	*dezessete*	deh-zeh-SEH-tchee
eighteen	*dezoito*	deh-ZOY-too
nineteen	*dezenove*	deh-zeh-NOH-vee

Notice that the combination of *–ss–* indicates a soft pronunciation of the [s] sound in English, not the [z] sound that is associated with *–s–*, which is common between vowels. The next set of numbers is from *vinte* (twenty) to *cem* (one hundred). When we need to express the combination of tens and units, we simply use the word *e* (and) in between the numbers. See the following examples.

▼ NUMBERS TWENTY TO ONE HUNDRED

twenty	*vinte*	VEEN-tchee
twenty-one	*vinte e um, uma*	VEEN-tchee-ee-UHN, -UHN-ah
twenty-two	*vinte e dois, duas*	VEEN-tchee-ee-DOYSH, -DOO-ahsh
twenty-three	*vinte e três*	VEEN-tchee-ee-TREYSH

thirty	*trinta*	TREEN-tah
forty	*quarenta*	kwa-REHN-tah
fifty	*cinqüenta*	sin-KWEN-tah
sixty	*sessenta*	seh-SEHN-tah
seventy	*setenta*	seh-TEHN-tah
eighty	*oitenta*	oy-TEHN-tah
ninety	*noventa*	noh-VEHN-tah
one hundred	*cem*	SEH-in

After *cem* (one hundred), any combination of 100 plus another unit, such as 101, results in a change to *cento* (hundred) plus the word *e* followed by the unit. The same is repeated after each case. See the following examples.

one hundred and one	*cento e um, uma*	SEHN-too-ee-UHN, -UHN-ah
one hundred and ten	*cento e dez*	SEHN-too-ee-DEYSH
one hundred and eleven	*cento e onze*	SENH-too-ee-OHN-zee
one hundred and twenty-one	*cento e vinte e um, uma*	SEHN-too-ee-VEEN-tchee-ee-UHN, -UHN-ah

Starting at two hundred and up to nine hundred, the numbers have a masculine and a feminine form. These depend on what follows, whether it is a masculine or a feminine noun. So, "two hundred students" could be *duzentos alunos* (two hundred [male or mixed] students) or *duzentas alunas* (two hundred [female] students). And don't forget that the rule for one and two still apply, with their two forms. So, there could be *duzentas e trinta e uma páginas* (two hundred and thirty-one pages), where the word "page" is feminine, and thus the number one is expressed in the feminine form. See the next set of numbers here.

▼ NUMBERS TWO HUNDRED TO NINE HUNDRED

two hundred	*duzentos, duzentas*	doo-ZEHN-toos, doo-ZEHN-tahs
three hundred	*trezentos, trezentas*	treh-ZEHN-toos, treh-ZEHN-tahs
four hundred	*quatrocentos, quatrocentas*	kwa-troh-ZEHN-toos, kwa-troh-ZEHN-tahs

five hundred	*quinhentos, quinhentas*	keen-NHEN-toos, keen-NHEN-tahs
six hundred	*seiscentos, seiscentas*	seys-SEHN-toos, seys-SEHN-tahs
seven hundred	*setecentos, setecentas*	seh-the-SEHN-toos, seh-the-SEHN-tahs
eight hundred	*oitocentos, oitocentas*	oy-too-SEHN-toos, oy-too-SEHN-tahs
nine hundred	*novecentos, novecentas*	noh-vee-SEHN-toos, noh-vee-SEHN-tahs

After those, the number *mil* (one thousand) shows no variation; that is, there is no feminine counterpart. However, if the number ends in one, such as in one thousand and one, there is the normal feminine form of one, depending on the noun. An example is *mil e uma páginas* (one thousand and one pages), where the word "page" is feminine. Following are more examples.

one thousand nine hundred	*mil e novecentos*	meel-ee-noh-vee-SEHN-toos
one thousand nine hundred and two	*mil novecentos e dois*	meel-noh-vee-SEHN-toos-ee-DOYSH
one thousand nine hundred and twenty-two	*mil novecentos e vinte e dois*	meel-noh-vee-SEHN-toos-ee-VEEN-tchee-ee-DOYSH

Notice that if there is a need to use *e* (and) after the hundreds, then the first *e* is dropped. Remember that in the case of years that relate to the last millennium, we don't say "nineteen hundred" but rather "one thousand, nine hundred," and so forth.

Alert

In Portuguese (and in most other languages), a period is used after the thousands. So the number 1,400 in English is expressed as 1.400 in Portuguese. The reverse also happens in the case of fractions. The number *pi* is expressed as 3,1416 . . . with a comma, not a period, in Brazil!

You might not use the words *um milhão* (one million) or *um bilhão* (one billion) in Brazil, since inflation has been curbed in the past decades. But you might need to use them when referring to populations. These words match the English closely, unlike in Spanish dialects, where one billion is expressed as "one thousand million." Make sure to use the preposition *de* after these words and before nouns, such as in *dois milhões de pessoas* (two million people).

Exercise: Translation Using Numbers

Now let's try some practice. Write in the numbers in Portuguese followed by a translation of the words. Check your answers in Appendix C.

1. 15 notebooks: _____
2. 83 books: _____
3. 379 professors: _____
4. 761 female students: _____
5. 1.006 cars: _____
6. 432.578 people: _____

Ordinal Numbers

Ordinal numbers are used when you want to talk about sequences, such as first, second, third, and so on. Use these numbers to refer to kings, emperors, and popes, such as D. Pedro II, pronounced *Dom Pedro segundo* (Pedro the Second), the second emperor of Brazil. The following are the ordinal numbers in Portuguese:

▼ ORDINAL NUMBERS

Portuguese	English	Portuguese	English
primeiro	first	*oitavo*	eighth
segundo	second	*nono*	ninth
terceiro	third	*décimo*	tenth
quarto	fourth	*décimo-primeiro*	eleventh
quinto	fifth	*décimo-segundo*	twelfth
sexto	sixth	*vigésimo*	twentieth
sétimo	seventh		

You might also hear *trigésimo* (thirtieth) and *quadragésimo* (fortieth) in more elevated sequences. As you can see from the previous table, at the eleventh number, you start with the word *décimo*, add a dash, and then add the ordinal number of the corresponding unit, such as in *décimo-quinto* (fifteenth). Make sure to match the ordinal number to the noun(s) it modifies, depending on gender. So, you should say *décimo-sexto andar* for "sixteenth floor," which is masculine, and *décima-sexta cláusula* for "sixteenth clause," which refers to a feminine noun.

Essential

The common abbreviations used for ordinal numbers (1st, 2nd, and 3rd) are different in Portuguese, as can be expected. When expressing abbreviated ordinal numbers, use the superscripts 1° (*primeiro*) or 1ª (*primeira*), depending on the gender of the noun. Use the same symbols for all sequences: 2° (*segundo*), 2ª (*segunda*), and so on.

Exercise: Using Ordinal Numbers

Okay, now let's see how you fare with an ordinal numbers exercise. Rewrite the expressions using the numbers for the following items. Check your answers in Appendix C.

1. *A 7ª maravilha do mundo* (the seventh wonder of the world)

   _____

2. *O 4° ciclo do inferno* (the fourth ring of hell)

   _____

3. *A 1ª lição* (the first lesson)

   _____

4. *A 5ª dinastia* (the fifth dynasty)

   _____

5. *O 20° tenista do ranking mundial* (the twentieth tennis player of the world ranking)

   _____

Days of the Week

One of the most unique aspects of the Portuguese language has to do with the names of weekdays. We express the days of the week by using ordinal numbers followed by the word *feira*. The following table more clearly explains the origin of the names of the weekdays.

▼ **WEEKDAYS**

English	Portuguese	Origin	Literal Translation
Sunday	*domingo*	Domenica	Day of the Lord
Monday	*segunda-feira*	Feria Secunda	Second Holy Day
Tuesday	*terça-feira*	Feria Tertia	Third Holy Day
Wednesday	*quarta-feira*	Feria Quarta	Fourth Holy Day
Thursday	*quinta-feira*	Feria Quinta	Fifth Holy Day
Friday	*sexta-feira*	Feria Sexta	Sixth Holy Day
Saturday	*sábado*	Shabbat	The Sabbath

This distinctive way of expressing weekdays came about because of a very influential bishop named Martinho de Dume, also known as Martinho de Braga. During his tenure as Bishop of Braga, he considered it undignified for good Christians to say the names of weekdays by their original pagan names—*Lunae dies* (Day of the Moon), *Martis dies* (Day of Mars), *Mercurii dies* (Day of Mercury), *Jovis dies* (Day of Jovis or Jupiter), *Veneris dies* (Day of Venus), *Saturni dies* (Day of Saturn), and *Solis dies* (Day of the Sun). So, starting from Sunday, he devised the names *Prima Feria*, *Secunda Feria*, and so forth, for the days of the Holy Week. The current word *feira* is a linguistic corruption of *Feria*, which meant "Holy Day" or holiday, a day on which people should not work. Later, the first day (*Prima Feria*), or Sunday, was changed to *Domenica*, which is Latin for the "Day of the Lord." This meaning is also kept in Spanish, Italian, and French.

To know what day it is, you should ask *Que dia (da semana) é hoje?* (What day [of the week] is today?) The answer could be *É sexta!* (It's Friday!) Also, when asked *Quando você vai à igreja?* (When do you go to church?), the answer could be *no domingo* (on Sunday). For the other days of the week, use the contraction *na* for the weekdays, as in *na segunda*, *na terça*, *na quarta*, and so on, and use *no sábado* to express "on Saturday."

Essential

To form the plural of the days of the week, you should add an *–s* to both parts of the word: for example, *segundas-feiras* (Mondays) and *quartas-feiras* (Wednesdays). In spoken Portuguese it is very common to drop the word *–feira* and simply say *Eu estudo português nas terças e quintas* (I study Portuguese on Tuesdays and Thursdays).

Talking about Time

Que horas são? is the expression used to ask what time it is in Portuguese. If you are answering about a singular time (that is, if it's a certain hour, on the dot), you should say *São* _____ *horas*. We use the verb *são* (are) because the noun *horas* (hours) is in the plural form. But between 1:00 A.M./P.M. and 1:59 A.M./P.M. you should say *É uma hora* plus any minutes. Also use *É* if the time is noon or midnight.

Here are some examples.

▼ **TELLING TIME IN PORTUGUESE**

English	Portuguese
It's (twelve) noon.	*É meio-dia.*
It's (twelve) midnight.	*É meia-noite.*
It's 1:00 P.M.	*É uma hora (em ponto).*
It's 2:00 P.M.	*São duas horas.*
It's 2:15 P.M.	*São duas e quinze.*
It's 2:20 P.M.	*São duas e vinte.*
It's 6:30 P.M.	*São seis e meia./São seis e trinta.*
It's 6:40 P.M.	*São vinte para as sete./São seis e quarenta.*
It's 6:45 P.M.	*São quinze para as sete./São seis e quarenta e cinco.*

Notice that it is not necessary to say *horas* or *minutos* when telling time. In order to say that it's the time "on the dot," say *em ponto*. In addition, it is possible to say either "it's twenty minutes to four" or "it's three forty"; both ways are acceptable in colloquial speech. In Portuguese, speakers do not use the symbols A.M. and P.M., so they need to indicate the time of the day by using some extra words.

da manhã (in the morning)
da tarde (in the afternoon)
da noite (in the evening)
da madrugada (in the small hours of the morning)

It is also very common to use the twenty-four-hour clock, or what is commonly known as "military time," instead of the added phrases *de manhã, da tarde*, and so on, in order to avoid confusion between morning, afternoon, and evening hours. Here are some examples:

The concert starts at 10 P.M. (*O concerto começa às vinte e duas horas.*)
The movie starts at 3:30 P.M. (*O filme começa às quinze e trinta.*)
The class ends at 5:45 P.M. (*A aula termina às dezessete e quarenta e cinco.*)

As you can see from these examples, to say when something ends or starts you have to use the contraction *às* (at) plus the time. If it's one o'clock, use the singular *à* (at) plus the time. For example, to answer the question *Quando começa a peça de teatro?* (When does the play start?) a person might answer *Começa às vinte horas* (It starts at 8 P.M.).

The Months and Seasons

The months, or *os meses* in Portuguese, are very easy to learn because they sound a lot like their English equivalents. See the following list:

▼ THE MONTHS

Portuguese	English
janeiro	January
fevereiro	February
março	March
abril	April
maio	May
junho	June
julho	July
agosto	August
setembro	September
outubro	October
novembro	November
dezembro	December

Notice that the months are not written in capital letters, as they are in English. All days except the first of the month—*É primeiro de agosto* (It's the first of August)—are expressed with ordinal numbers, as in *É vinte e seis de julho* (It's July 26). In Portuguese the day comes first, followed by the month, so the example in the previous sentence is how you might answer the question *Que dia é hoje?* (What day is today?)

The months are usually associated with seasons, and since Brazil is below the equator, these happen in different months as compared to the United States. See the following.

▼ THE SEASONS IN BRAZIL

Season	English	Months
o verão	the summer	*dezembro, janeiro, fevereiro*
o outono	the fall	*março, abril, maio*
o inverno	the winter	*junho, julho, agosto*
a primavera	the spring	*setembro, outubro, novembro*

Since parts of Brazil are very tropical, the changing of the seasons is not nearly as evident as it is in countries such as the United States or Canada. In fact, sometimes in the northeastern parts of Brazil there is basically a raining or monsoon season, followed by a drought or dry season. When traveling abroad to countries below the equator, always check with the available online resources to find out which "season" they are in.

Exercise: Holidays

Write out the dates in Portuguese for the following holidays. Check your answers in Appendix C.

1. *O Dia da Indepedência dos Estados Unidos* (Independence Day):

   _____

2. *O Dia dos Namorados* (Valentine's Day):

   _____

3. *O dia de São Patrício* (Saint Patrick's Day):

   _____

4. *O (Dia de) Natal* (Christmas Day):

   _____

CHAPTER 9

First Conjugation Verbs

Verbs are one of the most important parts of the grammar of a language. Once you learn how to conjugate the basic verbs, you will start making a lot of sense. In this chapter you will learn the first conjugation, or the formation of verbs that end in *–ar* in the infinitive. We will start with regular verbs and move on to verbs with prepositions. Using all these verbs with the vocabulary of "going places" will help you form great sentences in Portuguese!

Regular *–AR* Verbs

There are four main categories of verbs in Portuguese, and the first and most important one of them is the group of verbs that end in *–ar* in the infinitive (for example, *fal**ar*** [to speak]). The infinitive can be understood as the "default" form of the verb, or the form that can change depending on the grammatical context. In English, this is comparable to the "to" form, as in "to walk" or "to speak." The other categories are the verbs that end in *–er* (*com**er*** [to eat]), *–ir* (*dorm**ir*** [to sleep]), and a smaller category of verbs that end in *–or* (*comp**or*** [to compose]). We will review these other categories in the next chapters. For now, look at the following conjugation, which is the model that should be followed for all verbs that end in *–ar*, in the present tense.

▼ *FALAR* (TO SPEAK) IN THE PRESENT TENSE

Portuguese	English
eu falo	I speak
você fala	you speak [one person]
ele/ela fala	he/she speaks
nós falamos	we speak
vocês falam	you (all) speak [more than one person]
eles/elas falam	they speak

Notice that *elas* refers to "they" as in all females, and *eles* refers to all males or a mixed group of persons. The conjugation for *tu* is not mentioned in the previous table (*tu falas* [you speak]) because if you use *você* (you) in order to address one person, you will be understood by all speakers. You might hear the *tu* form, and people will probably conjugate it using the *você* ending, *tu fala* (you speak), though this is considered ungrammatical by many educated speakers. Here is a list of common verbs that end in *–ar*:

▼ COMMON VERBS ENDING IN *–AR*

Portuguese	English
acabar	to finish
achar	to find, to think
ajudar	to help
colocar	to put, to place
começar	to start
comprar	to buy
descansar	to rest
estudar	to study
ficar	to be (situated), to stay
jogar	to play (a sport or a game)
morar	to live
pagar	to pay
tocar	to play (an instrument), to touch
tomar	to drink
trabalhar	to work
viajar	to travel

In order to learn these verbs, try to first memorize them by putting the verbs into lists or categories. Can you divide the previous list into "things that I do often" and "things that I rarely do"? How about dividing the list into "action verbs" and "mental verbs"? Whatever categories you choose to organize the verbs, the important thing is that you find a way to process and arrange these new pieces of information in your brain. Once you have done this, it will be easier to retrieve the information later.

Exercise: Fill in the Blank

Complete the blanks with the correct form of the verb, depending on the subject. Check your answers in Appendix C.

1. *A criança* _____ *futebol.* (The child plays soccer.)
2. *Os jovens* _____ *clarinete.* (The youngsters play clarinet.)
3. *Nós* _____ *português e inglês.* (We speak Portuguese and English.)
4. *Você* _____ *pão todo dia?* (Do you buy bread every day?)
5. *Vocês* _____ *no Brasil?* (Do you [pl.] live in Brazil?)

Exercise: Make a Match

Match the sentence with its missing verb by writing the letter in the blank space.

1. *O concerto* _____ *às cinco horas.*
2. *Você* _____ *basquete?*
3. *Nós* _____ *em Ipanema.*
4. *Eu* _____ *a conta, sempre!*
5. *Os alunos* _____ *muitas horas por dia.*

(a) *estudam* (study)
(b) *pago* (pay)
(c) *joga* (play)
(d) *moramos* (live)
(e) *começa* (starts)

Verbs with Prepositions

Some verbs that end in *–ar* have prepositions that normally go with them. It is possible that they do not correspond to the same prepositions, or do not even need those prepositions, in English. Here are a selected few:

▼ **VERBS THAT NEED PREPOSITIONS**

Portuguese	English
chamar de	to call [someone or something a name]
entrar em	to enter
gostar de	to like
olhar para	to look at
precisar de	to need

It should be noted that the use of *chamar de* is not as common as the more frequent use of *chamar-se*, the reflexive verb used to introduce oneself. In the latter, you don't need a preposition, just the reflexive pronoun, as in *Como você se chama?* (What do you call yourself?) and *Eu me chamo José* (I call myself José). Also important is the fact that the prepositions often "contract" with articles to make up some interesting words:

Ele entra ***num*** *carro.* [*em + um = num*] (He gets into a car.)
Elas gostam ***da*** *música.* [*de + a = da*] (They like the music.)
Eu preciso ***dum*** *lápis.* [*de + um = dum*] (I need a pencil.)

Exercise: Conjugate the Verb

Try your hand at this exercise for prepositional verbs in Portuguese. Conjugate the verb in parentheses and make any changes needed. Check your answers in Appendix C.

Model: *Você (gostar de) a aula de português?* (Do you like the Portuguese class?) > *Você* **gosta da** *aula de português?*

1. *Ele (precisar de) o dicionário.* (He needs the dictionary.)

_____

2. *Você (chamar) essa fruta (de) laranja?* (You call this fruit an orange?)

   _____

3. *Eles (gostar de) a comida.* (They like the food.)

   _____

4. *Os alunos (entrar em) a biblioteca.* (The students enter the library.)

   _____

5. *Eu não (entrar em) um banco sem documentos.* (I don't enter a bank without documents.)

   _____

Vocabulary: Going Places

In order to use most of these new verbs, you should learn the names of many places in Portuguese. In this section we will find out the places where you can do things such as *comprar* (to buy), *jogar* (to play), and *estudar* (to study). Let's now match verbs and places!

▼ **COMMON PLACES**

Portuguese	English
o açougue	the butcher shop
a banca de revista	the newsstand
o banco	the bank
o cabelereiro	the hairdresser
a farmácia/a drogaria	the drugstore
a feira	the street market
o lava a seco	the dry cleaners
a livraria	the bookstore
a loja	the store
a padaria	the bakery
o restaurante	the restaurant
a papelaria	the stationery store
o salão de beleza	the beauty salon
a sapataria	the shoe store
o shopping	the mall
o supermercado	the supermarket

As you can see, many words are cognates; for example, *banco* (bank), *farmácia* (pharmacy), and *restaurante* (restaurant). There are some words that come from the English language, such as *shopping*, which means "mall," and the phrase *cyber café*. The *açougue* is not a common place anymore because most *supermercados* sell fresh meat and poultry in more hygienic conditions. But you can still find some *açougues* in many cities and towns. There are many *bancas de revistas* (newsstands) all over big cities in Brazil where you can buy the latest magazines and newspapers. They also sell phone cards, which are needed in order to use the public phones. In drugstores, usually only pharmaceutical products are sold, except for the occasional soap or lotion. There are many *padarias* (bakeries) around, sometimes two on the same street, and you can buy fresh bread there every day. These *padarias* double as *pastelarias* (pastry shops), where you can also buy all kinds of baked goods. Most men still go to the *barbeiro* (barber) instead of the *cabelereiro* (hairdresser) to get a haircut. And most establishments advertise themselves as *unisex*, meaning they can take care of both sexes, just to make sure that the male clientele also patronize them. Nowadays, supermarkets in Brazil sell fresh fruits and vegetables. But you can still find Saturday or mid-week *feiras* (street markets) in most cities, where you can buy anything from edibles to arts and crafts. Finally, the word *loja* applies to any store, so you can say *loja de sapatos* for a shoe store or *loja de roupa* for a clothing store. The following is a list of places and some of the products that are usually associated with these places:

- *Supermercado: queijo* (cheese), *pão* (bread), *leite* (milk), *ovos* (eggs), *feijão* (beans), *arroz* (rice)
- *Padaria: pão* (bread), *bolos* (cakes), *bolachas* (crackers), *leite* (milk), *queijo* (cheese), *presunto* (ham), *frios* (cold cuts)
- *Livraria: livros* (books), *revistas* (magazines), *CDs*, *jornais* (newspapers)
- *Papelaria: papel* (paper), *canetas* (pens), *lápis* (pencils), *cartões* (cards)
- *Banca: jornais* (newspapers), *revistas* (magazines), *cartões telefônicos* (phone cards)
- *Farmácia: remédios* (medicine), *perfumes* (perfume), *loções* (lotions)

Exercise: Where Can I Buy . . . ?

Notice that many foods or products can be bought in a variety of places. Now try to determine where you can buy these products in the following exercise. Write down a couple of places where you can buy these products. Check your answers in Appendix C.

1. *pão* (bread): _____, _____
2. *revistas* (magazines): _____, _____
3. *leite* (milk): _____, _____
4. *frutas* (fruit): _____, _____
5. *bolos* (cakes): _____, _____

Vocabulary: Routine Activities

In a normal day in Brazil, many activities that you perform might be first conjugation verbs. Take a look at some of them here.

▼ **ROUTINE ACTIVITIES**

Portuguese	English
acordar(–se)	to wake up
almoçar	to have lunch
brincar com os filhos	to play with the children
escovar os dentes	to brush (the) teeth
descansar	to rest
jantar	to have dinner
levantar(–se)	to get up (from bed)
pegar os filhos	to pick up the children
tomar café (da manhã)	to have breakfast (literally to drink coffee in the A.M.)
tomar banho	to take a shower
trabalhar	to work
voltar pra casa	to go back home

Notice that all of these verbs end in *–ar,* but that does not mean that all routine verbs do so. There are plently of verbs about routine—*assistir* *televisão* (to watch television), *ir para a cama* (to go to bed), *fazer a barba* (to shave)—that end in another way and thus belong to the second or third conjugations. You will see these verbs in later chapters.

Exercise: Put Them in Order

Try to put these sentences in a logical sequence by writing the numbers in the correct order in the spaces provided. Check your answers in Appendix C.

1. *Anne almoça com os amigos.* _____
2. *Anne brinca com os gatos.* _____
3. *Anne volta para casa.* _____
4. *Anne trabalha na universidade.* _____
5. *Anne se acorda às 8 da manhã.* _____

CHAPTER 10

Second Conjugation and Beyond

After the first conjugation comes the second. In this chapter you will learn how to conjugate the verbs that end in *–er*, *–ir*, and even the less common *–or*. We will also practice with very common second conjugation verbs, which are a bit irregular. We will finish up with the vocabulary related to family and family relations so that you can use the just-learned verb *ter* (to have) with these words. Have fun!

Regular *–ER* and *–IR* Verbs

Verbs that end in *–er* when written in the infinitive are called the "second conjugation." By the same token, verbs that end in *–ir* are named "third conjugation." Beyond that, there are some verbs in Portuguese that end in *–or* in the infinitive. Now that you know how the verbs of the first conjugation are written, here are the verbs from the second and third conjugations.

▼ ***COMER* (TO EAT) IN THE PRESENT TENSE**

Portuguese	English
eu como	I eat
você come	you eat [one person]
ele/ela come	he/she eats
nós comemos	we eat
vocês comem	you (all) eat [more than one person]
eles/elas comem	they eat

As with the verb *falar* (to speak) of the first conjugation, the *tu* (you [singular]) form is conjugated as *tu comes* (you eat). Again, it is not necessary to learn this form because if you use *você*, you will be understood. But you might hear the *tu* form in some parts of Brazil. What about the third conjugation? The good news is that except for the *nós* form, it is exactly the same as the second conjugation. See the following table.

▼ *ABRIR* (TO OPEN) IN THE PRESENT TENSE

Portuguese	English
eu abro	I open
você abre	you open [one person]
ele/ela abre	he/she opens
nós abrimos	we open
vocês abrem	you (all) open [more than one person]
eles/elas abrem	they open

The conjugation rule states that in order to say verbs correctly, you have to drop the *–er* or *–ir* of the infinitive and add the previous endings, according to the subject. Following are lists of common verbs that end in *–er* and *–ir* and follow this same rule.

▼ COMMON VERBS ENDING IN *–ER*

Portuguese	English	Portuguese	English
aprender	to learn	*escrever*	to write
atender	to answer the phone, to wait on	*ler*	to read
beber	to drink	*querer*	to want
comer	to eat	*receber*	to receive
compreender	to understand, to comprehend	*responder*	to answer
correr	to run	*vender*	to sell
entender	to understand	*viver*	to live
escolher	to choose		

▼ **COMMON VERBS ENDING IN *–IR***

Portuguese	English	Portuguese	English
aplaudir	to applaud	*impedir*	to impede
assistir (a)	to attend, to watch	*investir*	to invest
competir	to compete	*partir*	to leave
conseguir	to achieve, to get	*permitir*	to allow
construir	to construct	*reagir*	to react
curtir	to enjoy [slang]	*rir*	to laugh
dormir	to sleep	*transferir*	to transfer
exigir	to demand		

Just as you did with the previous chapter, try to put these verbs into separate categories, such as active versus passive verbs or even positive versus negative verbs. Categorizing new vocabulary according to your own worldview helps you to truly learn a language.

Exercise: Fill in the Verb

Try your hand at these exercises to practice your verbs even more. Fill in the blanks with the correct form of the verb, depending on the subject. Check your answers in Appendix C.

1. *A criança* _____ *o sanduíche.* (The child eats the sandwich.)
2. *Os jovens* _____ *o filme.* (The youngsters watch the movie.)
3. *Nós* _____ *oito horas por dia.* (We sleep eight hours a day.)
4. *Você* _____ *nos Estados Unidos?* (Do you live in the United States?)
5. *Vocês* _____ *às perguntas?* (Do you [pl.] answer the questions?)

Exercise: The Right Match

Match the sentence with its missing verb by writing the letter in the blank space.

1. *Minha amiga* _____ *o telefone imediatamente.* (a) *comemos* (eat)
2. *Essa livraria* _____ *livros e revistas?* (b) *parto* (leave)
3. *Nós sempre* _____ *neste restaurante.* (c) *riem* (laugh)
4. *Eu* _____ *amanhã para o Rio!* (d) *vende* (sell)
5. *Os amigos* _____ *muito com a comédia.* (e) *atende* (answer)

Special –*IR* Verbs

All the verbs similar to *servir* (to serve) and *dormir* (to sleep), which have these same vowels before the last syllable, undergo a special change, aside from the regular conjugation. This change is regular for all of these types of verbs in the first person singular or the *eu* (I) form. Following is a model of this conjugation.

▼ SPECIAL VERB: *SERVIR* (TO SERVE)

Portuguese	English
eu sirvo	I serve
você serve	you serve
ele/ela serve	he/she serves
nós servimos	we serve
vocês servem	you (all) serve
eles/elas servem	they serve

Other verbs that follow the same model are: *mentir*, meaning "to tell a lie" (*eu minto*); *preferir*, meaning "to prefer" (*eu prefiro*); *repetir*, meaning "to repeat" (*eu repito*); and *seguir*, meaning "to follow" (*eu sigo*).

The next table shows the other special –*ir* verb.

▼ SPECIAL VERB: *DORMIR* (TO SLEEP)

Portuguese	English
eu durmo	I sleep
você dorme	you sleep
ele/ela dorme	he/she sleeps

nós dormimos	we sleep
vocês dormem	you (all) sleep
eles/elas dormem	they sleep

A few verbs have the vowel *–u–* in the infinitive, and their conjugation is somewhat of the flipside of the previous ones. Instead of only the *eu* form changing, every other form changes, while *eu* and *nós* keep the same regular vowel of the infinitive. Here is a model of this kind of verb.

▼ **SPECIAL VERB: *SUBIR* (TO GO UP)**

Portuguese	English
eu subo	I go up
você sobe	you go up
ele/ela sobe	he/she goes up
nós subimos	we go up
vocês sobem	you (all) go up
eles/elas sobem	they go up

Exercise: Regular and Special Verbs

Let's see what you have learned. Try to complete the following exercise. Fill in the blanks with the correct conjugations of the verbs in parentheses. Check your answers in Appendix C.

1. *O garçom* _____ *a cerveja no restaurante, e eu* _____ *vinho em casa. (servir)*
2. *Eu* _____ *as escadas e a secretária* _____ *pelo elevador. (subir)*
3. *Meus amigos* _____ *oito horas por dia, mas eu só* _____ *seis horas. (dormir)*
4. *A aluna* _____ *as frases, e eu* _____ *a tarefa de casa. (repetir)*
5. *Eu não* _____ *muito, mas minha irmã* _____ *demais! (mentir)*

To Go and to Come: *Ir* and *Vir*

Two very common verbs in Portuguese (as well as in English) are *ir* (to go) and *vir* (to come). They can be used with direction prepositions, *a* or *para*, both meaning "to" or "toward." Here is a sample dialogue:

Q: Márcia: *Oi, Júlio, tudo bem?* (Hi Júlio, how is it going?)
A: Júlio: *Tudo bem, Márcia.* (All right, Márcia.)
Q: Márcia: *Para onde você* ***vai****?* (Where are you going?)
A: Júlio: ***Vou*** *para o clube, fazer ginástica.* (I'm going to the gym, to do a workout.)
Q: Márcia: *Que legal, você gosta do clube?* (Great, do you like the gym?)
A: Júlio: *Eu adoro, mas não* ***vou*** *com freqüência.* (I love it, but I don't go often.)
Q: Márcia: *Eu também não.* (Neither do I.)
A: Júlio: *Então* ***vamos*** *juntos?* (So let's go together?)
Q: Márcia: *Opa, tá combinado!* (Hey, it's a date!)

Here is the full conjugation for the verb *ir* (to go).

▼ **THE VERB *IR* (TO GO)**

Portuguese	English
eu vou	I go
você vai	you go
ele/ela vai	he/she goes
nós vamos	we go
vocês vão	you (all) go
eles/elas vão	they go

You will use this verb a lot in Portuguese. In addition, much like in English, this verb is used in constructing the future tense.

▼ **FUTURE TENSE WITH *IR***

Ir [conjugated]	VERB [infinitive]	Translation
eu vou	*falar*	I'm going to speak
você vai	*dormir*	You're going to sleep
nós vamos	*beber*	We're going to drink
elas vão	*jogar*	They're going to play

Use the present tense of the verb *ir* and add the infinitive of the other verb, as in English "going to + verb," and you're done! There is another future tense in Portuguese, which is not a combination of verbs, but a "one-word" tense. We will look at that conjugation in upcoming chapters. At this point, just know that the future tense with *ir* is the most common future structure spoken. This same kind of future tense can also be expressed using the previous structure and the verb *vir* (to come). Here is the full conjugation of this verb in the present tense.

▼ **THE VERB *VIR* (TO COME)**

Portuguese	English
eu venho	I come
você vem	you come
ele/ela vem	he/she comes
nós vimos	we come
vocês vêm	you (all) come
eles/elas vêm	they come

In English you could also imply future tense if you say "I'm *coming* to see," for example, as well as "I'm going to see." In Portuguese the same is true for the verb *vir* (to come). But most of the time you will use this verb by itself to ask where people come from, as in the following dialogue.

Q: Jonas: *De onde você* ***vem****?* (Where are you coming from?)
A: Cleuza: *Eu?* ***Venho*** *da feira, e você?* (Me? I'm coming from the market, how about you?)

Q: Jonas: ***Venho*** *do banco.* (I'm coming from the bank.)
A: Cleuza: *Ótimo, então você tem mais dinheiro do que eu.* (Great, so you have more money than I do.)

The most important aspect to remember is that the verb *vir* (to come) is usually followed by the preposition *de* (from), which in combination with an article—*o* or *a*—changes, as the previous dialogue indicates.

Exercise: Using *Ir* and *Vir*

Now try to see how much you got from this famous pair of verbs. Fill in the blanks with the appropriate verb and form. Check your answers in Appendix C.

1. *Eu* _____ *do cabelereiro.* (I come from the hairdresser.)
2. *As garotas* _____ *para a casa.* (The girls go/are going home.)
3. *Nós* _____ *do banco.* (We come from the bank.)
4. *Meus amigos* _____ *para a escola todo dia.* (My friends go to school every day.)
5. *Eu* _____ *para o trabalho de carro.* (I go to work by car.)
6. *Os vizinhos* _____ *do parque.* (The neighbors come from the park.)

To Have: *Ter*

Two verbs that are very common and used in Portuguese are *ter* (to have) and *ver* (to see). *Ter* in particular can be used in many different situations. See the full conjugation in the present tense here:

▼ **THE VERB *TER* (TO HAVE)**

Portuguese	English
eu tenho	I have
você tem	you have

Portuguese	English
ele/ela tem	he/she has
nós temos	we have
vocês têm	you (all) have
eles/elas têm	they have

Notice that the verb is actually irregular, as compared to the other *–er* verbs. But since it is so frequently used, it is learned very fast. The pronunciation for the third person singular *tem* (has) and plural *têm* (have) are exactly the same. As in English, this verb conveys the notion of possession of or relationship to either a concrete or abstract entity. See the following examples.

A professora tem muitos alunos. (The teacher has a lot of students.)
Eu tenho um livro interessante. (I have an interesting book.)
Meus amigos têm meu número de telefone. (My friends have my phone number.)
A aluna tem uma prova amanhã. (The student has an exam tomorrow.)

Aside from expressing possession of or relationship to, this verb is also used when describing people, in sentences such as *Ele tem olhos verdes* (He has green eyes) and *Ela tem cabelo castanho* (She has brown hair), for example.

There is also an impersonal usage of *ter.* By impersonal we mean that there is no clear subject, and the sentence is normally translated as "there is/are." This usage is also referred to as the "existential" use of *ter.* Use this verb when you want to report on what "exists" in some place or situation, as in the following sample sentences:

Tem um livro em cima da mesa. (There is a book on the table.)
Tem muitos alunos na sala de aula. (There are many students in the classroom.)
Tem muita gente no banco. (There are a lot of people in the bank.)
Tem uma padaria aqui perto. (There is a bakery near here.)

Notice that the verb does not change, regardless of the number of the noun that follows; it's always the third person singular form, *tem*.

Finally, the verb *ter* can be used within a structure to mean "obligation." In this case, it is very similar to the structure in English "have to," as in the examples that follow:

▼ OBLIGATION: *TER QUE* + VERB

[subject]	*Ter* [conjugated]	*que*	Verb [infinitive]
Eu	*tenho*	*que*	*comer verduras.*
I have to eat vegetables.			
Você	*tem*	*que*	*assinar os documentos.*
You have to sign the documents.			
Nós	*temos*	*que*	*dormir oito horas.*
We have to sleep eight hours.			

Notice that the first verb, *ter*, is conjugated according to the person. The second verb is not conjugated—it's in the infinitive.

Exercise: Using *Ter*

Fill in the blanks with the correct form of the verb *ter* (to have). Check your answers in Appendix C.

1. *Eu* _____ *dois carros.* (I have two cars.)
2. *Minha amiga* _____ *pouca paciência.* (My friend has little patience.)
3. *Nós* _____ *uma casa no Rio.* (We have a house in Rio.)
4. *Eles não* _____ *aula na sexta.* (They don't have class on Friday.)
5. *O menino* _____ *olhos azuis.* (The boy has blue eyes.)
6. _____ *duas janelas na sala.* (There are two windows in the room.)

Vocabulary: Family Relations

One of the most useful batches of vocabulary you will learn in a second language includes the names of family relations. The following are some of the basic words:

▼ **FAMILY RELATIONS**

Portuguese	English	Portuguese	English
pai	father	*avó*	grandmother
papai	dad, daddy	*vovó*	grandma, granny
mãe	mother	*neto*	grandson
mamãe	mom, mommy	*neta*	granddaughter
filho	son	*bisavô*	great-grandfather
filha	daughter	*bisavó*	great-grandmother
irmão	brother	*sobrinho*	nephew
irmã	sister	*sobrinha*	niece
primo	cousin (male)	*padrasto*	stepfather
prima	cousin (female)	*madrasta*	stepmother
tio	uncle	*padrinho*	godfather
tia	aunt	*madrinha*	godmother
avô	grandfather	*afilhado*	godson
vovô	grandpa	*afilhada*	goddaughter

Remember, as with any other list of words in a second language, try to put them in categories. Perhaps list the relations that you have and the ones that you do not. Another practice tip is to list the names of all your family members according to their family relation. The following is a list of additional relatives:

▼ **MORE RELATIONS**

Portuguese	English
marido, esposo	husband
mulher, esposa	wife
sogro	father-in-law
sogra	mother-in-law

Portuguese	English
genro	son-in-law
nora	daughter-in-law
cunhado	brother-in-law
cunhada	sister-in-law
namorado	boyfriend
namorada	girlfriend
noivo	fiancé, groom
noiva	fiancée, bride

Always use family relations along with a possessive adjective: Say *meu pai* for "my father" and *minha mãe* for "my mother." The plural of these words usually takes the masculine form: *Meus pais* means "my parents" (not "my fathers"), *meus avós* means "my grandparents," and *meus filhos* means "my children," including both males and females. If only females are included, then use the feminine plural form, as in *minhas filhas* (my daughters), *minhas netas* (my granddaughters), *minhas sobrinhas* (my nieces), and so forth. Be careful with a common false cognate that stumps students: *Meus parentes* means "my relatives," not my parents.

What about a person's marital status? In Brazil the *estado civil* has to do with a person's civil status before the law. Here are some basic vocabulary words to help convey civil status:

▼ CIVIL STATUS

Portuguese	English
solteiro, solteira	single
casado, casada	married
separado, separada	separated
divorciado, divorciada	divorced
viúvo, viúva	widower, widow

One important thing to remember is that in Portuguese we do not use the "apostrophe" to express possession. So, if you want to say, for example, "my brother's wife," you would have to say *a esposa do meu irmão* or "the spouse of my brother," literally. Make sure that when you do so, you make any changes to the preposition *de* (of), as in the example *a irmã da minha mãe* (the sister of my mother, or, my aunt).

Exercise: Who Is It?

Complete the blanks with the correct family name. Check your answers in Appendix C.

1. *O filho do meu filho é o meu* _____.
2. *A irmã da minha mãe é a minha* _____.
3. *Os filhos dos meus tios são os meus* _____.
4. *A mãe da minha mãe é a minha* _____.
5. *Os pais dos meu pai são os meus* _____.
6. *O marido da minha irmã é o meu* _____.

CHAPTER 11

Important Verbs to Know

Though you've already become acquainted with a number of Portuguese verbs, there are some verbs that are important enough to be introduced separately. They are *haver* (to exist/to be), *fazer* (to do), *acabar* (to finish), and the duo *saber* and *conhecer* (to know). You'll become a whiz in Portuguese once you master these frequently used verbs.

To Be or to Exist: *Haver*

One of the most common verbs in Portuguese (as well as in English) is the verb "to have." In the previous chapter you learned how to use *ter* in expressing possession, obligation, or simply existence. The verb *haver* used to have the same function of *ter* in many instances, but now it has a more specialized usage. Here are the conjugations of *haver*:

▼ **THE VERB *HAVER***

Conjugated	Verb Tense	English
há	present indicative	there is/there are
havia	imperfect	there was/there were
houve	preterite	there was/there were
haverá	future	there will be
tinha havido	present perfect	there had been
haja	present subjunctive	there is/are
houvesse	imperfect subjunctive	there was/were
houver	future subjunctive	there will be
haveria	conditional	there would be

You will probably only use a couple of these forms initially. The verb does not have the traditional subject pronoun conjugations, and it basically expresses the idea of "there is/there are," also called the existential use. Third person singular forms are used in both singular and plural contexts, as in the following examples.

Há *muitas pessoas na rua.* (There are lots of people in the street.)
Não ***houve*** *possibilidade de vê-lo.* (There was no possibility to see him.)
Haja *paciência com aquele menino!* ([One should] have patience with that boy!)

The verb *haver* is also used as an auxiliary verb in compound verbal phrases, but it is less used nowadays in Brazilian Portuguese. Examples are *eu havia feito* (I had done), which is normally said with the verb *ter* in conversational Brazilian Portuguese, as in *eu tinha feito* (I had done). In some more traditional grammars, both verbs are listed as helping verbs in the same compound structures! Here are some more examples with the verb *haver*:

Ela ***havia*** *feito um bolo.* (She had made a cake.)
Eles ***haviam*** *comprado um carro.* (They had bought a car.)

Alert

The form of the verb following *haver* is called the past participle. This form also exists in English, such as "done" and "written." Sometimes both the past and the past participle are the same form: "put." This might produce confusion for English speakers, but the past participles in Portuguese are very different and will be explained in a later chapter.

To Make or to Do: *Fazer*

One of the most useful verbs in Portuguese is the verb *fazer*, which is used in many idiomatic expressions. Following are the conjugations for this irregular (but very common) verb:

▼ **THE VERB *FAZER* (TO MAKE, TO DO)**

Subject	Present	English	Preterite	English
eu	*faço*	I do	*fiz*	I did
você	*faz*	you do	*fez*	you did
ele/ela	*faz*	he/she does	*fez*	he/she did
nós	*fazemos*	we do	*fizemos*	we did
vocês	*fazem*	you (plural) do	*fizeram*	you (plural) did
eles/elas	*fazem*	they do	*fizeram*	they did

Here is a sample dialogue using this verb:

Ele fez o dever de casa? (Did he do the homework?)
Sim, fez. E você? (Yes, he did. And you?)
Eu ainda não fiz. (I didn't do it yet.)
Vamos fazer juntos? (You want to do it together?)
Sim, mas faz tanto sol lá fora! (Yes, but it's so sunny outside!)

Expressions with *Fazer*

You might have noticed that in the last dialogue we expressed the weather with the verb *fazer.* Here are other weather or climate expressions that take this verb:

▼ **EXPRESSING WEATHER WITH *FAZER***

Portugese	English
Faz (muito) sol.	It's (very) sunny.
Faz (muito) frio.	It's (very) cold.
Faz (muito) calor.	It's (very) hot.

Not all expressions of weather employ the verb *fazer.* Here are other expressions:

▼ **EXPRESSING WEATHER**

Portuguese	English
Neva (muito).	It snows (a lot).
Chove (muito).	It rains (a lot).
Venta (muito).	It is windy (a lot).

Other expressions with the verb *fazer* probably make very little sense when translated literally to English. Here are some of those expressions, which are very common in Brazilian Portuguese:

▼ **EXPRESSIONS WITH *FAZER***

Portuguese	English
fazer anos	to celebrate one's birthday
fazer a barba	to shave
fazer de conta	to pretend; literally, to make count
fazer compras	to shop; literally, to make purchases
fazer falta	to be missed; to lack
fazer greve	to go on strike
fazer as pazes	to make peace

Exercise: Multiple Choice

Choose one of the multiple choices for each question. Check your answers in Appendix C.

1. The workers are getting very low wages, so . . .
   a. *eles fazem greve.*
   b. *eles fazem a barba.*
   c. *eles fazem anos.*
   d. *eles fazem de conta.*

2. My nephew is having all of his friends over for a party.
   a. *Ele faz de conta.*
   b. *Ele faz greve.*
   c. *Ele faz anos.*
   d. *Ele faz falta.*

3. He has that five o'clock shadow, so . . .
   a. *ele decide fazer de conta.*
   b. *ele decide fazer greve.*
   c. *ele decide fazer compras.*
   d. *ele decide fazer a barba.*

4. Maria has practically nothing in the fridge, so . . .
   a. *ela vai fazer de conta.*
   b. *ela vai fazer compras.*
   c. *ela vai fazer anos.*
   d. *ela vai fazer a barba.*

5. They were mad at each other, but not anymore. That means that . . .
   a. *eles fizeram de conta.*
   b. *eles fizeram as pazes.*
   c. *eles fizeram compras.*
   d. *eles fizeram greve.*

To Know: *Saber* and *Conhecer*

In Portuguese there are two verbs that express the idea of "knowing." The verb *saber* is used when you want to express the notion that you know a piece of information that can be reproduced, such as a set of numbers. For example, *ela sabe o meu número de telefone* (she knows my phone number). Similarly, if you say *eles sabem cantar a canção do Roberto Carlos* (they know how to sing Roberto Carlos's song), that means that they have the skill to do it. On the other hand, the verb *conhecer* is used when you want to communicate that you are familiar or acquainted with a person, place, or object. For example, if you say *nós conhecemos o nordeste do Brasil* (we know the northeast of Brazil), this means that you are acquainted with that geographical location, because you perhaps visited there, and so on. The same verb is used when talking about people you know, because you are familiar or acquainted with them.

Alert

Both of these verbs are regular *–er* verbs, except for the first person singular, or the *eu* (I) form: *eu sei* and *eu conheço* (I know). The rest of the subject pronouns follow the same endings for regular verbs, that is *sabe, sabemos, sabem,* and *conhece, conhecemos,* and *conhecem.*

Following is a chart that helps you see the different usages of *saber* and *conhecer*:

▼ WHEN TO USE *SABER* AND *CONHECER*

Use *Saber*: Before information, such as numbers, dates **Example:** *Ela sabe a hora.* (She knows the time.)
Use *Saber*: Before particles *que* (that), *qual* (which), *quando* (when) **Example:** *Eu sei que . . .* (I know that . . .)
Use *Saber*: Before a verb in the infinitive (*–r*) **Example:** *Ela sabe cozinhar.* (She knows how to cook.)
Use *Conhecer*: Before people **Example:** *Você conhece Teresa?* (Do you know Teresa?)
Use *Conhecer*: Before places **Example:** *Eles conhecem o Rio.* (They know Rio.)
Use *Conhecer*: Before familiar objects **Example:** *Nós conhecemos esse livro.* (We know this book.)

It is important to understand that there are gray areas in the usage of these verbs, and that native speakers might use them interchangeably in some contexts. Also, in some situations, a poem or piece of music, for example, could become more than just familiar (*conhecer*), and be recited or played perfectly, by heart (*saber*). See how well you know these verbs now.

Exercise: Choose the Verb

Circle the verb that should be used in the sentence. Check your answers in Appendix C.

1. *Elas* ***sabem/conhecem*** *bem a capital do Brasil.* (They know Brazil's capital really well.)
2. *Você* ***sabe/conhece*** *andar de bicicleta?* (Do you know how to ride a bike?)
3. *Nós* ***sabemos/conhecemos*** *os nossos vizinhos.* (We know our neighbors.)
4. *Vocês* ***sabem/conhecem*** *aquela música do Gil?* (Do you guys know that song by Gil?)
5. *Maristela* ***sabe/conhece*** *que Magdale é atriz.* (Maristela knows that Magdale is an actress.)

Exercise: Fill in the Blank

Fill in the blanks with the correct form of either *saber* or *conhecer.* Check your answers in Appendix C.

1. *Eu* _____ *Lisboa, a capital de Portugal.*
2. *Vocês* _____ *o Rio Capibaribe?*
3. *Minha esposa e eu* _____ *dirigir muito bem.*
4. *Eu* _____ *que preciso estudar mais.*
5. *Os nossos amigos* _____ *que estamos juntas.*

More Special Verbs

Some second conjugation verbs are indeed very special because, just like *saber* and *conhecer,* they include a modification in the first person singular, *eu* (I) form. Check out these irregular verbs, and try to find some consistency in them.

ouvir (to hear)

- *eu* ***ouço***
- *você/ele/ela ouve*
- *nós ouvimos*
- *vocês/eles/elas ouvem*

pedir (to ask for)

- *eu* ***peço***
- *você/ele/ela pede*
- *nós pedimos*
- *vocês/eles/elas pedem*

perder (to lose)

- *eu* ***perco***
- *você/ele/ela perde*
- *nós perdemos*
- *vocês/eles/elas perdem*

Notice that the forms are very similar, especially the third person singular forms, such as *pede* (he asks for) and *perde* (he loses). This is particularly true if the final syllable /r/ is not clearly pronounced in speech.

The next set of verbs are from the first, second, and third conjugations.

dar (to give)

- *eu* ***dou***
- *você/ele/ela dá*
- *nós damos*
- *vocês/eles/elas dão*

sair (to leave)

- *eu* ***saio***
- *você/ele/ela sai*
- *nós saímos*
- *vocês/eles/elas saem*

dizer (to say)

- *eu* ***digo***
- *você/ele/ela diz*
- *nós dizemos*
- *vocês/eles/elas dizem*

trazer (to bring)

- *eu* ***trago***
- *você/ele/ela traz*
- *nós trazemos*
- *vocês/eles/elas trazem*

pôr (to put, place)

- *eu* ***ponho***
- *você/ele/ela põe*
- *nós pomos*
- *vocês/eles/elas põem*

In these lists, only the verbs in bold represent some kind of unexpected deviation from the regular conjugation. But notice that even with their irregularities, these verbs have some kind of system, be it the insertion of a *–g–* (*digo, trago*) or the leaving out of an *–e–*, making the form end in a *–z* (*diz, traz*). As you learn these verbs, try to use them in real-life situations, such as the ones included in the following exercises.

Exercise: Translate

Translate the following sentences to Portuguese. Check your answers in Appendix C.

1. She loses the keys frequently.

   _____

2. Mário always asks for *guaraná* at the restaurant.

   _____

3. Sabrina never tells the truth.

   _____

4. We bring the books to school.

   _____

5. Mário and Maria put the cups on the table.

   _____

Exercise: Make a Match

Match the sentences on the left with the verbs that fit in the blanks. Check your answers in Appendix C.

1. *Eu* _____ *as chaves do carro.*		(a) *saio*
2. *Eu* _____ *música muito alto.*		(b) *digo*
3. *Eu* _____ *os livros para a aula.*		(c) *ponho*
4. *Eu* _____ *a verdade à mamãe.*		(d) *ouço*
5. *Eu* _____ *o lápis na mesa.*		(e) *trago*
6. *Eu* _____ *de casa muito cedo.*		(f) *perco*

CHAPTER 12

Verb Tenses: An Overview

By now you've had a pretty solid introduction to the Portuguese language. You've learned a lot of vocabulary, how to handle certain social situations, and when to use some of the more important verbs in the language. Now it's time to focus on verb tenses. This chapter covers the present tense, the preterite and imperfect past tenses, and the future and conditional tenses. Use this chapter as your verb reference!

Present Tense

The present tense in Portuguese, as in any other language, is necessary to express ideas of habitual activities, to state the present situation, and even to explain what is happening at the time of speech. Sometimes we use the present tense to talk about future actions, if it is allowed by the context. Following is a chart with the present tenses of all the verb conjugations in Portuguese.

▼ THE PRESENT TENSE: REGULAR ENDINGS

Subject	–ar	–er	–ir
eu	*falo*	*como*	*durmo*
você	*fala*	*come*	*dorme*
ele/ela	*fala*	*come*	*dorme*
nós	*falamos*	*comemos*	*dormimos*
vocês	*falam*	*comem*	*dormem*
eles/elas	*falam*	*comem*	*dormem*

To conjugate a verb, simply drop the infinitive endings (*–ar, –er, –ir*) and add the endings that are in bold, according to the grammatical subject. Do this for all verbs, as long as they follow the regular pattern. The previous table shows clearly that there is some consistency when it comes to the present tense, if you do not count the irregular first person singular forms from the last chapter—*ouço* (I hear), *peço* (I ask for), *saio* (I leave), *dou* (I give). For one thing, the *você* (you) and *ele/ela* (he/she) forms are the same. The *vocês* (you [pl.]) and *eles/elas* (they) forms are also written exactly the same. If you look across the table, you will see that all third person singular forms end in a vowel and that all of the third person plural forms end in the consonant *–m*. In addition, all the *nós* (we) forms end in *–mos*, which makes it easier to identify the subject by looking at the end of the verb.

Essential

Portuguese is a "pro-drop" language, which means that because there is such rich verb morphology (there are so many different verb endings), we do not need to say the subject pronoun in order to be understood, unlike in English, where you need to state the subject explicitly all of the time. Learning verb endings is essential to speaking Portuguese fluently.

Preterite Tense

The two past tenses in Portuguese convey ideas of actions and states in the past before the time of utterance, or before what is conceived as the present. They relate not only to actions but also to conditions and situations in the past. The preterite tense is used when speakers try to convey ideas that relate to punctual actions in the past, usually within a clearly defined point in time. So, if you say *Eu visit**ei** o Brasil no ano passado* (I visited Brazil last year), you have identified an action that happened in the past, within a certain time frame. Here are the regular endings for verbs in the past, in the three major conjugations:

▼ THE PRETERITE TENSE: REGULAR VERBS

Subject	*–ar*	*–er*	*–ir*
eu	*fal**ei***	*com**i***	*dorm**i***
você	*fal**ou***	*com**eu***	*dorm**iu***
ele/ela	*fal**ou***	*com**eu***	*dorm**iu***
nós	*fal**amos***	*com**emos***	*dorm**imos***
vocês	*fal**aram***	*com**eram***	*dorm**iram***
eles/elas	*fal**aram***	*com**eram***	*dorm**iram***

Like the present tense, the preterite tense, aside from its seemingly diverse list of endings, has its own internal consistency. The first person has the same ending for the *–er* and *–ir* conjugations, and the second and third persons share the exact same endings. The *nós* form is the same as the present, but should be understood as relating to past actions according to the context of the sentence or situation. Finally, both the second and third person plural are the same.

Alert

Be careful! The *–eu* ending for the *você/ele, ela* forms (*ele comeu* [he ate]) is often used by students for the first person, *eu*. It would be so very nice if it could be done in this way! But unfortunately, the past tense forms for the first person end in either *–ei* or *–i* (*eu falei* [I spoke]; *eu comi* [I ate]) as you may have noticed in the table.

There are several verbs, very common ones in fact, that do not follow this regular system. They are listed here and should each be learned individually.

▼ THE PRETERITE TENSE: IRREGULAR VERBS

Changes in the First Person Only	
Verb	**Conjugation**
chegar (to arrive)	*cheguei, chegou, chegamos, chegaram* (arrived)
explicar (to explain)	*expliquei, explicou, explicamos, explicaram* (explained)
dançar (to dance)	*dancei, dançou, dançamos, dançaram* (danced)

Changes in All Persons	
Verb	Conjugation
poder (to be able to)	*pude, pôde, pudemos, puderam* (was/were able to)
querer (to want)	*quis, quis, quisemos, quiseram* (wanted)
saber (to know)	*soube, soube, soubemos, souberam* (knew)
trazer (to bring)	*trouxe, trouxe, trouxemos, trouxeram* (brought)
ver (to see)	*vi, viu, vimos, viram* (saw)
vir (to come, arrive)	*vim, veio, viemos, vieram* (came, arrived)

The first three verbs in the previous table have only one change in the first person singular, *eu* (I). Even so, the change is only there to make sure that the pronunciation does not change in the conjugated forms. If the *–u–* was not inserted in *cheguei*, the *–g–* next to the *–ei* would have sounded like the *g* in the English word "gel" and not like in the English word "gal." The same principle was followed in the phonetic change to *–qu–* in the *expliquei* form. The other verbs listed have overall changes in all grammatical persons. The last two verbs, *ver* (to see) and *vir* (to come), are very similar in the past tense and must be learned together, especially the first person singular *vim* (I came) versus *vi* (I saw), where the only difference is a nasal versus an oral vowel.

Imperfect Tense

In Portuguese, as in other Romance languages, there is a separate past tense to relate to conditions and situations in the past not covered by the preterite. The imperfect tense is used to refer to habitual and continuous actions in the past, and there are other usages too. Thus, the verb tense is difficult to translate in English because it could have at least three interpretations. For example, if I say *Eu andava*, that sentence could mean "I walked," "I would walk," "I used to walk," or "I was walking." Many Portuguese grammars are dedicated to the presentation of this verb tense and how it relates to the preterite. Following is the conjugation for the imperfect verb tense:

▼ THE IMPERFECT TENSE: REGULAR VERBS

Subject	–ar	–er	–ir
eu	*falava*	*comia*	*dormia*
você	*falava*	*comia*	*dormia*
ele/ela	*falava*	*comia*	*dormia*
nós	*falávamos*	*comíamos*	*dormíamos*
vocês	*falavam*	*comiam*	*dormiam*
eles/elas	*falavam*	*comiam*	*dormiam*

As can be seen in the previous table, the verb tense is very regular, despite its name being "imperfect." As far as verb tenses go, this one is very student-friendly. For one, the first three grammatical persons are conjugated exactly the same. Second, the first person plural has an accent across the board, in all conjugations. Finally, the *vocês* and *eles* forms are also exactly alike, as in all other conjugations. The trick with this verb is to concentrate on its many usages, which can be very distinct. However, there are some irregular imperfect verbs:

▼ THE IMPERFECT TENSE: IRREGULAR VERBS

Verb	Conjugation
ser (to be)	*era*, *éramos*, *eram* (were, used to be)
ter (to have)	*tinha*, *tínhamos*, *tinham* (had, used to have)
vir (to come)	*vinha*, *vínhamos*, *vinham* (came, used to come)
pôr (to put)	*punha*, *púnhamos*, *punham* (put, used to put)

These are among the few irregular verbs in the imperfect tense, which makes it a very "regular" and consistent verb tense. Notice that three out of four verbs have the *–nh–* combination, making it easier to identify this tense. The next section goes into more detail about the differences between the "preterite" and the "imperfect."

The Preterite Versus the Imperfect

So, how do you know when to use one past tense or the other? The following is a handy list of guidelines, along with some examples.

▼ PRETERITE VERSUS IMPERFECT USAGE

Preterite	Imperfect
Punctual Actions	Continuous Actions
Time frame is often indicated	Time frame is less important or nonexistent
Action often happens only once	Action happens over and over, or is ongoing
Many times used with action verbs	Many times used with nonaction verbs
Used in narratives, consecutive actions	Used in descriptions, with simultaneous actions or conditions
Not used to tell time	Used to tell time in the past
Not used for age	Used to refer to age in the past

This table will help you to draw a distinction between the two tenses. Other clues to figuring out the correct verb to use are the adverbs (from Latin *ad–* [next to] and *verbum* [verb]). Adverbs are words that are placed close to verbs and modify their meaning, such as "eat fast," where "fast" modifies or "adds to" the meaning of "eat." There are adverbs or adverbial expressions that are more used with each type of past tense. Here is a list:

▼ ADVERBS AND ADVERBIAL EXPRESSIONS WITH PAST TENSES

Mostly Used with Preterite	Mostly Used with Imperfect
ontem (yesterday)	*sempre* (always)
na semana passada (last week)	*ao mesmo tempo* (at the same time)
no mês passado (last month)	*enquanto* (while)
no ano passado (last year)	*quando era pequeno* (when I was little)
de repente (all of a sudden)	*quando era adolescente* (when I was a teenager)
naquele dia (that day)	*todos os dias* (every day)
naquele mês (that month)	*todos os meses* (every month)
naquele ano (that year)	*todos os anos* (every year)

Note that these are not mutually exclusive, that is, I could use the imperfect tense with *naquele dia*, as long as I mean that something happened continuously. So, I could say *Naquele dia chovia muito* (That day it was raining a lot). However, it is true that these expressions are mostly used with the verb tense under which they are listed. Try your hand at these exercises for the use of preterite and imperfect.

Preterite or Imperfect? Exercise A

Circle either the preterite or the imperfect form so that the sentence makes sense. Check your answers in Appendix C.

1. *Quando eu era criança,* ***comi/comia*** *muito chocolate.*
2. *Ontem nós* ***vimos/víamos*** *um filme interessante.*
3. ***Choveu/chovia*** *um pouco quando saímos do cinema.*
4. *Meu pai sempre nos* ***levou/levava*** *para o parque.*
5. *Estava no banho e de repente minha irmã me* ***ligou/ligava****.*
6. *Em Illinois* ***fez/fazia*** *um frio horrível.*

Preterite or Imperfect? Exercise B

Fill in the blanks with the conjugated form of the verb in parentheses. Check your answers in Appendix C.

1. *No mês passado eu* _____*(ir) para Aruba.*
2. *Todos as manhãs, minha irmã e eu* _____*(ir) à praia.*
3. *Na adolescência, nós nos* _____*(acordar) muito cedo.*
4. *Anteontem nós nos* _____*(acordar) tarde.*
5. *Minha esposa* _____*(cozinhar) ontem à noite.*
6. *Minha avó* _____*(cozinhar) todos os dias.*

Future Tenses

There are at least two straightforward ways to express the future in Portuguese. One way is more colloquial, that is, used more often in everyday speech. The other way to express the future is seen more often in print but can also be heard in more formal interactions. Let's first present the more colloquial version of the future tense:

▼ **FUTURE TENSE WITH TWO VERBS**

ir (to go)	verb [infinitive]
eu vou	*andar* (I'm going to walk)
você vai	*comer* (you are going to eat)
ela vai	*dormir* (she is going to sleep)
nós vamos	*falar* (we are going to speak)
vocês vão	*beber* (you (pl.) are going to drink)
elas vão	*assistir* (they are going to watch)

Make sure that the second verb is always in the infinitive, or in other words, in the /–r/ ending, which could be construed as its "default" form. The first verb is the verb *ir* (to go) and is conjugated for the grammatical subject in question. Here is a sample dialogue with the future tense:

Q: Júlia: *Você vai viajar para o Brasil em dezembro?* (Are you going to travel to Brazil in December?)
A: Fernanda: *Não, eu e Jane vamos visitar os pais dela em Washington.* (No, Jane and I will visit her parents in Washington.)
Q: Júlia: *Então quanto tempo você vai ficar lá?* (So, how long will you stay there?)
A: Fernanda: *Acho que vou ficar lá uns dois dias, mas Jane vai voltar somente na outra semana.* (I think I'll stay there a couple of days, but Jane will be back only the following week.)
Q: Júlia: *Que bom, então ela vai ter mais tempo com os pais.* (Great, so she'll have more time with her folks.)
A: Fernanda: *Pois é!* (Right!)

The other way of expressing the future is to use the regular future tense. This is done by keeping the infinitives and adding extra endings, depending on the grammatical subject. This is comparable to the English "will" + verb. Here is the regular future tense in Portuguese:

▼ **THE FUTURE TENSE**

andar (to walk)	*comer* (to eat)	*dormir* (to sleep)
*eu and**arei***	*eu com**erei***	*eu dorm**irei***
*você and**ará***	*você com**erá***	*você dorm**irá***

andar (to walk)	*comer* (to eat)	*dormir* (to sleep)
*ele and**ará***	*ele com**erá***	*ele dorm**irá***
*nós and**aremos***	*nós com**eremos***	*nós dorm**iremos***
*vocês and**arão***	*vocês com**erão***	*vocês dorm**irão***
*eles and**arão***	*eles com**erão***	*eles dorm**irão***

Here is a sample dialogue that includes some of the future tense forms:

Q: Professor: *Vocês **entregarão** as tarefas na segunda.* (You will turn in the homework on Monday.)
A: Aluno: *E quando **teremos** a primeira prova?* (And when will we have the first test?)
Q: Professor: *A primeira prova **será** em uma semana.* (The first test will be in one week.)
A: Aluno: *E o exame final? Quantas perguntas **serão** incluídas?* (And the final exam? How many questions will be included?)
Q: Professor: *Haverá cem perguntas de múltipla escolha no exame.* (There will be one hundred multiple choice questions in the exam.)
A: Aluno: *Ah, só? Que bom!* (Oh, that's it? Great!)

Conditional Tense

The conditional is very similar to the future tense, but it denotes the possibility of something happening in the future once a certain condition or stipulation is met. It is comparable to the English "would" + verb. The conditional is used more in colloquial speech than the regular future tense.

▼ **THE CONDITIONAL TENSE**

andar (to walk)	*comer* (to eat)	*dormir* (to sleep)
*eu and**aria***	*eu com**eria***	*eu dorm**iria***
*você and**aria***	*você com**eria***	*você dorm**iria***
*ele and**aria***	*ele com**eria***	*ele dorm**iria***
*nós and**aríamos***	*nós com**eríamos***	*nós dorm**iríamos***
*vocês and**ariam***	*vocês com**eriam***	*vocês dorm**iriam***
*eles and**ariam***	*eles com**eriam***	*eles dorm**iriam***

There is a lot of regularity in this verb tense, as you can see from the singular forms, which are all the same. Here are some sample sentences with the conditional tense:

Fabiana falou que ***mandaria*** *o cartão postal.* (Fabiana said that she would send the postcard.)
Mário e Isabela ***chegariam*** *a tempo se o trem fosse mais rápido.* (Mário and Isabela would arrive on time if the train was faster.)
Se tivesse mais caipirinha, meus amigos e eu ***beberíamos*** *mais.* (If there were more Brazilian rum, my friends and I would drink more.)

Practice with the Future and Conditional Tenses

Now let's see if you can remember what you've learned about the future and conditional tenses. Complete the following exercises and check your answers in Appendix C.

Future and Conditional Verbs: Exercise A

Translate the following sentences using the *ir* + verb future tense.

1. I'm going to call you tomorrow.

   _____

2. We are going to visit Brazil in the summer.

   _____

3. You are going to write a book?

   _____

Future and Conditional Verbs: Exercise B

Fill in the blanks with the verb in parentheses using the future tense.

1. *O advogado* _____*(solicitar) uma audiência amanhã.*
2. *A prova* _____*(ter) cinco perguntas de ensaio.*
3. *Nós* _____*(acompanhar) as crianças até o parque.*

Future and Conditional Verbs: Exercise C

Fill in the blanks using the conditional tense.

1. *Se fosse mais cedo, nós* _____ *(sair) para dar uma volta.*
2. *Ele disse à Maria que* _____ *(chegar) tarde.*
3. *As meninas* _____ *(levantar) mais cedo se pudessem.*

CHAPTER 13

More Verbs

There is more to Portuguese than just conjugating regular verbs. Sometimes we have to contend with using two verbs together, past participles, the passive voice, or reflexive verbs. You'll learn how to put all these new verb structures together in this chapter.

Using Two Verbs Together

It is very common to use two verbs together, not only in English, but also in many other languages, Portuguese included. The first situation, which was previously mentioned, is the future tense with *ir* (to go). The important thing to remember is to conjugate the first verb and leave the second verb in the infinitive. Here are some examples:

*Nós **vamos visitar** o Brasil no ano que vem.* (We're going to visit Brazil next year.)
*Eu **vou fazer** exercícios amanhã!* (I'm going to exercise tomorrow!)
*Você **vai sair** hoje à noite?* (Are you going to go out tonight?)
*Eles **vão pôr** a mesa para as visitas.* (They will set the table for the guests.)

Here are other expressions that require two verbs in Portuguese. In all of these, you conjugate the first verb and add another verb in (you guessed it) the infinitive. The formula looks like this: *querer* + infinitive

(Portuguese) = "want" + infinitive (English). The following table shows this pattern clearly:

Portuguese	English
Queremos desejar um Feliz Natal a todos.	We want to wish a Merry Christmas to all.
Quero ver esse filme neste fim de semana.	I want to see this movie this weekend.
Vocês querem ir ao barzinho?	Do you guys want to go to the club?
Ele quis impor sua vontade.	He wanted to impose his will.

Use this pattern to express wishes and desires. As long as the first verb *querer* is conjugated and the next verb is in the infinitive, you are in good shape. This pattern can be used in the present to express future meaning (for example, *Quero sair amanhã* [I want to go out tomorrow]), but it could also be used in the past tense (for example, *Eu quis visitá-lo* [I wanted to visit him]) to express a wish that was not completed or realized. Here's another formula: *ter* + *vontade de* + infinitive = "feel like –ing."

Portuguese	English
Eu tive vontade de sentar-me.	I felt like sitting.
Nós temos vontade de sair.	We feel like going out.
Vocês têm vontade de fazer exercícios?	Do you (pl.) feel like exercising?
Ela tem vontade de compor.	She feels like composing.

This pattern is used when you want to relate to things that you want to do or feel like doing. The word *vontade* means "will" or "desire." An alternative construction is to say *estou com vontade de* (I feel like), which is also a bit difficult to translate in a literal sense.

Using Two Verbs Together: Exercise A

Fill in the blanks with conjugated forms of the verb *querer* or *ter* depending on the structure of the sentence. Check your answers in Appendix C.

1. *A minha irmã* _____ *ir para a Inglaterra no ano que vem.* (My sister wants to go to England next year.)
2. *Eu* _____ *vontade de comer doce depois das quatro da tarde.* (I feel like eating sweets after four in the afternoon.)
3. *Os meus primos* _____ *visitar o Museu de Arte Moderna de São Paulo.* (My cousins wanted to visit the Modern Art Museum in São Paulo.)
4. *A minha amiga Júlia e o marido* _____ *sair para jantar na sexta-feira à noite.* (My friend Júlia and her husband want to go out to eat on Friday night.)
5. *Nós os brasileiros sempre* _____ *vontade de ir à Disneylândia de férias.* (We Brazilians always feel like going to Disneyland for vacation.)

Here are more "two-verb" structures common in Portuguese:

▼ ***ACABAR DE* (PAST) + INFINITIVE** **"HAVE JUST" + VERB**

Portuguese	English
Ele acabou de chegar.	He has just arrived.
Vocês acabaram de ligar?	Have you guys just called?
Nós acabamos de ver o filme.	We have just seen the movie.

The literal translation for this expression in English is "finished doing," from the verb *acabar* "to finish," but the best way to say it would be "have just [done something]." Again, the first verb is conjugated and the second verb stays the same, in the infinitive form. This next structure also uses the infinitive.

▼ ***TER* + *QUE* + INFINITIVE** **"HAVE TO" + VERB**

Portuguese	English
Eu tenho que terminar o livro.	I have to finish the book.
Ela tem que fazer compras.	She has to go shopping.
Nós temos que ir ao banco.	We have to go to the bank.

This pattern is used to convey the idea of obligation, as you have seen in Chapter 10. It might be useful to avoid translating *ter que* literally, since you would end up with "I have to that"! Simply remember that this pattern is used to relate to things you must or have to do. This next structure relates to "abilities" and "skills."

▼ ***PODER* + INFINITIVE** **"CAN/IS ABLE TO" + VERB**

Portuguese	English
Pode sentar!	You can sit down!
Eu posso fazer exercícios fáceis.	I can do easy exercises.
Nós podemos sair hoje à noite.	We can go out tonight.

The verb *poder* is conjugated and the following verb, which describes the ability, is in the infinitive. At the same time, this structure can also refer to "permission," more commonly translated in English with the modal verb "may," as in *Eu posso entrar?* (May I come in?)

Using Two Verbs Together: Exercise B

Translate the following sentences, using the information you learned in the previous pages. Check your answers in Appendix C.

1. Elvis has just left the building.

   _____

2. May I go now?

   _____

3. Maria can run for a long time.

   _____

4. The teacher has to correct the tests.

   _____

5. We have just finished reading the paper.

   _____

6. Can you go out tonight?

   _____

7. They can come in.

   _____

Past Participles

Past participles are verbal forms that are used in combination with the verb *estar* (to be) to denote the resulting effect of an action or condition. The comparable sentence in English would be "is/are [done]." Of course, the other tenses are also used; for example, "was/were [done]" or "will be [done]," and so forth.

Alert

Past participles in English usually end in "–ed" and are similar to the past tense form: "talked" and "have talked." However, there are some that end in "–en," such as "written" and "given"; use of these forms is decreasing in English, especially in colloquial speech. On the other hand, past participles are very frequently used in Portuguese.

The following table shows how to arrive at the past participle form of the verb.

▼ PAST PARTICIPLE ENDINGS ACCORDING TO VERB CONJUGATION

–ar verbs > drop the *–ar* ending and add *–ado* (*–ados*, *–ada*, *–adas*)
–er verbs > drop the *–er* ending and add *–ido* (*–idos*, *–ida*, *–idas*)
–ir verbs > drop the *–ir* ending and add *–ido* (*–idos*, *–ida –idas*)

However, there are some irregular past participles in Portuguese.

▼ IRREGULAR PAST PARTICIPLES

abrir (to open)	*aberto* (opened)
cobrir (to cover)	*coberto* (covered)
dizer (to say)	*dito* (said)
escrever (to write)	*escrito* (written)
entregar (to hand, to give)	*entregue* (handed, given)
fazer (to make, to do)	*feito* (made, done)
ganhar (to win)	*ganho* (won)
gastar (to spend)	*gasto* (spent)

morrer (to die)	*morto* (died)
pagar (to pay)	*pago* (paid)
pôr (to put, to set)	*posto* (put, set)
ver (to see)	*visto* (seen)
vir (to come, to arrive)	*vindo* (come, arrived)

The following are sample sentences with the *estar* + past participle construction.

***estar* + past participle**	**English**
O restaurante está aberto.	The restaurant is open.
A porta está fechada.	The door is closed.
Os cheques estao assinados.	The checks are signed.
As mesas estão postas.	The tables are set.

Notice that with the past participle after the verb *estar* (to be), there needs to be agreement with the subject. For example, *mesas* (tables) is a feminine and plural word, so the past participle needs to match these two categories and end in *–as*, which is the feminine plural form. There are four different forms for the past participle, unless it ends in *–e*, in which case the masculine and feminine forms are the same and the word varies only in number (i.e., *entregues* "given").

Exercise: Past Participles

Fill in the blanks with the correct form of the past participle of the verb in parentheses. Check your answers in Appendix C.

1. *As portas estavam* _____ *(abrir).* (The doors were open.)
2. *O mecânico está muito* _____ *(ocupar).* (The mechanic is very busy.)
3. *O que está* _____ *(escrever) ali?* (What is written there?)
4. *A mesa está* _____ *(pôr) para o jantar.* (The table is set for the dinner.)

5. *Os bancos estão* _____ *(cobrir) de neve.* (The benches are covered with snow.)

Passive Voice

Past participles are also used with the verb *ser* (to be) to denote the passive voice. To understand the passive voice, first you need to understand the active voice. In a sentence in the active voice, the subject and the agent are the same, as in the sentence "The boy closed the door." In this case, "the boy" is both the subject of the sentence and the agent, in other words, the entity that completes the verbal action. On the other hand, the passive voice sentence would express the same idea, but in a different way: "The door was closed by the boy." In this sentence, "the door" is the subject of the sentence, not "the boy." In fact, in this sentence the subject is the "recipient" of the verbal action. To summarize, an active sentence is one in which the subject is also the agent of the action, while a passive sentence is one in which the subject is the recipient of the verbal action. Speakers use the passive voice in order to focus attention away from the agent of the action. You might not want to call attention to the fact that "the boy" was the agent of the action, but you do want to emphasize the fact that the action actually occurred. Using the passive voice allows you to shift focus away from the agent, which can be mentioned or not (i.e., you can simply say "the door was closed" and not mention "by the boy").

Here are some passive voice sentences in Portuguese:

▼ PASSIVE VOICE EXAMPLES

Portuguese	English
A mesa foi posta pelas empregadas.	The table was set by the maids.
Os livros foram escritos pelas poetas.	The books were written by the poets.
As portas foram fechadas.	The doors were closed.
O ladrão foi pego.	The thief was caught.

Most, but not all, passive voice sentences are written in the past tense. There can be passive sentences written in the present or future. For example: *Como pessoa famosa, ele* ***é reconhecido*** *todos os dias* (As a celebrity, he **is recognized** every day). Or even: *O aniversário dele vai ser comemorado no restaurante* (His birthday will be celebrated in the restaurant).

Exercise: Passive Voice

Translate the following sentences. Check your answers in Appendix C.

1. The two men were seen near here.

   _____

2. The money was spent very fast.

   _____

3. What was said yesterday?

   _____

4. The food was consumed by the birds.

   _____

Reflexive and Reciprocal Verbs

Some verbs in Portuguese are called "reflexive" while others are "reciprocal." Reflexive verbs reflect an action that is done by the agent to itself. They can be translated to English by using the reflexive pronouns "–self" and "–selves," as in *eu me chamo* (I call myself). By the same token, reciprocal verbs can be translated to English by using the construction "each other." In this case, the action is done by one entity to another entity, which in turn does the same action to the original entity, as in the expression *se beijam* (they kiss each other). In Portuguese, reflexive and reciprocal verbs are conjugated by using reflexive pronouns, as listed here.

▼ **REFLEXIVE AND RECIPROCAL PRONOUNS**

Pronoun + Verb	English
eu ***me*** *chamo*	I call myself
você ***se*** *chama*	you call yourself
ele/ela ***se*** *chama*	he/she calls him/herself
nós ***nos*** *chamamos*	we call ourselves
vocês ***se*** *chamam*	you (pl.) call yourselves
eles/elas ***se*** *chamam*	they call themselves

Notice that the pronoun is placed before the verb and that the pronouns serve for both reflexive and reciprocal ideas.

Alert

Not all reflexive verbs in Portuguese have a corresponding English reflexive verb. In the case of *chamar-se* (to call oneself), the translation works out fine, but there are reflexive verbs in Portuguese that are not reflexive in English, such as *levantar-se* (to get up).

Here is a list of common reflexive verbs in Portuguese:

▼ **COMMON REFLEXIVE VERBS**

Verb	English
lavar-se	to wash oneself
vestir-se	to put on clothes, to dress oneself
olhar-se	to look at oneself
pentear-se	to brush/comb oneself
sentar-se	to seat oneself
divertir-se	to entertain oneself, to have fun
deitar-se	to go to bed, to retire
machucar-se	to hurt oneself
reunir-se	to get together

In order to conjugate the verb, you must drop the *-se* and add one of the reflexive pronouns according to the grammatical subject. So *deitar-se* would be conjugated as *eu me deito* (I go to bed) for the first person singular.

Reflexive Verbs with Prepositions

Some reflexive verbs are used with prepositions in a sentence. Here's a list of these verbs:

▼ REFLEXIVE VERBS WITH PREPOSITIONS

Verb	English
aproveitar-se de	to take advantage of
convencer-se de	to convince oneself of
esquecer-se de	to forget + infinitive
lembrar-se de	to remember + infinitive
queixar-se de	to complain about
rir-se de	to laugh at
decidir-se a	to decide + infinitive
dedicar-se a	to dedicate oneself to
acostumar-se com	to get used to
parecer-se com	to look like
casar-se com	to marry
preocupar-se com	to worry about
surpreender-se com	to be surprised

Notice that not all verbs are translated with the same proposition (some can be translated as "at," "about," or "with"). In addition, some verbs such as "to marry" and "to be surprised" do not require a preposition at all in English.

Practice with Reflexive and Reciprocal Verbs

Now let's see what you can remember about using reflexive and reciprocal verbs. Try out the following two exercises and then check your answers in Appendix C.

Reflexive and Reciprocal Verbs: Exercise A

Match Column A (expressions) with Column B (verbs).

1. *Eles* _____ *na igreja.*
2. *Nós* _____ *muito na festa.*
3. *Minha amiga* _____ *com a família.*
4. *Meu irmão* _____ *com meu pai.*
5. *Os alunos* _____ *do livro sempre.*
6. *Eu* _____ *às 11 da noite.*

(a) *me deito*
(b) *se preocupa*
(c) *nos divertimos*
(d) *se queixam*
(e) *se parece*
(f) *se casaram*

Reflexive and Reciprocal Verbs: Exercise B

Translate the following sentences to Portuguese.

1. The professor dedicates herself to teaching.

_____

2. Our neighbor was surprised with the visit.

_____

3. The man laughed at the situation.

_____

4. I look like my father.

_____

CHAPTER 14

Negative Words and Constructions

There are many times when you want or need to negate, refuse, or just plain say no to something. When the waiter asks you if you'd like to order more food, you might be too full. If a friend invites you out on a night when you already have plans, you'll need to kindly refuse and possibly suggest an alternate plan. Those types of situations are covered in this chapter; you'll learn how to make negative sentences, become familiar with common negative expressions, and discover how to distinguish between the negative and the positive.

How to Say No

The word for "no" in Portuguese is *não*, a one-syllable word with a nasal diphthong that sometimes takes practice to pronounce. In order to say a sentence in the negative, simply put the word *não* before the verb. This is very different from English, where negative sentences are constructed with a system of auxiliary verbs (don't, didn't, haven't, etc.). See the following table to understand the simplicity of Portuguese.

Essential

In order to pronounce the word *não* correctly, try saying the word "now" in English but try to make it nasal, as you would if you said "huh?"

▼ **SENTENCES IN THE NEGATIVE**

Portuguese	English [many possibilities]
Eu não tenho um cachorro.	I don't have a dog.
Ela não quer conversar.	She doesn't want to talk.
Nós não podemos acreditar.	We can't believe this.
Vocês não souberam da verdade?	You guys didn't find out the truth?
Você não deve fazer isso.	You shouldn't do that.

As you can see, the Portuguese system is pretty straightforward. The negative is simply made by placing the negative word *não* before the verb. No alterations or auxiliary verbs are needed. What if you want to say "never" or "nobody"? Read more to find out.

▼ **MORE NEGATIVE WORDS IN PORTUGUESE**

Word	Example	English
Nunca	*Eu nunca estive em Manaus.*	I've never been to Manaus.
Nada	*Nada a declarar.*	Nothing to declare.
Ninguém	*Ninguém chegou na hora.*	Nobody arrived on time.
Nem . . . nem	*Nem um nem outro.*	Neither one nor the other.
Nenhum	*Nenhum artigo foi perdido.*	Not one article was lost.
Nenhuma	*Nenhuma pessoa ficou lá.*	Not one person stayed there.

What if this is still not enough? Read on to find out how to put sentences together in the negative.

Two Negatives Make a Negative

In English the rule is to say only one negative word per sentence ("I saw no one" or "I didn't see anyone"). Double negatives are a big no-no, unless you speak a dialect of English in which they are accepted in conversation ("I didn't see nobody"). Portuguese is similar to these nonstandard English dialects, because two negatives are not only allowed; they are the rule! Here is a list of negative words used together:

▼ **DOUBLE NEGATIVES IN PORTUGUESE**

Portuguese	English
Eu não faço exercício nunca.	I don't exercise ever.
Eu não digo nada.	I don't say anything.
Eu não vejo ninguém.	I don't see anyone.
Eu não tenho nenhum (nenhuma) . . .	I don't have any . . .

Use *nenhum* before masculine words, such as *nenhum problema* (any problem), and *nenhuma* before feminine words, such as *nenhuma sugestão* (any suggestion). How do you answer in the negative when asked a "yes-no" question? Here are several possibilities:

Você vai para o cinema amanhã? (Are you going to the movies tomorrow?)
ANSWER 1: *Não, não vou.* No, I'm not (going).
ANSWER 2: *Não, não vou não.* No, I'm not (going).
ANSWER 3: *Não, vou não.* No, I'm not (going).

There are subtleties to the answers, but they all mean the same thing. Answers 1 and 2 are spoken by more educated speakers, mostly in formal contexts. Answer 3 is considered more colloquial, informal speech, if not ungrammatical by some. Be prepared to hear all these possibilities in Brazilian Portuguese.

Common Negative Expressions

There are many expressions that are negative but that might not seem so at first glance from an English-language perspective. Here are some of them:

▼ **NEGATIVE EXPRESSIONS**

Portuguese	English	Situation
Pois não?	Yes? May I help you?	When answering the phone, door, or asking if you need help.
Pois não.	Sure.	When agreeing (!) to do something.

Portuguese	English	Situation
Absolutamente!	Absolutely not! No way!	When refusing or disagreeing.
Sei lá!	Who knows? I don't know!	When denying that you know something.
Não tem importância.	No problem.	When reassuring someone that it was nothing.
De jeito nenhum.	No way.	When refusing or rejecting something.

Make sure you train your ears and tongue to understand as well as use these expressions. Pay attention to interactions among Brazilians when they use these expressions, especially in restaurants and supermarkets.

Here are some examples of the usage of negative words in typical conversation in Brazilian Portuguese:

Q: *Oi, tudo bem?* (Hi, is everything all right?)
A: *Não, tudo mal!* (No, everything's bad!)
Q: *Por que? O que aconteceu?* (Why? What happened?)
A: *Não recebi dinheiro ontem.* (I didn't get any money yesterday.)
Q: *Ontem foi dia de pagamento?* (Yesterday was payday?)
A: *Não era anteontem, mas eles não me nem um tostão!* (No, it was the day before, but they didn't give me one cent!)
Q: *Nada?* (Nothing?)
A: *Nadinha mesmo.* (Nothing at all.)
Q: *Nossa, que coisa. E agora?* (Wow, that's amazing. And now?)
A: *Não sei o que fazer. Você tem algum dinheiro para me emprestar?* (I don't know what to do. Do you have any money to lend me?)
Q: *Não, de jeito nenhum. Não tenho nada mesmo.* (No, not at all. I don't have anything, really.)
A: *Não faz mal.* (It's all right.)

Exercise: Practice with Negatives

Fill in the blanks with the best negative word in Portuguese. Check your answers in Appendix C.

1. *Eu* _____ *me lembro de* _____ *da escola primária.* (I don't remember anyone from elementary school.)
2. *A minha amiga Anne* _____ *se acorda antes das dez da manhã.* (My friend Anne never gets up before ten in the morning.)
3. *Sofia* _____ *tem* _____ *contra seus colegas de trabalho.* (Sofia has nothing/doesn't have anything against her coworkers.)
4. *Nós* _____ *fizemos* _____ *exercício hoje.* (We did not do any exercises [or: not one exercise] today.)
5. *Os escritores* _____ *completaram* _____ *página nesta semana.* (The writers did not complete any pages [or: not one page] this week.)

Positive Versus Negative

Comparing the positive versus the negative words is a good way to understand the differences in Portuguese and English. Here is a list of these expressions:

▼ POSITIVE VERSUS NEGATIVE WORDS

Positive	Negative
alguma coisa, algo (something)	*nada* (nothing)
alguém (somebody)	*ninguém* (nobody)
em algum lugar (somewhere)	*em lugar nenhum* (nowhere)
sempre (always)	*nunca, jamais, em tempo algum* (never)
também (also)	*também não* ([not] either, neither)
já (already)	*ainda não* (not yet)
ainda (still yet)	*não . . . mais* (not anymore)

Exercise: Positive to Negative

Change all the positive sentences into negative ones. Use the words that you just learned. Check your answers in Appendix C.

MODEL: *Eu **já** vi o filme.* (I already saw the movie.)
*Eu **ainda não*** vi *o filme.* (I did not see the movie yet.)

1. *Eu já fui no banco.* (I already went to the bank.)

   _____

2. *Você ainda tem medo de avião.* (You are still afraid of planes.)

   _____

3. *Tem alguém na sala.* (There is someone in the room.)

   _____

4. *Eles estão fazendo alguma coisa.* (They are doing something.)

   _____

5. *Elas sempre vão ao supermercado.* (They always go to the supermarket.)

   _____

Exercise: Negative to Positive

Change all the negative sentences into positive ones.

1. *Eles não encontraram nada em casa.* (They did not find anything at home.)

   _____

2. *Eu não vi ninguém na festa.* (I didn't see anybody at the party.)

   _____

3. *Nós não o vimos em lugar nenhum.* (We did not see him anywhere.)

   _____

4. *Você jamais telefona à noite.* (You never call at night.)

   _____

5. *Eu ainda não terminei o capítulo.* (I did not finish the chapter yet.)

   _____

CHAPTER 15

Questions and Exclamations

How do you ask questions in Portuguese? In this chapter, you'll learn the answer to this question and more. This chapter covers the most useful interrogative words and question tags and ends with interjections. You will also learn how to show surprise in Portuguese. Read on!

How to Ask Questions

In Portuguese, asking questions does not require complicated inversion rules as French does or the use of auxiliaries and inversion as English does. For the most part, questions are asked by using a rising intonation at the end of the utterance. Following are some examples of "yes-no" questions:

▼ **QUESTIONS IN PORTUGUESE**

Portuguese	Literal English Translation	English Equivalent
Você vai para o cinema?	You going to the movies?	Are you going to the movies?
As meninas já chegaram?	The girls already come?	Have the girls come already?
A conversa foi boa?	The talk was good?	Was the talk good?
Eu ligo pra você?	I call you?	Should I call you?

In order to ask a question in Portuguese, simply raise the tone of the last word in the utterance. In very colloquial speech in English this is also done. Have you ever heard people say "You're going?" instead of "Are you going?" These two sentences have similar meanings, at least superficially. The first example, "You're going?", implies that the speaker is surprised about the fact the listener is leaving, as suggested by contextual evidence. The second sentence, "Are you going?", is simply a yes-no question that shows that the speaker really wants information that is not contextually available. In any case, Portuguese speakers use the first type of sentence to ask a yes-no question.

Interrogative Words

Not all questions are yes-no questions. Some questions begin with a "question word" or interrogative word (also called a "wh-question" because in English the interrogative word begins with those letters). If you use an interrogative word, you don't need to use the rising intonation at the end of the utterance. The presence of the word itself will suffice. These are the most common interrogative words in Portuguese:

▼ **INTERROGATIVE WORDS FOLLOWED BY NOUNS**

Portuguese	Example	English
que?	*Que filme você quer ver?*	Which film do you want to see?
qual?	*Qual blusa você vai comprar?*	Which blouse will you buy?
quantos?	*Quantos irmãos você tem?*	How many siblings do you have?
quantas?	*Quantas irmãs você tem?*	How many sisters do you have?

The interrogative *o que*? (what?) is said in a longer form—*o que é que . . .* ? or more literally, "What is it that . . . ?"—but it means the same thing. There is not much difference between *que* and *qual* (which), except that when using *qual* (or *quais*, the plural form), there is an implicit choice between two or more possibilities. And make sure to pay attention to the gender of the noun that follows either *quantos* [masc.] or *quantas* [fem.].

Other interrogative words are followed by verbs, not nouns. These are listed here.

▼ INTERROGATIVE WORDS FOLLOWED BY VERBS

Portuguese	Example	English
o que?	*O que você estuda?*	What do you study?
como?	*Como vai?*	How are you?
quanto?	*Quanto custa isso?*	How much does this cost?
quando?	*Quando é a festa?*	When is the party?
onde?	*Onde você pôs as chaves?*	Where did you put the keys?
aonde?	*Aonde ela está indo?*	Where is she going to?
por que?	*Por que você foi embora?*	Why did you leave?

In this group, notice that these interrogatives are followed by either a verb (*vai, custa*) or a subject and a verb (*você pôs, ela está*). Sometimes inversion is allowed in the first case, when the interrogative is followed only by the verb. So, for some interrogative-word questions you can say *Quando seu filho nasceu?* or *Quando nasceu seu filho?* (When was your son born?), and they mean the same thing.

Here is a typical conversation between a reporter and a famous person in Brazil.

Q: *Olá, como vai?* (Hi, how are you?)
A: *Bem, obrigada, e você?* (Well, thanks, and you?)
Q: *Muito bem, agora que você está aqui conversando conosco. Quanto tempo você vai ficar em São Paulo?* (Very well, now that you are here talking to us. How long will you stay in São Paulo?)
A: *Uns dois dias, promovendo o filme.* (A couple of days, promoting the movie.)
Q: *Quando é a estréia do filme?* (When is the release of the movie?)
A: *Já nessa semana que vem!* (Already this next week!)
Q: *Você gostou de trabalhar com o diretor?* (Did you like working with the director?)
A: *A melhor parte é que ele é um profissional.* (The best part is that he is such a professional.)

Q: *Você acha que o filme terá sucesso internacional?* (Do you think the movie will have international success?)
A: *Acho que sim, tem um apelo para a gente jovem.* (I think so, it has an appeal to younger people.)
Q: *Qual foi a parte mais difícil de interpretar para você?* (What was the most difficult part about acting for you?)
A: *Acho que a parte dramática é mais fácil que a comédia.* (I think the dramatic roles are easier than the comedic roles.)
Q: *Como anda a família, tudo bem?* (How's the family doing, all right?)
A: *Tudo em ordem.* (Everything is fine.)
Q: *Aonde vocês vão passar as férias?* (Where will you guys go for vacation?)
A: *Não posso dizer, é segredo de estado!* (I can't tell, it's a state secret!)
Q: *Você promete voltar ao nosso programa antes do final do ano?* (Do you promise to come back to our show before the end of the year?)
A: *Claro que sim, com o maior prazer!* (Of course, it will be my pleasure!)
Q: *Um grande abraço e obrigada!* (A big hug to you, and thanks!)

Exercise: Interrogative Words

Fill in the blanks with the most appropriate question word. Check your answers in Appendix C.

1. _____ *é seu aniversário?* (. . . is your birthday?)
2. _____ *custa essa blusa?* (. . . is this blouse?)
3. _____ *você quer ir hoje?* (. . . do you want to go today?)
4. _____ *ele foi tão cedo?* (. . . he left so early?)
5. _____ *você mora?* (. . . you live?)
6. _____ *se diz em português?* (. . . you say it in Portuguese?)
7. _____ *você acha disso?* (. . . do you think of that?)

Exercise: Asking Questions

Write a question for the following answers in Portuguese.

1. _____ *? Eu me chamo Daniel.*

2. _____? *Eu moro no Rio de Janeiro.*
3. _____? *Eu tenho três irmãos.*

Question Tags

Question tags are words that are said at the end of utterances in order to make a question. English has a very complex set of so-called "tag-questions" because of all the many auxiliary and modal verbs in the language (do, should, can, etc.). It is possible to also use the original verb in Portuguese to make a tag question, as in *Você visitou os Estados Unidos,* ***não visitou****?* (You visited the United States, didn't you?) However, it is far simpler (and more common) to use the expression *não é?* at the end of any declarative sentence to make a question. So, for example, you could say *Ele não comeu nada,* ***não é****?* (He did not eat anything, did he?)

Alert

In Brazilian Portuguese, speakers will very often reduce the expression *não é?* to the one-syllable *né?* Common sentences would be *Ela vai ligar depois, né?* (She will call later, won't she?), and so forth. Pay attention to this frequent abbreviation and use it yourself sometimes!

Exclamations

Exclamations are very common in any language, but in Portuguese the actual grammar constructions are a little different from exclamations in English. In English we say "what a . . . " followed by a comment. However, in Portuguese we only say *que* . . . followed by a comment, as in the following examples:

Que capítulo fácil! (What an easy chapter!)
Que país lindo! (What a beautiful country!)

The word *que* is also used in shorter expressions that simply include the adjective, such as:

Que lindo! (How beautiful!)

The other type of construction has to do with the one that can be translated to English as "how." In Portuguese we would use *que*, as in the following examples:

Que simpática (que) ela é! (How nice she is!)
Que bem (que) ele toca! (How well he plays!)

It should be noted here that the second *que* is optional, but very frequently heard in popular Brazilian Portuguese. In addition, we could also use the word *como* in order to convey the same meaning, as in these examples:

Como ela é simpática! (How nice she is!)
Como ele toca bem! (How well he plays!)

Another exclamatory word is *mas* (but), used as a type of reinforcement along with *que* and *como*:

Mas que chato! (What a bore!)
Mas como ele é persistente! (How persistent he is!)

Finally, there is also the use of *cada* (each, every), which can be exclamatory and translated in English as the word "such." Here is an example:

Ele me deu cada olhada! (He gave me such looks!)

Exercise: Translate Exclamations

Translate the following sentences to Portuguese. Check your answers in Appendix C.

1. What a pretty girl she is!

   _____

2. What an excellent hotel!

   _____

3. How badly he drives!

   _____

4. What horrible cold weather!

   _____

5. How interesting!

   _____

CHAPTER 16

The Future and Other Tenses

This chapter reviews the uses of the future and other tenses in Portuguese. One unique aspect of Portuguese is the personal infinitive, a rare flower indeed in the grammatical world. In addition, you will learn about impersonal assertions and finish off by discussing the weather and clothing using some of these grammar points!

The Present Versus the Future or the Preterite

You can use the present tense in Portuguese to denote a future event. For example, you might say *Eu vou ao banco* (I go to the bank) when you mean that you will in the near future, say the next day or in a couple of hours. It does not mean that "you always go to the bank," as the present tense usually means; that is, the present tense is not used to describe habitual actions in this case. Here is a dialogue where speakers use the present tense to denote the future:

Q: *Você* ***vai*** *amanhã para Brasília?* (You go tomorrow to Brasília?)
A: *Sim, a gente* ***sai*** *às duas da tarde.* (Yes, we leave at two in the afternoon.)
Q: *E quando vocês* ***voltam****?* (And when do you [pl.] come back?)
A: *Nós* ***voltamos*** *na semana que vem.* (We come back next week.)
Q: *Que legal, aproveitem!* (Great, enjoy!)
A: *Nós* ***vamos*** *sim!* (Yes, we will!)

Notice that the present tense can also be used with future meaning in English. The big difference between English and Portuguese has to do with the present progressive.

Essential

In English you can say "I'm leaving" to express an action in the future, as in "I'm leaving to Rio next month." But in Portuguese we could not use the *presente contínuo* to mean something in the future. We would have to use the future tense, and say either *Eu vou viajar para o Rio no mês que vem* (I'm going to travel to Rio next month) or *Eu viajarei para o Rio no mês que vem* (I will travel to Rio next month). But if you say *Eu estou viajando para o Rio* (I'm traveling to Rio), that means you are actually sitting on the plane talking to someone about what you are doing at that very moment!

What are the other uses of the present tense? One common use is in historical texts. It is possible to read a sentence such as *Naquele momento D. Pedro grita: 'Independência ou Morte!'* (At that moment, D. Pedro cries out "Independence or Death!") This sentence reveals a historical fact that happened in the early history of Brazil, when the son of the King of Portugal took sides and decided to fight for Brazilian independence. This tense is called the "historical present," and you might encounter it instead of the regular past tense—another similarity to English!

The Personal Infinitive

The similarities might just end there, as far as regular verb tenses go. The personal infinitive is a peculiarity of Portuguese that is not common in other languages. It deals with the use of an infinitive that has been modified to give more information about the agent of the action. An infinitive normally is not supposed to have any such information. Usually, we use a conjugated verb (with personal information) followed by an infinitive (bare of any personal data). Some examples are *Eu quero* ***comer*** *pão* (I want to eat bread), or *Você sabe* ***jogar*** *xadrez?* (Do you know how to play chess?), or even *Eles vão* ***dirigir*** *até a festa* (They will drive to the party).

Notice that the verbs in bold are infinitives, which means that they end in *–r*. The previous verb is conjugated according to the person or the subject. So, why add more information? This verb tense is used with impersonal expression when there might be some ambiguity of who is carrying out the action, as in the following examples:

A: *É importante estudar a gramática.* (It's important to study grammar.)
B: *É importante estudar**mos** a gramática.* (It's important [**for us**] to study grammar.)

Notice that in Example A there is no personal information of who might be doing "the studying." The sentence would generally be understood as an impersonal sentence that might apply to any subject. On the other hand, if I use Example B, I am being more specific as to who is going to be doing "the studying": It is "us"! Both sentences are grammatically correct; one just gives a little more information. How do you go about conjugating the personal infinitive? Here is a chart:

▼ **PERSONAL INFINITIVE**

–ar verbs *(lembrar)*	**–er verbs *(trazer)***	**–ir verbs *(dormir)***	**–or verbs *(pôr)***
eu lembrar	*eu trazer*	*eu dormir*	*eu pôr*
remember (me)	bring (me)	sleep (me)	put (me)
você lembrar	*você trazer*	*você dormir*	*você pôr*
remember (you)	bring (you)	sleep (you)	put (you)
ele lembrar	*ele trazer*	*ele dormir*	*ele pôr*
remember (he/she)	bring (he/she)	sleep (he/she)	put (he/she)
nós lembrarmos	*nós trazermos*	*nós dormirmos*	*nós pormos*
remember (us)	bring (us)	sleep (us)	put (us)
vocês lembrarem	*vocês trazerem*	*vocês dormirem*	*vocês porem*
remember (you [pl.])	bring (you [pl.])	sleep (you [pl.])	put (you [pl.])
eles lembrarem	*eles trazerem*	*eles dormirem*	*eles porem*
remember (they)	bring (they)	sleep (they)	put (they)

Notice that for the first three persons (the singular ones) there is no change in the infinitive. You can maybe say that the conjugation means adding nothing, or "zero." You will only know it is not a regularly conjugated verb because it will come right after the pronoun and it will be in the infinitive. Compare *Eu falo baixo* (I speak softly) with *É possível eu falar baixo* (It's possible for me to speak softly). The first sentence has a conjugated verb in the present and the second has a personal infinitive in it!

The personal infinitive is also used after certain prepositions, when they connect complex sentences, as in the following examples:

A fim de *eu terminar o livro, escrevi toda a noite.* (**So that** I would finish the book, I wrote the whole night.)
Antes de *eu jogar o papel fora, copiei a informação.* (**Before** throwing [I] away the paper, I copied the information.)
Até *eles compreenderem a lição, eles estudam.* (**Until** they comprehend the lesson, they study.)
Ao *abrirem o livro, vocês podem começar a ler.* (**Upon** opening [you (pl.)] the book, you may start to read.)
Depois de *eu entrar na casa, falo com os gatos.* (**After** entering [I] the house, I greet the cats.)
Para *ela terminar o trabalho, lhe deram mais tempo.* (**In order** for her **to** finish the work, they gave her more time.)
Sem *eles verem, abri a janela.* (**Without** them seeing, I opened the window.)

Essential

The personal infinitive is a rather cumbersome structure in English, as you can tell from the translations. However, it is very common in the everyday language of Brazilians. Make sure to master this verb form, because you will garner immense rewards if you do. For one thing, using it will help you to avoid using the dreaded subjunctive!

Now try your hand at the following exercises in the personal infinitive.

The Personal Infinitive: Exercise A

Rewrite the following sentences using the personal infinitive. Start with the impersonal expression—*É importante* (It's important), *É essencial* (It's essential)—and follow with the rest of the sentence, as in the model below. Check your answers in Appendix C.

MODEL: *Eu estudo todos os dias.* > *É importante* ***eu estudar*** *todos os dias.*
(I study every day.) > (It's important I study every day.)

1. *Eu lembro dos nomes dos alunos.* (I remember the names of the students.)
   É importante _____.
2. *Vocês dizem a verdade.* (You [pl.] tell the truth.)
   É essencial _____.
3. *Elas trazem os livros para a escola.* (They bring the books to school.)
   É imprescindível _____.
4. *Nós visitamos nossos avós.* (We visit our grandparents.)
   É necessário _____.
5. *Você e o Roberto põem a mesa.* (You and Robert set the table.)
   É bom _____.
6. *As meninas dormem cedo.* (The young girls sleep early.)
   É importante _____.

The Personal Infinitive: Exercise B

Complete the sentence with a verb in the personal infinitive. Check your answers in Appendix C.

1. *Antes de eu* _____ *(ligar), eu procurei o número.* (Before calling, I looked for the number.)
2. *Até eles* _____ *(chegar), nós esperamos.* (Until they arrived, we waited.)
3. *Depois de vocês* _____ *(comer), podem lavar os pratos.* (After eating, you (pl.) can wash the dishes.)

4. *Para você* _____ *(receber) os presentes, é preciso ser um bom menino.* (In order for you to receive the presents, you must be a good boy.)

Impersonal Assertions

As you saw in the previous section, impersonal expressions are part and parcel of more complex sentences in Portuguese. They are essential in constructing sentences with the personal infinitive and the subjunctive, a verb mood that you will see in subsequent chapters. Here are a few common impersonal expressions:

Portuguese	English
É bom.	It's good.
É essencial.	It's essential.
É importante.	It's important.
É necessário.	It's necessary.
É preciso.	It's necessary.
É triste.	It's sad.
É legal.	It's great.

Some expressions that are considered "impersonal" have to do with the use of the particle *se* in Portuguese. When used before a verb, it means that there is no specific subject, but rather that something "is done." Take a look at these examples:

Vende-se carro. (Car[s] is [are] sold [here].)
Conserta-se roupa. (Clothes are fixed [here].)
Fala-se português. (Portuguese is spoken [here].)

Additional impersonal forms might be associated with the weather, since there is no obvious subject in these expressions. Read on and find out how to say them in Brazilian Portuguese.

Discussing the Weather

How do you say "It's raining" in Portuguese? What about "It snows a lot here"? In this section you will learn how to discuss the weather in Portuguese.

Here is a list of common expressions that relate to the climate:

▼ WEATHER EXPRESSIONS

Portuguese	English
Faz (muito) frio.	It's (very) cold.
Faz frio no Sul do Brasil.	It's cold in the south of Brazil.
Faz (muito) calor.	It's (very) hot.
Faz calor no nordeste.	It's hot in the northeast.
Venta (muito).	It's (very) windy.
Venta muito em Fortaleza.	It's very windy in Fortaleza.
Neva (muito).	It snows (a lot).
Neva um pouco no Chile.	It snows a little in Chile.
Chove (muito).	It rains (a lot).
Chove muito em Belém.	It rains a lot in Belém.

Sometimes it is common to state how the weather is at the moment of speech. In this case you should use the verb *estar* (to be) plus the weather expression, as in the following examples:

▼ CURRENT WEATHER

Portuguese	English
Está fazendo frio hoje.	It's cold today.
Está fazendo calor hoje.	It's hot today.
Está ventando muito.	It's very windy.
Está nublado.	It's cloudy.
Está húmido!	It's humid!
Tem neblina na estrada.	There is fog on the road.
Tem relâmpago e trovoada.	There is lightning and thunder.
O tempo está feio!	The weather is ugly!/It will rain!
O tempo está bonito!	The weather is nice!

Alert

Even though you will not encounter a lot of bad weather in Brazil, remember that it is a tropical country, and it will probably rain unexpectedly. Also, be sure to understand the temperature readings, which are not in Fahrenheit, but rather in Celsius (i.e., freezing point is 0°C, same as 32°F). Hot weather is probably 40°C, or about 99°F. Fair weather is about 25°C or 75°F. Brazilians will feel cold at 15°C, or about 60°F!

Exercise: What's the Weather Like?

Now put your new knowledge to use! Translate the following sentences about the weather. Check your answers in Appendix C.

1. It's really hot in the Amazon.

   _____.

2. It does not snow in Brazil.

   _____.

3. It's hot in the north of Brazil.

   _____.

4. There is some fog on the road.

   _____.

5. The weather is nice today.

   _____.

The Vocabulary of Clothes

Since you just learned expressions for the weather, it is good to make connections with another important set of vocabulary, namely clothes! What kinds of clothes do you wear during the different seasons? What accessories do you have with you depending on the weather? In this section you will learn these vocabulary items and much more.

▼ ***ROUPA DE VERÃO/PRAIA* (SUMMER CLOTHES/BEACH WEAR)**

Portuguese	English
calção de banho	man's swim trunks
maiô	woman's swimsuit
biquini	bikini
shortes	shorts, short pants
saída de praia	cloth you wear around your waist as you leave the pool/beach
camiseta	T-shirt
camiseta sem manga	sleeveless shirt, tank top
sandálias	sandals
sandália japonesa	flip-flops

Here's a short list of accessories or products that you would wear or take with you to the beach:

▼ ***ACESSÓRIOS E PRODUTOS DE PRAIA* (BEACH ACCESSORIES AND PRODUCTS)**

Portuguese	English
óculos de sol, óculos escuros	sunglasses
bolsa de praia	beach bag
cadeira de praia	beach chair
sobrinha de praia	beach umbrella
bronzeador	tanning lotion
protetor solar	sunscreen

Essential

Brazilians don't usually read magazines or books when they go to the beach. The beach is a place to see and to be seen, and a place to flirt. It is the quintessential social hangout, where friends and acquaintances meet. When visiting a beach in Brazil, try to start up a conversation with a local beach-goer!

What about the clothes one might wear during the winter months? First of all, in Brazil the seasons are not as clearly delineated as in the United States. Because Brazil is a such a huge country, the north and northeast can have an array of tropical and subtropical climates while the south and southeast is more temperate. In any case, if you are visiting southern cities such as Rio de Janeiro and São Paulo in the winter months (June, July, and August for countries located below the Equator!), you should know the following vocabulary items:

▼ ***ROUPA DE INVERNO* (WINTER CLOTHES)**

Portuguese	English
botas	boots
luvas	gloves, mittens
chapéu, touca	hat
malha	sweater, sweatshirt
xale	scarf
casaco de frio	winter coat
casaco de couro	leather coat
impermeável	rain coat
jaqueta	jacket
pulôver	pullover, vest

Here is a typical conversation at a store where someone is trying to purchase clothes for the winter/autumn season:

Q: *Bom dia, senhora, em que posso servi-la?* (Good morning, ma'am, how can I help you?)
A: *Bom dia, estou procurando um pulôver.* (Good morning, I'm looking for a pullover.)
Q: *Pois não, nós temos aqui uma variedade para a senhora.* (Of course, here we have a great variety for you, ma'am.)
A: *Ah, sim, vocês têm algum sem manga?* (Oh, yes, do you have a vest?)
Q: *Sim, temos. São inclusive mais baratos.* (Yes, we sure do. In fact they are less expensive.)
A: *Ah, são lindos.* (Oh, they are beautiful.)

Q: *Quer experimentar esses?* (Do you want to try these on?)
A: *Quero, sim.* (I sure do.)
Q: *Então o lugar de experimentar fica logo ali. Qualquer coisa, pode falar comigo.* (The fitting rooms are right over there. If you need anything, just call me.)
A: *Muito obrigada.* (Thank you very much.)
Q: *Pois não, senhora.* (Sure, ma'am.)

Exercise: What Would You Wear?

Make a list of all the clothes and accessories you would wear according to the weather conditions. You can see some possible answers in Appendix C.

1. *Faz muito sol, a temperatura é de 38 graus Celsius.*

   _____

2. *Chove muito!*

   _____

3. *Está nevando.*

   _____

4. *Está um pouco frio, a temperatura é de 15 graus Celsius.*

   _____

5. *Você está em Copacabana!*

   _____

CHAPTER 17

Imperative and Subjunctive Constructions

The imperative and the subjunctive forms in Portuguese are intricate, but don't be intimidated by them! The imperative forms are the basis for the subjunctive constructions, which you will see later in this chapter. You will also learn the past subjunctive, as well as when to use the indicative and when to use the subjunctive. Have fun!

Imperative Constructions

When you want to have something done, you need a quick and easy way to express yourself. The English equivalent would be a verbal "command" or forceful request. In Portuguese, we use the imperative mode. Here are some examples of imperative constructions:

Ligue *para mim mais tarde.* [you] (Call me later.)
Comam *tudo!* [you (pl.)] (Eat everything!)
Abra *a janela, por favor!* [you] (Open the window, please!)
Trabalhem *mais rápido!* [you (pl.)] (Work faster!)

Notice that you usually give commands to either one person (you) or a group of people (you [pl.]). Normally we don't tell ourselves what to do, or even just ourselves and a group of people (i.e., we could say "let us [verb]" or "let me [see]," but that's not strictly a command or an imperative construction). So the imperative is relatively easy to learn because you only have to know two basic forms, singular and plural.

The following table shows how to write the imperative in Portuguese.

▼ IMPERATIVE OF *–AR* VERBS

Verb	First Person Form	Imperative	English
estudar (to study)	*estudo*	*Estude! Estudem!*	Study!
começar (to start)	*começo*	*Comece! Comecem!*	Start!
chegar (to arrive)	*chego*	*Chegue! Cheguem!*	Arrive!

In writing this verb, start with the first person singular, present indicative form of the verb. If the verb is *estudar* (to study), then the first person form is *estudo* (I study). Next, drop the last vowel and add the ending *–e* for singular forms or *–em* for plural forms. You are done! Now remember the rules in Portuguese about phonetic adjustments. Depending on the end vowels, you might have to add other letters to make the verbs sound alike, across conjugations. This is what happens to the verb *começar* (to start). In the first person form, this verb ends in *–o* and is preceded by the consonant *–ç–*. This makes the sound soft, like the [s] sound in "sat" or "sought." When the *–o* is dropped, and the *–e* is added, the *–ç–* can become *–c–*, because *–ce* produces the correct soft [s] sound. A somewhat similar situation occurs with the verb *chegar* (to arrive). In this case, it is necessary to include change with the combination *–gu–*; otherwise *–ge–* would sound like *gente* (people), with a soft consonantal sound.

Alert

Here we use the words "soft" and "hard" to describe consonants and vowels in Portuguese, but we need to make sure that everyone understands what we mean. By "soft" we mean sounds that are made with some friction of the air leaving the mouth, like the *j* in "jewel" or the *g* in "gist." By "hard" we mean sounds that are made with the sudden release of air, as in the *g* of "ghost."

Next, look at the imperative forms of verbs that end in *–er* and *–ir*.

▼ IMPERATIVES OF *–ER* AND *–IR* VERBS

Verb	First Person Form	Imperative	English
beber (to drink)	*bebo*	*Beba! Bebam!*	Drink!
fazer (to do)	*faço*	*Faça! Façam!*	Do!
trazer (to bring)	*trago*	*Traga! Tragam!*	Bring!
dormir (to sleep)	*durmo*	*Durma! Durmam!*	Sleep!
partir (to leave)	*parto*	*Parta! Partam!*	Leave!
pedir (to ask for)	*peço*	*Peça! Peçam!*	Ask for [it]!
vir (to come)	*venho*	*Venha! Venham!*	Come!

So, in this case, we drop the *–o* and add either *–a* or *–am* according to the number of listeners. Although they might look irregular, because they are based on the irregular first person form, these imperative verbs are actually very regular. Now, here's a list of the truly irregular imperative/command forms:

▼ IRREGULAR IMPERATIVES

Verb	Imperative	Example
dar (to give)	*Dê ! Dêem!*	*Me dê isso!* (Give me that!)
ser (to be)	*Seja! Sejam!*	*Sejam bonzinhos!* (Be nice [you (pl.)]!)
estar (to be)	*Esteja! Estejam!*	*Esteja aqui às nove!* (Be here at nine!)
ir (to go)	*Vá! Vão!*	*Vá embora!* (Go away!)
saber (to know)	*Saiba! Saibam!*	*Saiba que eu sou forte!* (Know [be aware] that I am strong!)

As you can see, there is no need to indicate the first person singular form of the present tense, since it does not matter for the purpose of creating these imperative verbs. They are all irregular from the start. These verbs are very handy when you want to communicate something immediately without a lot of subtlety.

If you would like to be a little more polite, you have to use what we call a present subjunctive. Read on.

Introducing the Subjunctive

The subjunctive scares a lot of language learners, especially those whose native language is not Italian, Spanish, or French. This of course includes English speakers, to whom the subjunctive seems unfamiliar and formal. The use of the subjunctive that is easiest for students to understand is the one that relates to "suggestion" or "want." You have just learned how to give a "command" for something you want done. Now you are going to achieve the same result, but you will do it in a more educated, polite way.

The other good news is that the forms of the subjunctive are the same as the commands you just learned! Look at the following comparative list of examples.

Limpe *a mesa!* (Clean the table!) [direct command]
Quero ***que*** *você* ***limpe*** *a mesa.* (I want you to clean the table.) [subjunctive]
Façam *o trabalho de casa!* (Do [you all] the homework!) [direct command]
Eu quero ***que*** *vocês* ***façam*** *o trabalho de casa.* (I want you all to do the homework.) [subjunctive]

Notice that the subjunctive forms happen when preceded by the word *que* (that). So you use the subjunctive form after the introduction of another subordinate clause that ends with the relative pronoun *que*. See the following table to get a clear picture of this subjunctive "map."

▼ **SUBJUNCTIVE CONSTRUCTION**

Expression of "Want"	*que*	[another subject]	Subjunctive Verb
Eu quero	*que*	*vocês*	*aprendam.*
Literal Translation: I want that you (pl.) learn.			
Eu preciso	*que*	*ela*	*me chame.*
Literal Translation: I need that she calls me.			
Eu sugiro	*que*	*você*	*estude mais.*
Literal Translation: I suggest that you study more.			
Eu desejo	*que*	*eles*	*saibam de tudo.*
Literal Translation: I desire that they know everything.			

Translating sentences from the Portuguese subjunctive to English is hard because English speakers don't usually say "We want that she learn." In fact, this sentence is a bit awkward. English speakers today are far more likely to say "We want her to learn." So, given the choice, English speakers would generally much rather use the infinitive rather than the subjunctive form.

Now, the previous complex sentences are written in the present tense. This means that both the first part of the sentence (the main clause, *quero* [I want]) and the second part (the *que*, or subordinate clause) are all in the present tense. But what if I wanted to say not "I long" but rather "I longed"? What would happen to the second part of the sentence? Read on to find out.

Past Subjunctive

The past subjunctive is used when the main clause is in the past and also requires you to play the "agreement game" again. Look at the following chart to get a better understanding:

▼ PAST SUBJUNCTIVE CONSTRUCTION

Expression of "Want"	que	[another subject]	Subjunctive Verb
Eu gostaria	*que*	*vocês*	*aprendessem.*
Translation: I wanted you (pl.) to learn.			
Eu precisava	*que*	*ela*	*me chamasse.*
Translation: I needed for her to call me.			
Eu sugeri	*que*	*você*	*estudasse mais.*
Translation: I suggested that you study more.			
Eu desejava	*que*	*eles*	*soubessem de tudo.*
Translation: I longed for them to know.			

Notice that the first verb is in either the preterite (*sugeri* [I suggested]) or in the imperfect (*precisava* [I needed]), or even in the conditional (*gostaria* [I wanted] or [would have liked]). All of these verb tenses imply that the desire existed before, and the next verb is a longing or unrealized event or action on the part of another agent.

You may also use the past subjunctive when you express doubt in the first clause. The verb that comes in the subordinate clause is in the past subjunctive, as in the following examples:

Duvidávamos que eles viessem. (We doubted that they would come.)
Não era certo que ela estivesse ali. (It was not certain that she was there.)

Finally, if there is a verb of emotion or surprise in the main clause, the next one in the subordinate is also in the past subjunctive:

Era surpreendente que ele ***tivesse*** *medo.* (It was suprising that he would be afraid.)
Fiquei triste que eles não ***telefonassem****.* (I was sad that they did not call.)

Future Subjunctive

Portuguese also has a verb mood called the future subjunctive. This construction works much the same way as other subjunctive forms. Use this verb with the words *se* (if), *quando* (when), and *enquanto* (while) in order to describe something that has not happened yet, as in the the following examples:

Podemos ir ao cinema, ***se*** *você* ***quiser****.* (We can go to the movies, if you want.)
Se fizer *frio, pomos o casaco.* (If it becomes cold, we'll put on the coat.)
Limpo a casa ***quando*** *ela* ***vier****.* (I'll clean the house when she comes.)
Quando *eu* ***puder****, ligo para você.* (When I can, I'll call you.)
Enquanto *eu* ***dormir****, não faça barulho.* (While I sleep, don't make any noise.)
Fique em casa ***enquanto*** *eu* ***estiver*** *fora.* (Stay home while I am out.)

Here is how you come up with the future subjunctive forms: First, start with the preterite tense form of *eles* (they) of any verb. For example, *falaram* (they spoke). Then remove the *–am* ending and add the following endings for the appropriate subject.

▼ CONJUGATING THE FUTURE SUBJUNCTIVE

if-clause	*–ar* verb	*–er* verb	*–ir* verb
	falaram	*comeram*	*dormiram*
Se eu	*falar*	*comer*	*dormir*
Se você	*falar*	*comer*	*dormir*
Se ele/ela	*falar*	*comer*	*dormir*
Se nós	*falarmos*	*comermos*	*dormirmos*
Se vocês	*falarem*	*comerem*	*dormirem*
Se eles/elas	*falarem*	*comerem*	*dormirem*

Notice that the first three persons (I, you, she/he) are conjugated by simply dropping the original ending and adding nothing. The next three persons are conjugated by adding some endings. Again, the same endings apply to all *–ar*, *–er*, and *–ir* verbs, respectively. Other subjunctive forms are *for* (be), *estiver* (be [located]), and *souber* (know).

Indicative or Subjunctive?

Sometimes it is difficult to decide whether to use one of the indicative tenses or the subjunctive tenses. In order to figure this out, ask yourself these questions: First, is the form in the main or the subordinate clause? If it's in the main clause, chances are you will need the indicative. Remember that most of the time the subordinate clause comes after the relative pronoun *que* (that). Second, ask yourself whether the action is a hypothetical or an action based on a condition. Chances are that such an action will be expressed in the subjunctive. If you are dealing with statements of fact, use the indicative. Here are some examples that will help you clarify these ground rules:

▼ **INDICATIVE VERSUS SUBJUNCTIVE EXAMPLES**

Indicative [fact]	Subjunctive [desire, doubt, request]
Você estuda muito.	*Eu quero que você estude muito.*
You study a lot.	I want to study a lot.
Ele tem um carro azul.	*Ele quer um carro que seja azul.*
He has a blue car.	He wants a car that is blue.
Elas foram ao banco.	*Eu queria que elas fossem ao banco.*
They went to the bank.	I wanted them to go to the bank.

Practice with the Subjunctive Forms

Now that you've had some experience with the subjunctive forms, let's see what you remember. The following exercises will test your knowledge and push you to determine which form should be used where. Check your answers in Appendix C when you're finished.

Subjunctive Forms: Exercise A

Write the verbs in parentheses in the subjunctive—present, past, or future.

1. *Eu preciso que vocês me* _____ (respond). (I need you to answer me.)
2. *Ela deseja que você lhe* _____ (give) *o livro.* (She wants you to give her the book.)
3. *Nós gostaríamos que ele* _____ (come) *mais cedo.* (We wanted him to come earlier.)
4. *Eles se surpreenderam que ela* _____ (was) *tão magra.* (They were surprised that she was so skinny.)
5. *Se não* _____ (be) *muito tarde, vou pegar o ônibus.* (If it is not too late, I will take the bus.)
6. *Enquanto ele* _____ (need) *de mim, eu vou ajudá-lo.* (While he needs me, I will help him.)

Subjunctive Forms: Exercise B

Indicative or subjunctive? Circle the correct verb.

1. *Se eu me* ***lembro/lembrasse*** *de tudo, seria mais fácil.* (If I remembered everything, it would be much easier.)
2. *Elas não se* ***esquecem/esqueçam*** *de nada.* (They do not forget anything.)
3. *Nós gostaríamos que eles* ***trouxeram/trousessem*** *a cerveja.* (We would like them to bring the beer.)
4. *É bom que eles* ***comem/comam*** *tudo.* (It's nice that they eat everything.)

Expressions with the Verb *Dar*

At this point in your language learning, it is important to add some idiomatic expressions that will help you sound more "native." These expressions do not necessarily follow subjunctive clauses, but they may. The important thing to learn is that this particular verb *dar* (to give) is very versatile in the Portuguese language.

▼ *DAR* (TO GIVE) EXPRESSIONS

Expression: *dar* (to be sufficient)
Example: *O dinheiro não dá para sair de ferias.* (The money is not enough for vacation.)

Expression: *Assim não dá!* (That's unacceptable!)
Example: *Mais que vinte dólares? Assim não dá!* (More than twenty bucks? That's not right!)

Expression: *dar certo* (to work out [well])
Example: *Faça assim que dá certo.* (Do it this way and it will work out.)

Expression: *dar em nada* (to fall through)
Example: *Tentei, mas não deu em nada.* (I tried, but it fell through.)

Expression: *dar um jeito/jeitinho* (to find a way)
Example: *Dá um jeitinho pra mim?* (Can you help me out/find a way for me?)

Expression: *dar em* [person] (to hit someone)
Example: *Ela deu no irmão dela.* (She hit her brother.)

Expression: *dar um passeio* (to go for a stroll/on an outing)
Example: *Vamos dar um passeio?* (Do you want to go out for a stroll?)

Expression: *dar um pulo* (to stop by)
Example: *Vou dar um pulo na casa dela.* (I'll make a quick stop by her house.)

Expression: *dá para/pra* [verb] (it's possible to/can [verb])
Example: *Dá pra entender isso?* (Can you understand that?)

Exercise: Using the Verb *Dar*

Now see if you can test your comprehension of these new expressions. Determine the best translation for the following sentences in English. Check your answers in Appendix C.

1. I made breakfast, but it didn't turn out well.

   _____

2. This is just not right!

   _____

3. I'll call a friend, and we'll find a solution.

   _____

4. The new venture fell through.

   _____

CHAPTER 18

Means of Communication

You have learned the difference between preterite and imperfect, practiced the subjunctive mood, and learned about Brazilian culture. Now you have some basic communication skills, not only to survive when you're visiting Brazil but also to really engage in meaningful conversations. By the end of this chapter, you'll feel even more confident about your language skills!

In Person

You will have lots of opportunities to converse in Portuguese when you get to Brazil, and in this chapter you will review some information that you have already learned but want to sharpen up. First, make sure to greet people correctly when you are in Brazil. Here are some familiar greetings:

Portuguese	English
Olá, como vai?	Hello, how are you?
Como vai o senhor?	How are you (sir)?
Como vai a senhora?	How are you (ma'am)?
Bem, obrigado.	Fine, thanks. [*obrigada* for female speakers]
Oi, tudo bem?	Hi, how's it going?
Tudo bom!	Great!
Tudo legal!/Tudo jóia!	Great! [a little slang]
E aí, tudo bem?	So, how's it going?

Portuguese	English
Mais ou menos.	So-so.
Tudo em ordem.	Everything is fine [literally "in order"].
Até logo./Até mais.	See you soon./See you later [literally "until"].
Tchau!	Bye!

One quick note on saying goodbye: Brazilians have adopted the word *tchau* from the Italian *ciao* (bye), pronouncing it very closely to the Italian, but with a Portuguese spelling. The original word in Portuguese for "goodbye" is *adeus*, which is still very common in European Portuguese. The diminutive *adeuzinho* is also heard among friends. If, however, a Brazilian says *adeus*, it usually has a serious connotation, as in "goodbye forever." So you might want to avoid saying that, especially after you have made some friends!

At a Social Gathering

Learning a language can be so much fun because you are able to make so many new friends from a different culture. In a social gathering, you have to master not only familiar greetings, but also ones that are a bit more formal in nature. Following are some examples of greetings and introductions that will help you with your newly acquired "social skills."

Q: Flávia: *Rodrigo, eu gostaria de te apresentar à Dona Maria.* (Rodrigo, I would like to introduce you to Mrs. Maria.) [The word *Dona* is an honorific, a sign of respect, and it is followed by one's first name.]
A: Rodrigo: *Muito prazer, Dona Maria.* (Nice to meet you, Mrs. Maria.)
Q: Flávia: *Dona Maria, eu gostaria de lhe apresentar ao meu amigo Rodrigo.* (Dona Maria, I would like to introduce you to my friend Rodrigo.)
A: Dona Maria: *Muito prazer, Rodrigo, você é o noivo da Flávia?* (Nice to meet you, Rodrigo, are you Flávia's fiancé?)

Other less formal examples are as follows:

Q: Michele: *Olá pessoal, eu gostaria de apresentar para vocês o meu amigo Robert.* (Hello guys, I would like to introduce you [pl.] to my friend Robert.)

A: Robert: *Prazer!* (My pleasure!)
Q: Felícia: *Oi Robert, tudo bem?* (Hi Robert, how's it going?)
A: Robert: *Tudo bem, mas estou morrendo de calor!* (Great, but I'm dying from this heat!)

Here are some more casual examples:

Q: Flávia: *Este é o meu amigo Patrício.* (This is my friend Patrício.)
A: Sílvio: *Esta é a minha esposa Isaura.* (This is my wife Isaura.)
Q: Flávia: *Encantada.* (Nice to meet you.)
A: Sílvio: *Muito prazer.* (My pleasure.)

Other responses to introductions include the following:

Igualmente. (Likewise.)
O prazer é (todo) meu. (The pleasure is [all] mine.)

Making Conversation in Portuguese

After introductions are done, the real conversation begins. Your host/hostess will probably say *bem-vindo* ("welcome" if you are a man) or *bem-vinda* ("welcome" if you are a woman). Once you have been introduced to people, you will have to carry on a conversation that goes beyond simple greetings. At times you might want to ask for clarification. Here are some useful guidelines.

Getting into the conversation with polite interruption:

perdão (excuse me; sorry)
por favor (please)
por obséquio (please [more formal])
por gentileza (please [more formal])

These expressions indicate you are not following the conversation:

Desculpa, não entendi. (Sorry, I didn't understand.)
Não escutei direito. (I didn't hear that well.)

Perdão, não compreendo. (Sorry, I don't understand.)

Here's how to express your confusion with a question:

Como? (What?)
Desculpa, o que o senhor/a senhora falou? (Pardon me, what did you say sir/ma'am?)
O que significa . . . ? (What does . . . mean?)
Quando se diz . . . ? (When do you say . . . ?)
Por que o senhor/a senhora disse que . . . ? (Why do you [sir/ma'am] say . . . ?)

Here's how to request that the speaker repeat what was said:

Por favor, o senhor/a senhora poderia repetir? (Please, could you repeat that [sir/ma'am]?)
Por gentileza, o senhor/a senhora poderia repetir o que disse? (Please, could you repeat what you said [sir/ma'am]?)
O senhor/a senhora poderia me fazer o favor de repetir? (Would the gentleman/the lady do me the favor of repeating that?)

When you are learning a new language, it may seem like people are speaking way too fast. This is because you are still learning the beginnings and ends of words, and they all seem to blend together. So you might want to ask speakers to slow down using the following expressions:

Desculpe, não falo português fluentemente. Você poderia falar mais devagar? (Sorry, I don't speak Portuguese fluently. Could you speak a little slower?)
Por favor, o senhor/a senhora poderia falar mais devagar? Eu não entendi da primeira vez. (Please, would the gentleman/the lady speak a little slower? I didn't get it the first time.)

Here are some other tips that you might find useful:

- Say *com licença* (excuse me) when you are passing through a crowd and need to get somewhere.
- Say *perdão!* or *desculpa!* (sorry!) if you need to apologize for bumping into someone.
- Say *com a sua licença* (excuse me) if you need to excuse yourself from the table.

Conversation Starters

Suppose that you have no idea as to how to start talking. Here are some topics that can help you:

o clima (the weather)
a situação econômica (the economic situation)
a situação internacional (the international situation)
os filmes que estão passando no momento (the movies currently showing)

Here are some questions to get conversations started with native speakers:

Que clima maravilhoso, não acha? (What wonderful weather, don't you think?)
Que tempo horrível lá fora, não? (What horrible weather outside, right?)
O que você acha? (What do you think?)
Que filmes você gosta de ver? (What movies do you like to see?)

Farewell

Everything must come to an end, and so do conversations. Here are some ways of saying "goodbye" in Portuguese.

Até logo! (See you later!)
Até mais! (See you soon!)
Até a próxima. (Until next time.)
Até amanhã. (Until tomorrow.)
Tchau! (Bye!)

Cultural Differences in Conversations

Brazilians normally like to talk about a variety of topics, such as the weather, fashion, and hotly debated or even controversial topics. The role of the United States in the world, and how this affects Brazilians worldwide, is a favorite among many university students and young people in general. The concept of "Brazilianness" or what it means to be "Brazilian" is another common topic of discussion. In that same vein, be prepared to answer many questions about what it really means to be an "American" or about your views on current world affairs. If talking about these topics makes you uncomfortable, say so! Brazilians will most likely not insist, and then will invite you to a party so you can learn more about their country!

Communication by Mail

Generally, Portuguese speakers write letters in a highly stylized fashion. Here are some guidelines for good letter writing.

As in English, the date is an essential part of the letter. In Portuguese the date usually goes on the top left-hand side of the paper. Take a look at how dates are expressed in Portuguese.

12 de maio de 2013
Boston, 12 de maio de 2013
Boston, 12/5/2013
12/5/2013

Letter headings depend on purpose and the intended reader. Most of the information will be on the left, unless it is displayed in the letterhead itself. In most formal business letters, the title of the recipient is indicated. If it is not, always start the letter with *Prezado Senhor* (Dear Sir) or *Prezada Senhora* (Dear Madam). If you do not know whom the letter addresses, such as all of those in an executive board, you can use *Prezados Senhores* (Dear Sirs). Notice that in Portuguese, abbreviations are not used when addressing the recipient.

For more personal or informal letters, you do not need to include the address, and the salutation is the next printed item. The most common salutations parallel those in English. Here are a few examples:

Meu querido José (My dear José)
Querido José (My dear José)
Meu caro José (My dear José)
Caro José (My dear José)
Minha querida Suzana (My dear Suzana)
Querida Suzana (My dear Suzana)
Minha cara Suzana (My dear Suzana)
Cara Suzana (My dear Suzana)
Meus queridos José e Suzana (My dear José and Suzana)
Queridos José e Suzana (My dear José and Suzana)
Meus caros José e Suzana (My dear José and Suzana)
Caros José e Suzana (My dear José and Suzana)

Common courtesy requires introductions in friendly letters. In business letters, introductions are not expected, since you want to be more efficient and get straight to the point. Here are some frequent introductions, from more informal to more formal:

Olá, Renato. Como vai? (Hello Renato, how are you?)
Eu estou te escrevendo para dizer que . . . (I am writing to let you know that . . .)
Desejo lhe comunicar que . . . (I would like to communicate that . . .)

The body of the letter is where you get to display your knowledge of Portuguese! There are no preset rules here, but make sure you keep on track, stick to the point, and remember to be consistent with your message.

The farewell of the letter also depends on how you started it. If you are writing a formal letter, stick to formal farewells. But if you are writing to a friend, it's always good to be friendlier at the end too. Here are some examples:

Atenciosamente (literally "Attentively," but better translated as "Cordially")
Saudações cordiais (literally "Cordial salutations," or better "Cordially")

Um forte abraço (literally "A strong hug," or better "A hug," but not too informal)
Com todo meu carinho (With all my affection)
Um abraço (A hug)
Beijos (Kisses)

Making Phone Calls

Communicating on the telephone is a lot harder for early learners because telephone conversations do not provide the visual clues usually associated with face-to-face conversations. However, learning some new words might help you to decipher what people are saying on the telephone.

▼ VOCABULARY: USING THE TELEPHONE

Portuguese	English
o aparelho (telefônico)	the telephone set
o gancho	the handset
o orelhão	the telephone booth [literally "the big ear" because of the design of public telephones in Brazil]
desligar o telefone	to hang up the phone
atender o telefone	to answer the phone
deixar um recado	to leave a message
a secretária (eletrônica)	the answering machine [literally "the electronic secretary"]
fazer um telefonema	to make a phone call
apertar, aperte	to press, press
o telefone sem fio	cordless phone
o sinal, dar sinal	dial tone, to have a dial tone

Here is some vocabulary relating to placing a phone call:

▼ VOCABULARY: MAKING A PHONE CALL

Portuguese	English
telefonista, ajuda ao assinante	operator, subscriber's assistance
o código de área	the area code
com cartão de crédito	with credit card
interurbano	long distance
ligação direta	direct call, person-to-person call
o catálogo telefônico	the phone book
o número de telefone	the phone number
chamada a cobrar	collect call
o código internacional	the country code

Some public phones still exist in Brazil, usually in an interesting design that looks like a huge yellow ear. To make a telephone call, you must buy a *cartão telefônico* or "phone card" because coins are not used in public phones anymore. You can buy phone cards at *bancas de revistas* or "newsstands." However, it is much more common to have people buy phone cards to add credit to their prepaid cell phones.

Here are some useful phrases that will help you to communicate on the phone in Portuguese:

Bom dia! (Good morning!)
Boa tarde! (Good afternoon!)
Boa noite! (Good evening! or Good night!)
Pronto! (Yes!)
Alô! (Hello!)
Quem fala? (Who's speaking?)

Here are some examples of how to introduce yourself:

Eu me chamo Flávia Cavalcanti. (My name's Flávia Cavalcanti.)
Sou o Senhor Silva. (I'm Mr. Silva.)
Meu nome é Madalena Alves. (My name is Madalena Alves.)

If the connection is not clear, and you would like more clarification, you might want to say the following:

Como se escreve (o seu nome)? (How do you write [your name]?)
O senhor/A senhora poderia me dizer como se escreve? (Can the gentleman/the lady tell me how it is written?)

Remember to spell your name slowly to listeners on the phone. Review how each of the letters are pronounced in Portuguese (refer to Chapter 2 for the alphabet). Also, be sure to describe each letter, if necessary. For example, in order to spell *Flávia*, say the following: "*F maiúscula* (capital F), *l, a com acento agudo* (acute accent), *v, i, a.*"

After the initial greeting, you might want to speak to someone on the phone. Here is how you do that:

Posso falar com o Senhor Barros? (Could I speak to Mr. Barros?)
Gostaria de falar com o Senhor Barros, por gentileza. (I would like to speak to Mr. Barros, please.)
Você poderia me transferir para a secção de atendimento ao consumidor, por favor? (Could you transfer me to the consumer's desk, please?)
O senhor poderia me fazer a gentileza de informar o Senhor Barros que a filha dele quer falar com ele? (Would you (the gentleman) do me the favor of informing Mr. Barros that his daughter would like to speak to him?)

Here are possible responses to your requests:

É da parte de quem? (Who is calling?)
Sim, pois não. Um momento, por favor. (Yes, of course. One moment, please.)
Desculpe a demora, senhora Ferreira. (Sorry for the wait, Ms. Ferreira.)
Um momentinho, vou fazer a transferência. (A [short] moment, I will make the transfer.)
Sinto muito, mas a doutora Maria Luiza não se encontra. (Sorry, but Dr. Maria Luiza is not in.)
Sinto muito, mas o senhor César está na outra linha. (Sorry, but Mr. César is on the other line.)

Sinto muito, mas a senhora Freitas está com um cliente. (Sorry, but Ms. Freitas is with a client.)
Deseja deixar recado, senhora/senhor? (Would you like to leave a message, ma'am/sir?)
Gostaria de esperar na linha, senhora/senhor? (Would you like to wait on the line, ma'am/sir?)
O senhor/A senhora pode telefonar mais tarde? (Would the gentleman/the lady like to call back later?)
O senhor/A senhora deseja falar com outra pessoa? (Would the gentleman/the lady like to speak to someone else?)

At this point, you may decide to leave a message (say *Posso deixar um recado, por favor?* meaning "Can I leave a message, please?") or call back at another time. Hopefully you will be able to connect and proceed with a conversation!

Vocabulary: *Ficar, Tornar-se, Fazer-se* (to Become)

Part of communicating better has to do with learning idiomatic expressions in the new language. Some of these expressions are seen in familiar verbs that have additional meanings. Three such verbs in Portuguese have the meaning of "to become": *ficar, tornar-se*, and *fazer-se*.

Ficar

In addition to meaning "to remain" and "to be located," *ficar* also can be used to mean "to get [emotion or state]." Here are some examples:

Ele ficou achateado com a notícia. (He got upset with the news.)
A rua ficava sempre deserta. (The street would always get deserted.)
Eles ficaram impressionados. (They became impressed.)

Tornar-se

The additional meaning here is that there is some intention on the part of the agent as far as the act of becoming, meaning that the person put some effort into this transformation. Here are some examples:

Bill Gates se tornou um dos homens mais rico do mundo. (Bill Gates became one of the richest men in the world.)
De repente elas se tornaram uns anginhos. (All of a sudden they became little angels.)
No final do semestre os alunos se tornam estudiosos. (At the end of the semester the students become dedicated.)

Fazer-se

This verb is used when referring to occupations, where the person took some time to gather the necessary tools or education to "become" the person with that professional identity. Here are some examples:

Amália se fez cantora de Fado. (Amália became a *Fado* singer.)
Anne e Júlia se fizeram professoras. (Anne and Júlia became professors.)
Depois de seis anos eu me fiz médica. (After six years I became a doctor.)

More Vocabulary: Expressions with *Estar com* and *Ter*

Some of the most important expressions in Portuguese are created with two very simple verbs: *estar com* (to be [emotion/state]) and *ter* (to have). In order to speak this language fluently, you must know these expressions.

▼ EXPRESSIONS WITH *ESTAR COM*

Portuguese	English	Example
estar com saudades	to be homesick	*Anne está com saudades de casa.*
estar com pena de	to be sorry for	*Júlia está com pena do gato dela.*
estar com pena que	to be sorry that	*Daniel está com pena que o gato está doente.*
estar com medo de	to be afraid of	*Cláudia está com medo do cachorro.*

Portuguese	English	Example
estar com medo que	to be afraid that	*Seu irmão está com medo que ela desmaie.*
estar com preguiça	to be feeling lazy	*Eu estou com preguiça de escrever.*
estar com dor de [part of body]	to have a/an [part of body] ache	*Ela está com dor de barriga.*

All of these expressions can be used with the verb *ter* as well. Just substitute the verb *ter* for the verbal expression *estar com* and the meaning is exactly the same. It is just a matter of which verb you would like to use.

However, there are some expressions that can only be used with *ter* (to have). They are as follows:

▼ EXPRESSIONS WITH *TER* (TO HAVE)

Expression: *ter jeito para* (to have a knack for)
Example: *Ele tem jeito pra desenho.* (He's got a knack for drawing.)

Expression: *ter a ver com* (to have to do with)
Example: *Isso tem a ver com os problemas sociais.* (This has to do with social problems.)

Expression: *não ter nada a ver com* (to have nothing to do with)
Example: *Isso não tem nada a ver com família.* (This has nothing to do with family.)

Expression: *não ter culpa de* [verb] (to not be guilty of [verb])
Example: *Ele não tem culpa de ser tão bonito.* (It's not his fault he's so handsome. [literally: he's not guilty for being . . .])

Communication Practice

Now it's time to see what you can remember from the lessons in this chapter. In the first exercise, you will decide if the sentences are formal or informal. In the second exercise, you'll decide what to say based on the context. Check your answers in Appendix C when you're finished.

Exercise: Formal or Informal?

Remember what you learned about communicating formally and informally? Decide if the sentence in the conversation is formal or informal.

1. *Alô!* _____
2. *Sinto muito, mas a doutora não se encontra.*
   _____
3. *Gostaria de esperar na linha, senhor?* _____
4. *Oi, posso falar com o Luís?* _____
5. *Gostaria de falar com o Senhor Gomes, por gentileza.*
   _____

Exercise: Communication Practice

Follow the English directions to decide what to say in Portuguese. Use the context you're given and write your answer in the space.

1. You want to let them know who you are.
   _____
   _____
2. You would like to speak to Mr. Barros.
   _____
   _____
3. You would like to leave a message.
   _____
   _____
4. You want to thank the person on the other line.
   _____
   _____

APPENDIX A

English to Portuguese Glossary

a lot
muito

abdominal
abdominal

able
capaz

absolutely not!
absolutamente!

abstinence
abstinência

acceptable
aceitável

accessible
accesível

accident
acidente

accommodating
acomodável

accountant
contador, contadora

achieve, to
conseguir

action
ação

actor
ator

actress
atriz

acute accent
acento agudo

address
endereço

admissible
admisível

adolescence
adolescência

adorable
adorável

affable
afável

affection
carinho

against
contra

airplane
avião

all
todos, todas

all, entire
todo, toda

allow, to
permitir

already
já

also
também

always
sempre

American
americano, americana

anaconda
sucuri

and
e

angel
anjo

Angola
Angola

Angolan
angolano, angolana

animal
animal

annex
anexo

anniversary
aniversário

annual
anual

answer the phone, to
atender o telefone

answer, to
responder

answering machine
secretária (eletrônica)

anxious
ansioso, ansiosa

any
qualquer

applaud, to
aplaudir

apple
maçã

approve, to
passar

April
abril

apron
avental

architect
arquiteto, arquiteta

ardor
ardor

area code
código de área

Argentina
Argentina

Argentinian
argentino, argentina

armadillo
tatu

aroused
excitado, excitada

arrest, to
prender

arrive, to
chegar

arrive, to
vir

art
arte

artist
artista

as much as
tanto... quanto

as... as
tão... quanto

ask for, to
pedir

asleep
dormindo

astral
astral

at the same time
ao mesmo tempo

atheist
ateu, atéia

athlete
atleta

athleticism
atletismo

attack
ataque

attend, to
assistir (a)

attention
atenção

attentively, cordially
atenciosamente

auditor
auditor

August
agosto

aunt
tia

Australia
Austrália

Australian
australiano, australiana

Austria
Áustria

Austrian
austríaco, austríaca

author
autor

automobile
automóve

autumn, fall
outono

average height
estatura mediana

avoidable
evitável

awake
acordado, acordada

backpack
mochila

bad
ruim

bag
bolsa

baggage
bagagem

bakery
padaria

bald
careca

bank
banco

bank teller
bancário

barbershop
barbeiro

basketball
basquetebol

bath
banho

be (situated), to
ficar

be able to, to
poder

be afraid, to
ter medo

be surprised, to
surpreender-se com

be windy, to
ventar

be, to
estar, ser

beans
feijão

beautiful
lindo, linda

beauty salon
salão de beleza

because
porque

become, to
ficar

beef
carne de boi

beer
cerveja

before
antes

behind
atrás, detrás de

Belgian
belga

Belgium
Bélgica

believe, to
acreditar

belt
cinto

better
melhor

big
grande

bill, account
conta

billfold
carteira

billion
bilhão

biodegradable
biodegradável

bird
pássaro

birthday
aniversário

black pepper
pimenta do reino

blasphemous
blasfemável

blind
cego

blond
louro, loura

blouse
blusa

blue
azul

board
quadro

boat, ship
nau, navio

bonbon
bombom

book
livro

bookstore
livraria

boring
chato, chata

both
ambos, ambas

bowsprit
proa

boy
menino

boyfriend
namorado

Brazil
Brasil

Brazilian
brasileiro, brasileira

bread
pão

brevity
brevidade

bride
noiva

bring, to
trazer

British
britânico, britânica

brother
irmão

brother-in-law
cunhado

brown
marrom

brush/comb (oneself), to
pentear-se

building
prédio

business partner
sócio, social

busy
ocupado, ocupada

but, however
porém

butcher shop
açougue

buy, to
comprar, fazer compras

bye
tchau

cake
bolo

calculating
calculável

call oneself, to
chamar-se

call, to
chamar, ligar

call (someone or something a name), to
chamar de

calm
tranqüilo, tranqüila

Canada
Canadá

Canadian
canadense

capital
capital

captain
capitão

car
carro

cardiac
cardíaco

cards
cartões

care
cuidado

careful (exclamation)
cuidado

cashew fruit
caju

cat
gato

catch, to
pegar

cathedral
catedral

celebrated
comemorado, comemorada

celebrity
pessoa famosa

censor
censor

center
centro

central
central

central-west
centro-oeste

chaos
caos

chapter
capítulo

cheap
barato, barata

cheese
queijo

chess
xadrez

chest
baú

child
criança

Chile
Chile

Chilean
chileno, chilena

China
China

Chinese
chinês, chinesa

chocolate
chocolate

choose, to
escolher

Christmas
Dia de Natal

church
igreja

circumflex accent
acento circunflexo

city
cidade

clarinet
clarinete

clarity
claridade

class
aula

classroom
sala de aula

clean
limpo, limpa

clearly
claramente

client
consumidor

climax
clímax

clinic
clínica

close, nearby
perto

clothes designer
costureiro, costureira

clothing store
loja de roupa

cloudy
nublado

club, gym
clube

coat
casaco

code
código, senha

coffee
café

cold
frio

cold cuts
frios

collect call
chamada a cobrar

Colombia
Colombia

Colombian
colombiano, colombiana

color
cor

comb
pente

come back, to
voltar

come, arrived
vindo

come, to
vir

comedian
comediante

comedy
comédia

comfortable
confortável

commercial
comercial

communicate, to
comunicar

communication
comunicação

compete, to
competir

competitors
concorrentes

complain about, to
queixar-se de

complete, to
completar

complex
complexo

compose, to
compor

composer
compositor

comprehend, to
compreender

comprehensible
compreensível

computer
computador

concert
concerto

conductor
condutor

conference
conferência

congested (by a cold)
constipado

conspirer
conspirador

consulate
consulado

consultant
consultor, consultora

consumed
consumido, consumida

consumer
consumidor

contruct, to
construir

conversation (colloquial)
bate-papo

convertible
conversível

convince oneself of, to
convencer-se de

cordial
cordial

cordially
saudações cordiais

cordless phone
telefone sem fio

corner
esquina

correct
certo

correct, to
corrigir

Costa Rica
Costa Rica

Costa Rican
costa-riquenho

cotton
algodão

counting
contagem

country code
código internacional

couple
casal

cousin (female)
prima

cousin (male)
primo

covered
coberto

cradle
berço

crazy
louco, louca

creature
criatura

credit
crédito

crime
crime, delito

cruel
cruel

Cuba
Cuba

cultural
cultural

culture
cultura

cup
xícara

curable
curável

curious
curioso

currency exchange agency
casa de câmbio

customer
freguês, freguesa

customs
alfândega

cycle, ring
ciclo

cyclist
ciclista

Czech
checo, checa

Czech Republic
República Checa

dad, daddy
papai

dance, to
dançar

dark-skinned
moreno, morena

daughter
filha

daughter-in-law
nora

day
dia

day after tomorrow
depois de amanhã

day before yesterday
anteontem

dear (formal)
prezado, prezada

dear (informal)
caro, cara, querido, querida

December
dezembro

decide to, to
decidir-se a

dedicate (oneself to), to
dedicar-se a

demand, to
exigir

dentist
dentista

desire, to
desejar

destroyer
destruidor

detector
detector

development
desenvolvimento

dial tone
sinal

dice
dado

dictionary
dicionário

died, dead
morto

dierisis
trema

difficult
difícil

digestible
digestível

direct call
ligação direta

director
diretor, diretora

dish
prato

divided
dividido

divorced
divorciado, divorciada

do, to
fazer

doctor
médico

document
documento

dog
cachorro, cão (male); cachorra, cadela (female)

dollars
dólares

domino
dominó

door
porta

dream
sonho

dress (oneself), to
vestir-se

dressmaker
costureiro, costureira

drink coffee, to
tomar café

drink, to
beber, tomar

drop
gota

drug, drugs
droga

drugstore
drogaria, farmácia

drunk
bêbado, bêbada

dry cleaners
lava a seco

duck
pato

durable
durável

Dutch
holandês, holandesa

dynasty
dinastia

early
cedo

earth, land
terra

easy
fácil

eat, to
comer

economic
econômico, econômica

Ecuador
Ecuador

Ecuadorian
equatoriano, equatoriana

editor
editor

educational
educacional

egg
ovo

Egypt
Egito

Egyptian
egípcio, egípcia

eight
oito

eight hundred
oitocentos, oitocentas

eighteen
dezoito

eighth
oitavo, oitava

eighty
oitenta

elderly
idoso, idosa

electric guitar
guitarra

electronic
eletrônico, electrônica

elegance
elegância

elegant
elegante

elementary school
escola primária

elephant
elefante

eleven
onze

eleventh
décimo-primeiro, décima-primeira

embarassed
envergonhado, envergonhada

embassy
embaixada

emotional
emocional

employee, maid
empregado, empregada

engineer
engenheiro, engenheira

England
Inglaterra

English
inglês, inglesa

enjoy, to
aproveitar

enjoy, to (slang)
curtir

enter, to
entrar em

entertain (oneself), to
divertir-se

envelope
envelope

error, mistake
erro

escape
fuga

essay, rehearsal
ensaio

essential
essencial, imprescindível

Europe
Europa

ever, never
jamais

exam
exame

excellent
excelente

exceptional
excepcional

excited
animado, animada

exclude, to
excluir

excuse me, sorry
com licença

exercise, to
fazer exercícios

exist, to
haver

exotic
exótico

expensive
caro

explain, to
explicar

explainable
explicável

explanations
explicações

eyeglasses
óculos

facing, in front of
defronte de

factory worker
operário, operária

falsifiable
falsificável

familiar, pertaining to family
familiar

family
família

famous
famoso, famosa

far from
longe de

fast
rápido, rápida

fat
gordo, gorda

fatal
fatal

father
pai

father-in-law
sogro

favor
favor

feat
façanha

February
fevereiro

federal
federal

fervor
fervor

few
poucos, poucas

fiancé
noivo

fiancée
noiva

fifteen
quinze

fifth
quinto, quinta

fifty
cinqüenta

find
arrumar

find, to
encontrar

find, to
achar

find (oneself), to
encontrar-se

finish, to
acabar, terminar

first
primeiro, primeira

five
cinco

five hundred
quinhentos, quinhentas

fix
arrumar

fluently
fluentemente

fly (insect)
mosca

fog
neblina

food
comida

forget to, to
esquecer-se de

fork
garfo

forklift
grúa

fortunately
felizmente

forty
quarenta

fossil
fóssil

four
quatro

four hundred
quatrocentos, quatrocentas

fourteen
catorze

fourth
quarto, quarta

France
França

French
francês, francesa

frequency
freqüência

Friday
sexta-feira

friend, partner
companheiro, companheira

frog
sapo

fundamental
fundamental

funny
engraçado, engraçada

future, future tense
futuro

garage
garagem

garlic cloves
dente de alho

German
alemão, alemã

Germany
Alemanha

gesture
gesto

get married, to
casar-se

get together, to
reunir-se

get used to, to
acostumar-se com

get, to
conseguir

gift
presente

girl
menina

girlfriend
namorada

give, to
dar

go on a short trip, to
dar uma volta

go on strike, to
fazer greve

go out (leave), to
sair

go to bed
deitar-se

go up, to
subir

go, to
ir

god
deus

goddaughter
afilhada

godfather
padrinho

godmother
madrinha

godson
afilhado

going-away party
festa de despedida

good
bom, boa

good afternoon
boa tarde

good evening
boa noite

good luck
boa sorte

good morning
bom dia

grammar
gramática

granddaughter
neta

grandfather
avô

grandma, granny
vovó

grandmother
avó

grandpa
vovô

grandson
neto

grave accent
acento grave

great
ótima

Great Britain
Grã-bretanha

great-grandfather
bisavô

great-grandmother
bisavó

Greece
Grécia

Greek
grego, grega

groom
noivo

guide
guia

gym
ginásio

hairdresser
cabelereiro

Haiti
Haiti

Haitian
haitiano, haitiana

ham
presunto

handed, given
entregue

handset
gancho

hang up the phone, to
desligar o telefone

hangover
ressaca

happiness
felicidade

happy
contente, feliz

have a good trip
boa viagem

have breakfast, to
tomar café

have dinner, to
jantar

have fun, to
divertir-se

have lunch, to
almoçar

have, to
haver

have, to
ter

have a dial tone, to
dar sinal

he
ele

hear, to
escutar, ouvir

heart
coração

Hebrew
hebreu, hebréia

hello
alô

help
socorro

help, to
ajudar

her (possessive)
dela

here
aqui

hey!
opa!

hi
oi, olá

himself/herself
si

his (possessive)
dele

Hindu
hindu

Holland
Holanda

homework
dever de casa

horrible
horrível

hospital
hospital

hot
calor

hot pepper sauce
pimenta malagueta

hotel
hotel

hour
hora

house
casa

how many
quantos, quantas

how much
quanto, quanta

hug
abraço

humid
húmido, húmida

humor
humor

hunt
caça

hurt (oneself), to
machucar-se

husband
marido

I
eu

idea
idéia

ideal
ideal

idealism
idealismo

identical
idêntico

identification tag
crachá

identity
identidade

illegal
ilegal

image
imagem

immediately
imediatamente

impede, to
impedir

importance
importância

important
importante

impose, to
impor

impossible
impossível

impressed
impressionado, impressionada

in
em

in front of
em frente de

in love
apaixonado, apaixonada

include, to
incluir

included
incluído, incluída

incomparable
incomparável

Independence Day
Dia da Independência

India
Índia

Indian
indiano, indiana

indoor soccer
futebol de salão

inevitable
inevitável

inferior
inferior

inform, to
informar

information
informação

inside
dentro de

insistence
insistência

inspector
inspetor

instructor
instrutor

intelligent
inteligente

international
internacional

Internet café
cyber café

introduce, to
apresentar

invent, to
inventar

inventor
inventor

invest, to
investir

Iran
Irã

Iranian
iraniano, iraniana

Iraq
Iraque

Iraqi
iraquiano, iraquiana

Ireland
Irlanda

Irish
irlandês, irlandesa

irritated
irritado, irritada

Israel
Israel

Israeli
israelense

Italian
italiano, italiana

Italy
Itália

Jamaica
Jamaica

Jamaican
jamaicano, jamaicana

January
janeiro

Japan
Japão

Japanese
japonês, japonesa

jealousy
ciúme

judge
juiz, juíza

July
julho

June
junho

kennel
canil

key
chave

king
rei

kiss
beijo

kiss (one another), to
beijar-se

knife
faca

know (information, skills), to
saber

know (people, places), to
conhecer

lack, to
fazer falta

lamentable
lamentável

last week
na semana passada

late
tarde

Latin America
América Latina

laugh, to
rir

laugh (at), to
rir-se de

lawyer
advogado, advogada

learn, to
aprender

leave a message, to
deixar um recado

leave, to
deixar

leave, to
partir

legume
legume

less
menos

lesson
lição

liberty
liberdade

library
biblioteca

lie, to
mentir

lightning
relâmpago

like, to
gostar de

likewise, same here
igualmente

liqueur
licor

Lisbon
Lisboa

listen, to
escutar, ouvir

live, to
viver

live, to (reside)
morar

local
local

long distance
interurbano

look like, to
parecer-se com

look (at oneself), to
olhar-se

look (at), to
olhar para

lose, to
perder

lotion
loção

love
amor

love, to
amar

luggage, baggage
bagagem

ma'am, lady
senhora

macaw
arara

made, done
feito

magazines
revistas

make, to
fazer

make a phone call, to
fazer um telefonema

make peace, to
fazer as pazes

mall
shopping

manager
gerente

map
mapa

March
março

married
casado, casada

match
fósforo

May
maio

may
poder

May I help you?
Pois não?

mechanic
mecânico

medicine, medication
medicina, remédios

melon
melão

mentor
mentor

Merry Christmas
Feliz Natal

message
recado

Mexican
mexicano, mexicana

Mexico
México

midnight
meia-noite

milk
leite

million
milhão

millionaire
milionário

minus
menos

mirror
espelho

miserable
miserável

miss, to
fazer falta

mister, sir
senhor

modern
moderno, moderna

mom, mommy
mamãe

moment
momento

Monday
segunda-feira

money
dinheiro

more
mais

mother
mãe

mother-in-law
sogra

motor, engine
motor

movie
filme

movies, cinema
cinema

Mozambique
Moçambique

multiple choice
múltipla escolha

museum
museu

music
música

musician
músico, música

my
meu, minha (plural: meus, minhas)

naked
nu, nua

name
nome

nap
cuchilo

napkin
guardanapo

national
nacional

natural
natural

nature
natureza

necklace
corrente, colar

need, to
precisar de

negotiable
negociável

neighbor
vizinho, vizinha

neighborhood
bairro

neither
também não

neither... nor
nem... nem

nephew
sobrinho

nervous
nervoso, nervosa

never
nunca

new
novo, nova

newspaper
jornal

newspaper seller
jornaleiro

newsstand
banca de revista

Nicaragua
Nicarágua

Nicaraguan
nicaragüense

nice
simpático

nice to meet you
encantado, encantada

nice to meet you
muito prazer

niece
sobrinha

nine
nove

nine hundred
novecentos, novecentas

nineteen
dezenove

ninety
noventa

ninth
nono, nona

no
não

nobody
ninguém

noise
barulho

noon, midday
meio-dia

normal
normal

north
norte

North America
América do Norte

northeast
nordeste

not one
nenhum, nenhuma

not yet
ainda não

notebook
caderno

nothing
nada

November
novembro

number
número

obvious
óbvio

October
outubro

office
escritório

official
oficial

official meeting
audiência

old
velho, velha

on top
em cima de

one
um, uma

one hundred and one
cento e um, uma

onion
cebola

open, to
abrir

opened
aberto

operator, directory assistance
telefonista, ajuda ao assinante

opposing
opositor

orange
laranja

organ
órgão

organizable
organizável

original
original

orphan
órfão

ostensible
ostensível

other
outro, outra

our
nosso, nossa

outside
fora

over, on top
sobre

overcome, to
passar

page
página

paid
pago

pain
dor

paintbrush
pincel

pale
pálido, pálida

Panama
Panamá

Panamanian
panamenho, panamenha

paper
papel

pardon, sorry
perdão

park
parque

partial
parcial

party
festa

pass, to
passar

passable
passável

past
passado, passada

pastor
pastor

patience
paciência

pay, to
pagar

peach
pêssego

pediatrician
pediatra

pen
caneta

pencil
lápis

people
gente

perfume
perfume

persistent
persistente

personal infinitive
infinitivo pessoal

pharmacist
farmacêutico, farmacêutica

phenomenal
fenomenal

Philippines
Filipinas

phone book
catálogo telefônico

phone card
cartão telefônico

phone number
número de telefone

photographer
fotógrafo, fotógrafa

phrase
frase

physical
físico

physicist
físico

pianist
pianista

pig's ear
orelha de porco

pig's foot
pé de porco

pig's tail
rabo de porco

pilot
piloto

pineapple
abacaxi

piranha
piranha

pity
dó

place
lugar

place, to
colocar, pôr

plane, leveled
plano

planet
planeta

play (a sport or game), to
jogar

play (an instrument), to
tocar

please
por favor

please (formal)
por gentileza, por obséquio

pleasure
prazer

Poland
Polônia

police
polícia

policeman
guarda

Polish
polonês, polonesa

poor
pobre

popular
popular

populated
populoso, populosa

pork
carne de porco

Portugal
Portugal

possible
possível

postcard
cartão postal

poster
cartaz

potent
potente

power
potência

presentable
presentável

president
presidente

press, to
apertare

pretend, to
fazer de conta

preterite tense
pretérito

pretty
bonito, bonito

problem
problema

profession
profissão

program
programa

progressive present
presente contínuo

proposal
proposta

protector
protetor

psychotherapist
analista

pub
barzinho

purple
roxo

purse
bolsa

put in jail
pôr na cadeia

put, set
posto

put, to
colocar, pôr

question
pergunta

radio
rádio

rain, to
chover

ranking
ranking

rational
racional

raw
cru, crua

react, to
reagir

read, to
ler

receive, to
receber

recognized
reconhecido, reconhecida

red
vermelho, vermelha

redhead, redheaded
ruivo, ruiva

reflect, to
refletir

reflector, reflecting
refletor

remember, to
recordar

remember to, to
lembrar-se

remembrance, souvenir
lembrança

reporter, journalist
jornalista

reptile
réptil

Republican
republicano, republicana

respectable
respeitável

rest, to
descansar

restaurant
restaurante

rested
descansado, descansada

retire, to
deitar-se

rice
arroz

rich
rico, rica

ride a bike, to
andar de bicicleta

rifle
fuzil

right, indeed
pois é

river
rio

root
raiz

rumor
rumor

run, to
correr

sad
triste

said
dito

saint
santo

Saint Patrick's Day
Dia de São Patrício

salesperson
vendedor, vendedora

salt
sal

same
mesmo

sandwich
sanduíche

satisfied
satisfeito, satisfeita

Saturday
sábado

say (imperative)
diga

say, to
dizer

scared
amedrontado, amendrontada

scheme, plan
esquema, complô

school
escola

sea, ocean
mar

second
segundo, segunda

secretary
secretária

section
seção

seductor
sedutor

see, to
ver

see you later
até mais

see you soon
até breve, até logo

see you tomorrow
até amanhã

seen
visto

sell, to
vender

sensational
sensacional

separated
separado, separada

September
setembro

serious
sério, séria

serve, to
servir

service
atendimento

set, to
pôr

seven
sete

seven hundred
setecentos, setecentas

seventeen
dezessete

seventh
sétimo, sétima

seventy
setenta

shave, to
fazer a barba

she
ela

shoe store
sapataria, loja de sapatos

short
baixo, baixa

sick
doente

sick, bored, boring
enjoado, enjoada

simple
simples

since
desde

sing, to
cantar

singer
cantor, cantora

single
solteiro, solteira

sinister
sinistro

sister
irmã

sister-in-law
cunhada

sit, to
sentar-se

situation
situação

six
seis

six hundred
seiscentos, seiscentas

sixteen
dezesseis

sixth
sexto, sexta

sixty
sessenta

size
tamanho

sky
céu

slave quarters
senzala

sleep, to
dormir

slowly
devagar

snow
neve

snow, to
nevar

so
assim

so many
tantos, tantas

so much
tanto, tanta

sober
sóbrio, sóbria

soccer
futebol

socialist
socialista

sofa
sofá

some, something
algum, alguma

someone
alguém

son
filho

song
música

song
canção

son-in-law
genro

sorry
desculpe, desculpa

so-so
mais ou menos

soup
sopa

south
sul

South America
América do Sul

southeast
sudeste

speak, to
falar

specialist
especialista

speech, language
fala

spend, to
gastar

sport
esporte

spouse
esposo, esposa

spring
primavera

stairs
escadas

start, to
começar

state
estado

statement
afirmação

stationery store
papelaria

stay, to
ficar

stepfather
padrasto

stepmother
madrasta

storage facility
armazém

store
loja

street
rua

street market
feira

street vendor
vendedor, vendedora ambulante

strong, stocky
forte

student
estudante

student center
centro estudantil

studious
estudioso, estudiosa

study, to
estudar

stunned
estupefato, estupefata

stupid
burro, burra

such
tal

suddenly, all of a sudden
de repente

sugarcane rum
cachaça

summer
verão

sun, sunny
sol

Sunday
domingo

superior
superior

supermarket
supermercado

Sure!, Of course!
Pois não!

surprising
surpreendente

Sweden
Suécia

Swedish
sueco, sueca

sweet
doce

Swiss
suíço, suíça

Switzerland
Suíça

systems analyst
analista de sistemas

table
mesa

take advantage of, to
aproveitar

take, to
tirar

talent
talento

talk (n.), conversation
conversa

tall
alto, alta

task, homework
tarefa

taxi
táxi

tea
chá

teacher, professor
professor, professora

telephone
telefone

telephone booth
orelhão

telephone call
telefonema

telephone set
aparelho (telefônico)

television
televisão

ten
dez

tennis player
tenista

tenor
tenor

tenth
décimo, décimo

test
prova

Thai
tailandês, tailandesa

Thailand
Tailândia

thank you
obrigado, obrigada

that
aquele, aquela

that (neutral, abstract)
aquilo

the
o, a, os, as

theirs
deles, delas

then
então

then, that
que

there, over there
lá

these
esses, essas

they, them
eles, elas

thin
magro, magra

think
achar

think, to
refletir

third
terceiro, terceira

thirteen
treze

thirty
trinta

this
esse, essa, este, esta

this (neutral, abstract)
isso

thorax
tórax

those
aqueles, aquelas

thousand
mil

three
três

three hundred
trezentos, trezentas

thunder
trovoada

Thursday
quinta-feira

tilde
til

time, climate
tempo

times (occasions)
vezes

tired
cansado, cansada

title
título

to
para

to you, him, her (indirect pronoun)
lhe

today
hoje

together
juntos, juntas

tomorrow
amanhã

too much
demais

touch, to
tocar

traditional
tradicional

traffic
trânsito

train
trem

transfer
transferência

transfer, to
transferir

trash
lixo

travel, to
viajar

traveler's checks
cheques de viagem

tree
árvore

trip
viagem

truck
caminhão

truth
verdade

Tuesday
terça-feira

turkey
peru

twelfth
décimo-segundo, décima-segunda

twelve
doze

twentieth
vigésimo, vigésima

twenty
vinte

twenty-one
vinte e um, vinte e uma

twenty-three
vinte e três

twenty-two
vinte e dois, vinte e duas

two
dois, duas

two hundred
duzentos, duzentas

type
tipo

ugly
feio, feia

uncle
tio

under
debaixo de, embaixo de

understand, to
entender

understand, to
compreender

usual
usual

vacation
ferias

Valentine's Day
Dia dos Namorados

valor
valor

value
valor

vegetable oil
óleo

vegetables
verduras

Venezuela
Venezuela

Venezuelan
venezuelano, venezuelana

very
muito

vinegar
vinagre

virgin
virgem

visit, to
visitar

voluntary, volunteer
voluntário

wait on, to
atender

waiter
garçom

waitress
garçonete

walk, to
andar

want, to
querer

war
guerra

wash, to
lavar

wash (oneself), to
lavar-se

watch, to
assistir (a)

way
jeito

we
nós

we (the people)
a gente

weak
fraco, fraca

weather
clima, tempo

Wednesday
quarta-feira

week
semana

weekend
fim de semana

welcome
bem-vindo, bem-vinda

well
bem

what, which
qual

what
que

when
quando

where
onde

where to, to where
aonde

while
enquanto

white
branco

who
quem

why
por quê

widow
viúva

widower
viúvo

wife, spouse
mulher

will
vontade

window
janela

wine
vinho

winter
inverno

wish, to
desejar

with
com

with credit card
com cartão de crédito

with you (pl.) (archaic)
convosco

won
ganho

wonder
maravilha

wonderful
maravilhoso, maravilhosa

wood
pau

work
trabalho

work, to
trabalhar

worried
preocupado, preocupada

worry about, to
preocupar-se com

worse, the worst
pior

Wow!
Nossa!

write, to
escrever

written
escrito

year
ano

yellow
amarelo, amarela

yes
sim

yesterday
ontem

yet
ainda

you
tu, você, vocês

you (pl.) (archaic)
vós

young
jovem

young boy (pejorative)
moleque

young man
rapaz

youngest offspring
caçula

youngster
jovem

your (familiar)
teu, tua, teus, tuas

your (formal)
seu, sua, seus, suas

yours (archaic)
vosso

zinc
zinco

Zulu
zulu

APPENDIX B

Portuguese to English Glossary

a, as
the (fem.)

a gente
we (the people)

abacaxi
pineapple

abdominal
abdominal

aberto
opened

abraço
hug

abril
April

abrir
to open

absolutamente!
absolutely not!

abstinência
abstinence

acabar
to finish

açaí
acai fruit, a wild berry found in the Amazon

ação
action

accesível
accessible

aceitável
acceptable

acento agudo
acute accent

acento circunflexo
circumflex accent

acento grave
grave accent

achar
to find, to think

acidente
accident

acomodável
accommodating

acordado, acordada
awake

Açores
also called the Azores, an archipelago or group of islands that belongs to Portugal

acostumar-se com
to get used to

açougue
butcher shop

acreditar
to believe

admisível
admissible

adolescência
adolescence, teenage years

adorável
adorable

advogado, advogada
lawyer

afável
affable

afilhada
goddaughter

afilhado
godson

afirmação
statement

agogô
two bells together, struck with a stick or squeezed together

agosto
August

ainda
yet

ainda não
not yet

ajudar
to help

Alemanha
Germany

alemão, alemã
German

alfândega
customs

algodão
cotton

alguém
someone

algum, alguma
some, something

almoçar
to have lunch

alô
hello

alto, alta
tall

amanhã
tomorrow

amar
to love

amarelo, amarela
yellow

Amazonas
a state in the north of Brazil

ambos, ambas
both

amendrontado, amendrontada
scared

América do Norte
North America

América do Sul
South America

América Latina
Latin America

americano, americana
American

amor
love

analista
psychotherapist

analista de sistemas
systems analyst

andar
to walk

andar de bicicleta
to ride a bike

anexo
annex

Angola
Angola

angolano, angolana
Angolan

animado, animada
excited

animal
animal

aniversário
birthday, anniversary

anjo
angel

ano
year

ansioso, ansiosa
anxious

anteontem
day before yesterday

antes
before

anual
annual

ao mesmo tempo
at the same time

aonde
where to, to where

apaixonado, apaixonada
in love

aparelho (telefônico)
telephone set

apertare
to press

aplaudir
to applaud

aprender
to learn

apresentar
to introduce

aproveitar
to take advantage of, to enjoy

aquele, aquela
that

aqueles, aquelas
those

aqui
here

aquilo
that (neutral, abstract)

arara
macaw

ardor
ardor

Argentina
Argentina

argentino, argentina
Argentinian

armazém
storage facility

arquiteto, arquiteta
architect

arroz
rice

arrumar
fix, find

arte
art

artista
artist

árvore
tree

às
to the (a + as contraction)

assim
so

assistir (a)
to attend, to watch

astral
astral

ataque
attack

até amanhã
see you tomorrow

até breve
see you soon

até logo
see you soon

até mais
see you later

atenção
attention

atenciosamente
attentively, cordially

atender
to answer the phone, to wait on

atender o telefone
to answer the phone

atendimento
service

ateu, atéia
atheist

atleta
athlete

atletismo
athleticism

ator
actor

atrás
behind

atriz
actress

audiência
official meeting

auditor
auditor

aula
class

Austrália
Australia

australiano, australiana
Australian

Áustria
Austria

austríaco, austríaca
Austrian

automóvel
automobile

autor
author

avental
apron

avião
airplane

avó
grandmother

avô
grandfather

azul
blue

bagagem
baggage, luggage

bairro
neighborhood

baixo, baixa
short

bambuzal
plantation of bamboo trees

banca de revista
newsstand

bancário
bank teller

banco
bank

Banco Central
Central Bank (the equivalent of the Federal Reserve)

banho
bath

barato, barata
cheap

barbeiro
barbershop

barulho
noise

barzinho
local pub

basquetebol
basketball

bate-papo
conversation, friendly chat (colloquial)

baú
chest

bêbado, bêbada
drunk

beber
to drink

beijar-se
to kiss one another

beijo
kiss

belga
Belgian

Bélgica
Belgium

bem
well

bem-vindo, bem-vinda
welcome

berço
cradle

berimbau
one-string African instrument

biblioteca
library

bilhão
one billion

biodegradável
biodegradable

bisavó
great-grandmother

bisavô
great-grandfather

blasfemável
blasphemous

blusa
blouse

boa noite
good evening

boa sorte
good luck

boa tarde
good afternoon

boa viagem
have a good trip

bolo
cake

bolsa
bag, purse

bom
good

bom dia
good morning

bombom
bonbon

bonito, bonito
pretty

Boniwa
indigenous language of Brazil

bonzinho, boazinha
very nice (about a person)

bossa nova
jazzy musical style that originated in the sixties in Brazil

branco
white

Brasil
Brazil

brasileiro, brasileira
Brazilian

brevidade
brevity

britânico, britânica
British

burro, burra
stupid

Caatinga
desert-like region of northeast Brazil

cabelereiro
hairdresser

caça
hunt

cachaça
sugarcane rum

cachorra
female dog

cachorro
dog

caçula
youngest offspring

caderno
notebook

café
coffee

caipirinha
a Brazilian cocktail made with limes, sugar, and sugarcane rum

caixa
a small drum with strings in the bottom that creates a sound like a snare drum

caju
cashew fruit

calculável
calculating

calor
hot

caminhão
truck

Canadá
Canada

canadense
Canadian

canção
song

caneta
pen

canil
kennel

cansado, cansada
tired

cantar
to sing

canto
I sing (present)

cantor, cantora
singer

cão
dog

caos
chaos

capaz
able

capital
capital

capitanias
territories awarded to Portuguese officials in the sixteenth century

capitão
captain

capítulo
chapter

capoeira
martial art that incorporates African dance

cardíaco
cardiac

careca
bald

carinho
affection

Carnaval
the equivalent of Mardi Gras, a week of festivities before Lent

carne de boi
beef

carne de porco
pork

carne seca
Brazilian beef jerky

caro, cara
expensive; dear (informal)

carro
car

cartão de crédito
credit card

cartão postal
postcard

cartão telefônico
phone card

cartaz
poster

cartões
cards

casa
house

casa de câmbio
currency exchange agency

casaco
coat

casado, casada
married

casal
couple

casar-se
to get married

castanho
brown, chestnut color

catálogo telefônico
phone book

catar (inf.)
to look for (colloquial)

catedral
cathedral

catorze
fourteen

cavaquinho
a small, four-string guitar-like instrument created in Portugal that later inspired the ukulele

cebola
onion

cedo
early

cego, cega
blind

cem
one hundred

censor
censor

cento e um, cento e uma
one hundred and one

central
central

centro
center

centro estudantil
student center

centro-oeste
central-west

certo
correct

cerveja
beer

céu
sky

chá
tea

chamada a cobrar
collect call

chamar
to call

chamar de
to call (someone or something a name)

chamar-se
to call oneself

chato, chata
boring

chave
key

checo, checa
Czech

chegar
to arrive

cheques de viagem
traveler's checks

Chile
Chile

chileno, chilena
Chilean

China
China

chinês, chinesa
Chinese

chocolate
chocolate

chover
to raïn

chucalho
a shaker instrument made by putting metal cans together and filling it with rocks, sand, or beans

churrasco
Brazilian barbecue

ciclista
cyclist

ciclo
cycle, ring

cidade
city

cinco
five

cinema
movies, cinema

cinema novo
Brazilian cinematic movement

cinqüenta
fifty

cinto
belt

ciúme
jealousy

claramente
clearly

claridade
clarity

clarinete
clarinet

clima
weather

clímax
climax

clínica
clinic

clube
club, gym

coberto
covered

código
code

código de área
area code

código internacional
country code

colocar
to put, to place

Colombia
Colombia

colombiano, colombiana
Colombian

com
with

com licença
excuse me, sorry

começar
to start

comédia
comedy

comediante
comedian

comemorado, comemorada
celebrated

comer
to eat

comercial
commercial

comida
food

companheiro, companheira
friends, partners

competir
to compete

completar
to complete

complexo
complex

complô
scheme

compor
to compose

compositor
composer

comprar
to buy

compreender
to understand, to comprehend

compreensível
comprehensible

computador
computer

comunicação
communication

comunicar
to communicate

concerto
concert

concorrentes
competitors

condutor
conductor

conferência
conference

confortável
comfortable

conhecer
to know (people, places)

conseguir
to achieve, to get

conspirador
conspirer

constipado
congested (by a cold)

construir
to contruct

consulado
consulate

consultor, consultora
consultant

consumido, consumida
consumed

consumidor
consumer, client

conta
bill, account

contador, contadora
accountant

contagem
act of counting

contente
happy

contra
against

conversa
conversation, talk (n.)

conversível
convertible, capable of being converted

convosco
with you (pl.) (archaic)

Copacabana
famous Brazilian beach located in Rio de Janeiro

cor
color

coração
heart

cordial
cordial

corrente, colar
necklace

correr
to run

corrigir
to correct

Costa Rica
Costa Rica

costa-riquenho
Costa Rican

costureiro, costureira
clothes designer, dressmaker

convencer-se de
to convince oneself of

crachá
identification tag

crédito
credit

criança
child

criatura
creature

crime
crime

cru, crua
raw

cruel
cruel

Cuba
Cuba

cuíca
drum-like instrument with a stiff string upon which the player slides his fingers up and down to produce a squeaky sound

cuidado
care; (be) careful (exclamation)

cultura
culture

cultural
cultural

cunhada
sister-in-law

cunhado
brother-in-law

curável
curable

curioso
curious

curtir
to enjoy (slang)

Curupira
human-like creature whose feet are backward; brings bad luck or death to those who see him

cyber café
Internet café

D. Pedro I
Dom Pedro I, the Emperor of Brazil

D. Pedro II
Dom Pedro II, son of D. Pedro I and Emperor of Brazil

dado
dice

dançar
to dance

dar
to give

dar sinal
to have a dial tone

dar uma volta
to go on a short trip

de repente
suddenly, all of a sudden

debaixo de
under

decidir-se a
to decide to

décimo, décimo
tenth

décimo-primeiro, décima-primeira
eleventh

décimo-segundo, décima-segunda
twelfth

dedicar-se a
to dedicate oneself to

defronte de
facing, in front of

deitar-se
to go to bed, to retire

deixar
to leave

deixar um recado
to leave a message

dela
her

dele
his

deles, delas
theirs

delito
crime

demais
too much

dente de alho
garlic cloves

dentista
dentist

dentro de
inside

depois de amanhã
day after tomorrow

descansado, descansada
rested

descansar
to rest

desculpe, desculpa
sorry

desde
since

desejar
to wish, to desire

desenvolvimento
development

desligar o telefone
to hang up the phone

destruidor
destroyer

detector
detector

detrás de
behind

deus
god

devagar
slowly

dever de casa
homework

dez
ten

dezembro
December

dezenove
nineteen

dezesseis
sixteen

dezessete
seventeen

dezoito
eighteen

dia
day

Dia da Independência
Independence Day

Dia de Natal
Christmas Day

Dia de São Patrício
Saint Patrick's Day

Dia dos Namorados
Valentine's Day

dicionário
dictionary

difícil
difficult

digestível
digestible

dinastia
dynasty

dinheiro
money

diretor, diretora
director

dito
said

divertir-se
to entertain oneself, to have fun

dividido
divided

divorciado, divorciada
divorced

dizer
to say

dó
pity

doce
sweet

documento
document

doente
sick

dois, duas
two

dólares
dollars

domingo
Sunday

dominó
domino

Dona
a title of respect for women, as in Dona Maria

dor
pain

dormindo
asleep

dormir
to sleep

doze
twelve

droga
drug, drugs

drogaria
drugstore

durável
durable

duzentos, duzentas
two hundred

e
and

econômica
economic

Ecuador
Ecuador

editor
editor

educacional
educational

egípcio, egípcia
Egyptian

Egito
Egypt

ela
she, her

ele
he, him

eles, elas
they, them

elefante
elephant

elegância
elegance

elegante
elegant

eletrônico, eletrônica
electronic

em
in

em cima de
on top

em frente de
in front of

embaixada
embassy

embaixo de
under

emocional
emotional

empregado, empregada
employee, maid

encantado, encantada
a pleasure, nice to meet you

encontrar
to find

encontrar-se
to find oneself

endereço
address

engenheiro, engenheira
engineer

engraçado, engraçada
funny

enjoado, enjoada
sick, bored, boring

enquanto
while

ensaio
essay, rehearsal

então
then

entender
to understand

entrar em
to enter

entregue
handed, given

envelope
envelope

envergonhado, envergonhada
embarassed

equatoriano, equatoriana
Ecuadorian

erro
error, mistake

escadas
stairs

escola
school

escola primária
elementary school

escolher
to choose

escrever
to write

escrito
written

escritório
office

escutar
to hear, to listen

especialista
specialist

espelho
mirror

esporte
sport

esposo, esposa
spouse

esquecer-se de
to forget to

esquema
scheme, plan

esquina
corner

esse, essa
this

essencial
essential

esses, essas
these

estado
state

estar
to be

estatura mediana
average height

este, esta
this

estudante
student

estudar
to study

estudioso, estudiosa
studious

estupefato, estupefata
stunned

eu
I

Europa
Europe

evitável
avoidable

exame
exam

excelente
excellent

excepcional
exceptional

excitado, excitada
aroused

excluir
to exclude

exigir
to demand

exótico
exotic

explicações
explanations

explicar
to explain

explicável
explainable

faca
knife

façanha
feat

fácil
easy

Fado
Portuguese musical style

fala
speech; language

falar
to speak

falsificável
falsifiable

família
family

familiar
familiar, pertaining to family

famoso, famosa
famous

farmacêutico, farmacêutica
pharmacist

farmácia
drugstore

fatal
fatal

favor
favor

fazer
to do, to make

fazer a barba
to shave

fazer as pazes
to make peace

fazer compras
to buy

fazer de conta
to pretend

fazer exercícios
to exercise

fazer falta
to miss, to lack

fazer greve
to go on strike

fazer um telefonema
to make a phone call

federal
federal

feijão
beans

feijoada
Brazilian black bean and pork stew

feio, feia
ugly

feira
street market

feito
made, done

felicidade
happiness

feliz
happy

Feliz Natal
Merry Christmas

felizmente
fortunately

fenomenal
phenomenal

ferias
vacation

fervor
fervor

festa
party

festa de despedida
going-away party

fevereiro
February

ficar
to be (situated), to become, to stay

filha
daughter

filho
son

Filipinas
Philippines

filme
movie

fim de semana
weekend

físico (adj.)
physical

físico (n.)
physicist

fluentemente
fluently

fora
outside

forte
strong, stocky

fósforo
match

fóssil
fossil

fotógrafo, fotógrafa
photographer

fraco, fraca
weak

França
France

francês, francesa
French

frase
phrase

freguês, freguesa
customer

freqüência
frequency

frio
cold

frios
cold cuts

fuga
escape

fundamental
fundamental

futebol
soccer

futebol de salão
indoor soccer

futuro
future, future tense

fuzil
rifle

gancho
handset

ganho
won

garagem
garage

garçom
waiter

garçonete
waitress

garfo
fork

gasto
spent

gato
cat

genro
son-in-law

gente
people

gerente
manager

gesto
gesture

ginásio
gym

gordo, gorda
fat

gostar de
to like

gota
drop

Grã-bretanha
Great Britain

gramática
grammar

grande
big

Grécia
Greece

grego, grega
Greek

grúa
forklift

Guanabara
beach/locality in Rio de Janeiro

guaraná
a tropical berry found in the Amazon; the main ingredient in a Brazilian soft drink

guarda
policeman

guardanapo
napkin

guerra
war

guia
guide

guitarra
electric guitar

guri
young boy; indigenous origin word

Haiti
Haiti

haitiano, haitiana
Haitian

haver
to exist, to have

hebreu, hebréia
Hebrew

hindu
Hindu

hoje
today

Holanda
Holland

holandês, holandesa
Dutch

hora, horas
hour, hours

horrível
horrible

hospital
hospital

hotel
hotel

húmido, húmida
humid

humor
humor

hundred
cem

ideal
ideal

idealismo
idealism

idéia
idea

idêntico, idêntica
identical

identidade
identity

idoso, idosa
elderly

igreja
church

igualmente
likewise, same here

ilegal
illegal

imagem
image

imediatamente
immediately

impedir
to impede

impor
to impose

importância
importance

importante
important

impossível
impossible

imprescindível
essential

impressionado, impressionada
impressed

incluído, incluída
included

incluir
to include

incomparável
incomparable

India
India

indiano, indiana
Indian

inevitável
inevitable

inferior
inferior

infinitivo pessoal
personal infinitive

informação
information

informar
to inform

Inglaterra
England

inglês, inglesa
English

insistência
insistence

inspetor
inspector

instrutor
instructor

inteligente
intelligent

internacional
international

interurbano
long distance

inventar
invent, to

inventor
inventor

inverno
winter

investir
to invest

Ipanema
famous beach in Rio de Janeiro

ir
to go

Irã
Iran

iraniano, iraniana
Iranian

Iraque
Iraq

iraquiano, iraquiana
Iraqui

Irlanda
Ireland

irlandês, irlandesa
Irish

irmã
sister

irmão
brother

irritado, irritada
irritated

Israel
Israel

israelense
Israeli

isso
this (neutral, abstract)

Itália
Italy

italiano, italiana
Italian

já
already

Jacarepaguá
locality in São Paulo

Jamaica
Jamaica

jamaicano, jamaicana
Jamaican

jamais
ever, never

janeiro
January

janela
window

jantar
to have dinner, dinner (n.)

Japão
Japan

japonês, japonesa
Japanese

jeito
way

joelho de porco defumado
smoked ham hocks

jogar
to play (a sport or a game)

jornal
newspaper

jornaleiro
newspaper seller

jornalista
reporter, journalist

jovem (adj.)
young

jovem (n.)
youngster

juiz, juíza
judge

julho
July

junho
June

juntos, juntas
together

lá
there, over there

lambada
African-inspired dance and musical style

lamentável
lamentable

lápis
pencil

laranja
orange

lava a seco
dry cleaners

lavar
to wash

lavar-se
to wash oneself

legume
legume, vegetable

leite
milk

lembrança
remembrance, souvenir

lembrar-se
to remember to

ler
to read

lhe
to you, him, her (indirect pronoun)

liberdade
liberty

lição
lesson

licor
liqueur

ligação direta
direct call

ligar
to call

limpo, limpa
clean

lindo, linda
beautiful

lingüiça
Brazilian chorizo or pepperoni

Lisboa
Lisbon

livraria
bookstore

livro
book

lixo
trash

local
local

loção
lotion

loja
store

loja de roupa
clothing store

loja de sapatos
shoestore

longe de
far from

louco, louca
crazy

louro, loura
blond

lugar
place

maçã
apple

machucar-se
to hurt oneself

Madeira
island in the Atlantic Ocean belonging to Portugal

madrasta
stepmother

madrinha
godmother

mãe
mother

magro, magra
thin

maio
May

mais
more

mais ou menos
so-so

mamãe
mom, mommy

Manaus
city in the north of Brazil, capital of the state of Amazonas

mapa
map

mar
sea, ocean

maravilha
wonder

maravilhoso, maravilhosa
wonderful

março
March

marido
husband

marrom
brown

mecânico
mechanic

medicina
medicine

médico
doctor

meia-noite
midnight

meio-dia
noon, midday

melão
melon

melhor
better, best

menina
girl

menino
boy

menos
minus

menos
less

mentir
to lie

mentor
mentor

mesa
table

mesmo
same

meu, minha (plural: meus, minhas)
my

mexicano, mexicana
Mexican

México
Mexico

mil
one thousand

milionário
millionaire

Minas Gerais
a state in the southeast of Brazil

miserável
miserable

Moçambique
Mozambique

mochila
backpack

moderno, moderna
modern

moleque
young boy; pejorative

momento
moment

morar
to live (reside)

moreno, morena
dark-skinned

morto
died

morto, morta
dead

mosca
fly (insect)

motor
motor, engine

MPB, Música Popular Brasileira
Brazilian popular music

mucama
young slave girl who fetches things

muito
a lot, very

muito prazer
nice to meet you

mulher
wife, spouse

múltipla escolha
multiple choice

museu
museum

música
music, song

música sertaneja
Brazilian country music

músico, música
musician

na semana passada
last week

nacional
national

nada
nothing

namorada
girlfriend

namorado
boyfriend

não
no

natural
natural

natureza
nature

nau, navio
boat, ship

neblina
fog

negociável
negotiable

nem... nem
neither... nor

nenhum, nenhuma
not one

nervoso, nervosa
nervous

neta
granddaughter

neto
grandson

nevar
to snow

neve
snow

Nheengatu
indigenous language of Brazil

Nicarágua
Nicaragua

nicaragüense
Nicaraguan

ninguém
nobody

noiva
fiancée, bride

noivo
fiancé, groom

nome
name

nono, nona
ninth

nora
daughter-in-law

Nordeste
northeast

normal
normal

norte
north

nós
we

Nossa!
Wow!

nosso, nossa
our

nove
nine

novecentos, novecentas
nine hundred

novembro
November

noventa
ninety

novo, nova
new

nu, nua
naked

nublado
cloudy

número
number

número de telefone
phone number

nunca
never

o, os
the (masc.)

obrigado, obrigada
thank you

óbvio
obvious

óculos
eyeglasses

ocupado, ocupada
busy

oficial
official

oi
hi

oitavo, oitava
eighth

oitenta
eighty

oito
eight

oitocentos, oitocentas
eight hundred

olá
hi

óleo
vegetable oil

olhar para
to look at

olhar-se
to look at oneself

onde
where

ontem
yesterday

onze
eleven

opa!
hey!

operário, operária
factory worker

opositor
opposing

orelha de porco
pig's ear

orelhão
telephone booth

órfão
orphan

organizável
organizable

órgão
organ

original
original

ostensível
ostensible

ótima
great

outono
autumn, fall

outro, outra
other

outubro
October

ouvir
to hear, to listen

ovo
egg

paciência
patience

padaria
bakery

padrasto
stepfather

padrinho
godfather

pagar
to pay

página
page

pago
paid

pagode
type of backyard samba typical of Rio

pai
father

pálido, pálida
pale

Panamá
Panama

panamenho, panamenha
Panamanian

pandeiro
large tambourine that is played fast and sometimes spun on one finger for show

pão
bread

papai
dad, daddy

papel
paper

papelaria
stationery store

para
to

parcial
partial

parecer-se com
to look like

parque
park

partir
to leave

passado, passada
past

passar
to pass, to overcome, to approve

pássaro
bird

passável
passable

pastor
pastor

pato
duck

pau
wood

pé de porco
pig's foot

pediatra
pediatrician

pedir
to ask for

pegar
to catch

pente
comb

pentear-se
to brush/comb oneself

perdã
pardon, sorry

perder
to lose

perfume
perfume

pergunta
question

permitir
to allow

Pernambuco
state in northeast Brazil

persistente
persistent

perto
close, nearby

peru
turkey

pêssego
peach

pessoa famosa
celebrity

pianista
pianist

piloto
pilot

pimenta do reino
black pepper

pimenta malagueta
hot pepper sauce

pincel
paintbrush

pior
worse, the worst

piranha
piranha

planeta
planet

plano
plane, leveled

pobre
poor

poder
to be able to, can, may

pois é
right, indeed

Pois não!
Sure!

Pois não?
May I help you?

polícia
police

polonês, polonesa
Polish

Polônia
Poland

popular
popular

populoso, populosa
populated

pôr
to put, to place

por favor
please

por gentileza
please (formal)

pôr na cadeia
put in jail

por obséquio
please (formal)

por quê
why

porém
but, however

porque
because

porta
door

Portugal
Portugal

possível
possible

posto
put, set

potência
power

potente
potent

poucos, poucas
few

prato
dish

prazer
pleasure

precisar de
to need

prédio
building

prender
to arrest

preocupado, preocupada
worried

preocupar-se com
to worry about

presentável
presentable

presente
gift

presente contínuo
progressive present

presidente
president

presunto
ham

pretérito
preterite tense

prezado, prezada
dear (formal)

prima
cousin (female)

primavera
spring

primeiro, primeira
first

primo
cousin (male)

proa
bow, front part of the ship

problema
problem

professor, professora
teacher, professor

profissão
profession

programa
program

proposta
proposal

protetor
protector

prova
test

punha
he/she would put (imperfect tense)

quadro
board

qual
what, which

qualquer
any

quando
when

quanto, quanta
how much

quantos, quantas
how many

quarenta
forty

quarta-feira
Wednesday

quarto, quarta
fourth

quatro
four

quatrocentos, quatrocentas
four hundred

que
then, that, what

queijo
cheese

queixar-se de
to complain about

quem
who

querer
to want

querido, querida
dear (informal)

quilombo
village of marooned slaves

quinhentos, quinhentas
five hundred

quinta-feira
Thursday

quinto, quinta
fifth

quinze
fifteen

rabo de porco
pig's tail

racional
rational

rádio
radio

raiz
root

ranking
ranking

rapaz
young man

rápido, rápida
fast

reagir
to react

real, reais
Brazilian currency

recado
message

receber
to receive

Recife
a city in northeast Brazil

reconhecido, reconhecida
recognized

recordar
to remember

refletir
to reflect, to think

refletor
reflector, reflecting

rei
king

relâmpago
lightning

remédios
medicines, medication

repenique
a medium-size drum, larger than a snare-drum, played with a stick and one hand

réptil
reptile

República Checa
Czech Republic

respeitável
respectable

responder
to answer

ressaca
hangover

restaurante
restaurant

reunir-se
to get together

revistas
magazines

rico, rica
rich

rio
river

Rio Capibaribe
Capibaribe River, a river in the state of Pernambuco

Rio Grande do Sul
a state in the south of Brazil

rir
to laugh

rir-se de
to laugh at

roxo
purple

rua
street

ruim
bad

ruivo, ruiva
redhead, redheaded

rumor
rumor

sábado
Saturday

saber
to know (information, skills)

sair
to go out, leave

sal
salt

sala de aula
classroom

salão de beleza
beauty salon

samba
a distinctly Brazilian musical style heavily influenced by the African drumming tradition

samba canção
also called the samba song, a slower samba piece with romantic lyrics put to music

samba enredo
fast, highly rhythmic samba with words and lyrics sung during Carnaval

Sambódromo
the place where samba schools

parade every year in Rio de Janeiro

sanduíche
sandwich

Santa Catarina
a state in the south of Brazil

santo
saint

sapataria
shoe store

sapo
frog

satisfeito, satisfeita
satisfied

saudações cordiais
cordially

seção
section

secretária
secretary

secretária (eletrônica)
answering machine (literally "the electronic secretary")

sedutor
seductor

segunda-feira
Monday

segundo, segunda
second

seis
six

seiscentos, seiscentas
six hundred

semana
week

sempre
always

senha
code

senhor
mister

senhora
ma'am, lady

sensacional
sensational

sentar-se
to sit

sentar-se
to sit oneself

senzala
slave quarters

separado, separada
separated

ser
to be

sério, séria
serious

servir
to serve

sessenta
sixty

sete
seven

setecentos, setecentas
seven hundred

setembro
September

setenta
seventy

sétimo, sétima
seventh

Seu
abbreviation for senhor, a title of respect

seu, sua (plural: seus, suas)
your

sexta-feira
Friday

sexto, sexta
sixth

shopping
mall

si
himself/herself

sim
yes

simpático
nice

simples
simple

sinal
dial tone

sinistro
sinister

sinto muito
I am terribly sorry

situação
situation

sobre
over, on top

sobrinha
niece

sobrinho
nephew

sóbrio, sóbria
sober

socialista
socialist

sócio, social
business partner

socorro
help

sofá
sofa

sogra
mother-in-law

sogro
father-in-law

sol
sun, sunny

solteiro, solteira
single

sonho
dream

sopa
soup

subir
to go up

sucuri
anaconda

sudeste
southeast

Suécia
Sweden

sueco, sueca
Swedish

Suíça
Switzerland

suíço, suíça
Swiss

sul
south

superior
superior

supermercado
supermarket

surdo
a large drum with a low but loud sound (surdo means "deaf" in Portuguese)

surpreendente
surprising

surpreender-se com
to be surprised

tá
short for está

tailandês, tailandesa
Thai

Tailândia
Thailand

tal
such

talento
talent

tamanho
size

também
also

também não
(not) either, neither

tamborim
a small, short drum played very fast with a stick

tanga
short bikini or loincloth

tanto, tanta
so much

tanto... quanto
as much as

tantos, tantas
so many

tão... quanto
as... as

tarde
late

tarefa
task, homework

tatu
armadillo

táxi
taxi

tchau
bye

telefone
telephone

telefone sem fio
cordless phone

telefonema
telephone call

telefonista, ajuda ao assinante
operator, directory assistance

televisão
television

tempo
time, climate

tempo
weather

tenista
tennis player

tenor
tenor

ter
to have

ter medo
to be afraid

terça-feira
Tuesday

terceiro, terceira
third

terminar
to finish

terra
earth, land

Tetra
fourth soccer championship

teu, tua (plural: teus, tuas)
your

tia
aunt

Tijuca
locality in Rio de Janeiro

til
tilde

tio
uncle

tipo
type

tirar
to take

título
title

tocar
to play (an instrument), to touch

todo, toda
all, entire

todos, todas
all

tomar
to drink

tomar café
to have breakfast, to drink coffee

tórax
thorax

trabalhar
to work

trabalho
work, paper

tradicional
traditional

tranqüilo, tranqüila
calm

transferência
transfer

transferir
to transfer

trânsito
traffic

trazer
to bring

trem
train

trema
dierisis

três
three

treze
thirteen

trezentos, trezentas
three hundred

trinta
thirty

triste
sad

Tropicália
psychedelic musical style created by Caetano Veloso and others in the seventies

trovoada
thunder

tu
you

Tukano
indigenous language of Brazil

Tupã
supreme being of the Tupi people

Tupi Guarani
indigenous language of Brazil

um milhão
one million

um, uma
one

usual
usual, or an extension of use

valor
value, valor

velho, velha
old

vendedor, vendedora
salesperson

vendedor, vendedora ambulante
street vendor

vender
to sell

Venezuela
Venezuela

venezuelano, venezuelana
Venezuelan

ventar
to be windy

ver
to see

verão
summer

verdade
truth

verduras
vegetables

vermelho, vermelha
red

vestir-se
to put on clothes, to dress oneself

vezes
times

viagem
trip

viajar
to travel

vigésimo, vigésima
twentieth

vinagre
vinegar

vindo
come, arrived

vinho
wine

vinte
twenty

vinte e dois, vinte e duas
twenty-two

vinte e três
twenty-three

vinte e um, vinte e uma
twenty-one

vir
to come, to arrive

virgem
virgin

visitar
to visit

visto
seen

viu
he/she saw (Preterite)

viúva
widow

viúvo
widower

viver
to live

vizinho, vizinha
neighbor

você
you

você, vocês
you

voltar
to come back

voluntário
voluntary, volunteer

vontade
will

vós
you (pl.) (archaic)

vosso
yours (archaic)

vovó
grandma, granny

vovô
grandpa

xadrez
chess

xícara
cup

Yara
proper name; Tupi divinity

zinco
zinc

zulu
Zulu

APPENDIX C

Answer Key

Chapter 1

Exercise: Suffixes

1. *incidente (incident)*
2. *mecânico (mechanical)*
3. *identidade (identity)*
4. *infelizmente (unfortunately)*
5. *resistência (resistance)*

Chapter 3

Exercise: What to Say?

1. *nome (name)*
2. *chamo/prazer (I call/pleasure)*
3. *onde (where)*
4. *Eu (I)*

Exercise: Goodbye!

1. *como (how)*
2. *obrigada (thank you)*
3. *Tudo (Everything)*
4. *mais or logo (later or soon)*

Exercise: Chapter Review

1. *Desculpe! or Perdão! (Sorry! or Pardon!)*
2. *Com licença. (Excuse me.)*
3. *Obrigada. or Obrigado. (Thank you.)*
4. *Poderia repetir, por favor? (Can you repeat, please?)*
5. *Falo um pouquinho (de português). (I speak a little [Portuguese].)*
6. *Como se diz isso em português? (How do you say this in Portuguese?)*

Chapter 4

Exercise: Practice with Gender

1. *o caderno (notebook)*
2. *a contagem (act of counting)*
3. *o caminhão (truck)*
4. *o armazém (storage facility)*
5. *o amor (love)*
6. *a ação (action)*
7. *o/a socialista (socialist)*
8. *o avental (apron)*
9. *o crachá (identification tag)*
10. *a alfândega (customs)*
11. *o esquema (scheme, plan)*
12. *a liberdade (liberty)*

Exercise: Addressing Others

1. *você (tu in some regions)*
2. *o senhor*
3. *o senhor*
4. *você (tu in some regions)*
5. *você (tu in some regions)*
6. *a senhora*

Exercise: Definite or Indefinite?

1. . . . *um lápis, um ca-derno e uma caneta.*
2. . . . *um livro de português.*
3. . . . *as suas canetas?*
4. . . . *chamaram o José . . .*
5. . . . *ter um ataque cardíaco!*

Exercise: Contractions

1. *Eu sou dos Estados Unidos.*
2. *Eu moro na residência estudantil.*
3. *Ela é de Cuba.*
4. *Eles são da Ilha da Madeira.*
5. *Eu estudo na universidade grande.*

Chapter 5

Exercise: Name the Nationalities

1. *Ela é alemã.*
2. *Ele é brasileiro.*
3. *Eles são russos.*
4. *Eles são italianos.*
5. *Ele é japonês.*

Exercise: Name That Profession!

1. *Ele é pianista. (He is a pianist.)*
2. *Ela é professora. (She is a professor.)*
3. *Ele é bancário. (He is a bank teller.)*
4. *Ela é juíza. (She is a judge.)*
5. *Ela é vendedora. (She is a salesperson.)*

Exercise: Choosing *Ser* or *Estar*

1. *Clarice está no hospital.*
2. *Ela é médica pediatra.*
3. *Ela é uma pessoa contente por natureza.*
4. *Clarice e Kadu são brasileiros.*
5. *Agora estão no Rio de Janeiro.*
6. *Kadu é estudante de medicina.*
7. *Ele está nervosa com os exames.*

Exercise: Now You Conjugate!

1. *Meus pais estão na Europa. (My parents are in Europe.)*
2. *O vermelho é uma cor linda. (Red is a beautiful color.)*
3. *Meu amigo Jonas é engenheiro civil. (My friend Jonas is a civil engineer.)*
4. *O livro de Português está encima da mesa. (The Portuguese book is on top of the table.)*
5. *Fortaleza fica (or está) no Nordeste do Brasil. (Fortaleza is located in the northeast of Brazil.)*
6. *São sete horas da noite. (It's seven o'clock at night.)*
7. *Nós estamos muito contentes com os nossos filhos. (We are very happy with our children.)*

Exercise: Time to Translate

1. *Ela está magra. (She is thin.)*
2. *Eles são professores. (also: Elas são professoras.) (They are teachers.)*
3. *Ele está furioso. (He is mad.)*
4. *Nós somos cubanos. (also: Nós somos cubanas.) (We are Cuban.)*
5. *Você está na cidade. (You are in the city.)*

Exercise: What's the Plural Form?

1. *corações (hearts)*
2. *canis (kennels)*
3. *pincéis (paintbrushes)*
4. *pães (breads)*
5. *órfãos (orphans)*
6. *difíceis (difficult) [plural adjective]*
7. *cantores (singers)*
8. *tórax (thorax) [plural is written the same as singular]*

Chapter 7

Exercise: Transforming Adjectives

1. *francês (French): francesa*
2. *indiano (Indian): indiana*
3. *nu (naked): nua*
4. *ateu (atheist): atéia*
5. *jornaleiro (newspaper seller): jornaleira*
6. *japonês (Japanese): japonesa*
7. *israelense (Israeli): (same as masculine)*
8. *colombiano (Colombian): colombiana*

Exercise: Put It All in Order

1. *um carro vermelho (a red car)*
2. *umas casas novas (some new houses)*
3. *todos (os) meus amigos (all my friends)*
4. *o aluno inteligente (the intelligent student)*
5. *uma blusa laranja (an orange blouse)*
6. *ambos os livros (both of the books)*
7. *a minha amiga ([the] my friend)*
8. *um carro novo (a new car)*

Exercise: Comparing Unequal Elements

1. *Rita é mais inteligente que Teresa. (also: Teresa é mais burra que Rita.)*
2. *Marta é mais nova que Rodrigo. (also: Rodrigo é mais velho que Marta.)*
3. *Amaro é mais baixo que Cláudio. (also: Cláudio é mais alto que Amaro.)*
4. *Jorge é mais gordo que Maria. (also: Maria é mais magra que Jorge.)*
5. *Bill é mais rico que Donald. (also: Donald é mais pobre que Bill.)*

Exercise: Comparing Equal Elements

1. *Jorge é tão feio quanto Vicente.*
2. *Martha é tão rica quanto Donald.*
3. *O Porsche tem tanta potência quanto o Ferrari.*
4. *Meu computador tem tantos problemas quanto o seu.*
5. *Gilberto tem tanto talento quanto Chico.*

Exercise: Fill in the Superlative

1. *O futebol é o esporte mais popular do Brasil.*
2. *Brasília é a capital mais moderna da América Latina.*
3. *Amália Rodrigues é a melhor cantora de Fado de Portugal.*

Exercise: Who Owns It?

1. *my pen: minha caneta*
2. *your book: seu caderno*
3. *my friends: meus amigos (also: minhas amigas)*
4. *our parents: nossos pais*
5. *your backpack: sua mochila*
6. *our house: nossa casa*
7. *your notebooks: seus cadernos*
8. *my sisters: minhas irmãs*

Exercise: Translation

1. *Their (female) classes: as aulas delas*
2. *His computer: o computador dele*
3. *Her pencil: o lápis dela*
4. *Their (male) house: a casa deles*
5. *Her books: os livros dela*
6. *Their (female) car: o carro delas*
7. *His glasses: os óculos dele*
8. *Her purse: a bolsa dela*

Chapter 8

Exercise: Translation Using Numbers

1. *15 notebooks: quinze cadernos*
2. *83 books: oitenta e três livros*
3. *379 professors: trezentos e setenta e nove professores*
4. *761 female students: setencentas e sessenta e uma alunas*
5. *1.006 cars: mil e seis carros*
6. *432.578 people: quatrocentas e trinta e duas mil, quinhentas e setenta e oito pessoas*

Exercise: Using Ordinal Numbers

1. *A sétima maravilha do mundo (the seventh wonder of the world)*
2. *O quarto ciclo do inferno (the fourth ring of hell)*
3. *A primeira lição (the first lesson)*
4. *A quinta dinastia (the fifth dynasty)*
5. *O vigésimo tenista do ranking mundial (the twentieth tennis player of the world ranking)*

Exercise: Holidays

1. *O Dia da Indenpendência dos Estados Unidos (Independence Day): 4 (quatro) de julho.*
2. *O Dia dos Namorados (Valentine's Day): 14 (catorze) de fevereiro*

3. *O Dia de São Patrício (Saint Patrick's Day): 17 (dezessete) de março.*
4. *O (Dia de) Natal (Christmas Day): 25 (vinte e cinco) de dezembro.*

Chapter 9

Exercise: Fill in the Blank

1. *A criança joga futebol. (The child plays soccer.)*
2. *Os jovens tocam clarinete. (The youngsters play clarinet.)*
3. *Nós falamos português e inglês. (We speak Portuguese and English.)*
4. *Você compra pão todo dia? (Do you buy bread every day?)*
5. *Vocês moram no Brasil? (Do you [pl.] live in Brazil?)*

Exercise: Make a Match

1. *O concerto (e) começa às cinco horas.*
2. *Você (c) joga basquetebol?*
3. *Nós (d) moramos em Ipanema.*
4. *Eu (b) pago a conta, sempre!*
5. *Os alunos (a) estudam muitas horas por dia.*

Exercise: Conjugate the Verb

1. *Ele precisa do dicionário. (He needs the dictionary.)*
2. *Você chama essa fruta de laranja? (You call this fruit an orange?)*
3. *Eles gostam da comida. (They like the food.)*
4. *Os alunos entram na biblioteca. (The students enter the library.)*
5. *Eu não entro num banco sem documentos. (I don't enter a bank without documents.)*

Exercise: Where Can I Buy . . . ?

1. *pão (bread): padaria, supermercado, mercearia*
2. *revistas (magazines): banca de revistas, livraria*
3. *leite (milk): supermercado, padaria*
4. *frutas (fruit): feira, supermercado*
5. *bolos (cakes): pastelaria, padaria, supermercado*

Exercise: Put Them in Order

1. *Anne almoça com os amigos. (3)*
2. *Anne brinca com os gatos. (5)*
3. *Anne volta para casa. (4)*
4. *Anne trabalha na universidade. (2)*
5. *Anne se acorda às 8 da manhã. (1)*

Chapter 10

Exercise: Fill in the Verb

1. *A criança come o sanduíche. (The child eats the sandwich.)*
2. *Os jovens assistem o filme. (The youngsters watch the movie.)*
3. *Nós dormimos oito horas por dia. (We sleep eight hours a day.)*
4. *Você vive nos Estados Unidos? (Do you live in the United States?)*
5. *Vocês respondem às perguntas? (Do you [pl.] answer the questions?)*

Exercise: The Right Match

1. *Minha amiga (e) atende o telefone imediatamente.*
2. *Essa livraria (d) vende livros e revistas?*
3. *Nós sempre (a) comemos neste restaurante.*
4. *Eu (b) parto amanhã para o Rio!*
5. *Os amigos (c) riem muito com a comédia.*

Exercise: Regular and Special Verbs

1. *O garçom serve a cerveja no restaurante, e eu sirvo vinho em casa.*
2. *Eu subo as escadas, e a secretária sobe pelo elevador.*
3. *Meus amigos dormem oito horas por dia, mas eu só durmo seis horas.*
4. *A aluna repete as frases, e eu repito a tarefa de casa.*
5. *Eu não minto muito, mas minha irmã mente demais!*

Exercise: Using *Ir* and *Vir*

1. *Eu vim do cabelereiro. (I come from the hairdresser.)*
2. *As garotas vão para a casa. (The girls go/are going home.)*
3. *Nós vimos do banco. (We come from the bank.)*
4. *Meus amigos vão para a escola todo dia. (My friends go to school every day.)*
5. *Eu vou para o trabalho de carro. (I go to work by car.)*
6. *Os vizinhos vêm do parque. (The neighbors come from the park.)*

Exercise: Using *Ter*

1. *Eu tenho dois carros. (I have two cars.)*
2. *Minha amiga tem pouca paciência. (My friend has little patience.)*
3. *Nós temos uma casa no Rio. (We have a house in Rio.)*
4. *Eles não têm aula na sexta. (They don't have class on Friday.)*
5. *O menino tem olhos azuis. (The boy has blue eyes.)*
6. *Tem duas janelas na sala. (There are two windows in the room.)*

Exercise: Who Is It?

1. *O filho do meu filho é o meu neto.*
2. *A irmã da minha mãe é a minha tia.*
3. *Os filhos dos meus tios são os meus primos.*
4. *A mãe da minha mãe é a minha avó.*
5. *Os pais dos meu pai são os meus avós.*
6. *O marido da minha irmã é o meu padrastro.*

Chapter 11

Exercise: Multiple Choice

1. *The workers are getting very low wages, so . . .*
   a. eles fazem greve.
2. *My nephew is having all of his friends over for a party.*
   c. Ele faz anos.
3. *He has that five o'clock shadow, so . . .*
   d. ele decide fazer a barba.

4. *Maria has practically nothing in the fridge, so . . .*
   b. *ela vai fazer compras.*
5. *They were mad at each other, but not anymore. That means that . . .*
   b. *eles fizeram as pazes.*

Exercise: Choose the Verb

1. *Elas conhecem bem a capital do Brasil. (They know Brazil's capital really well.)*
2. *Você sabe andar de bicicleta? (Do you know how to ride a bike?)*
3. *Nós conhecemos os nossos vizinhos. (We know our neighbors.)*
4. *Vocês conhecem aquela música do Gil? (Do you guys know that song by Gil?)*
5. *Maristela sabe que Magdale é atriz. (Maristela knows that Magdale is an actress.)*

Exercise: Fill in the Blank

1. *Eu conheço Lisboa, a capital de Portugal.*
2. *Vocês conhecem o Rio Capibaribe?*
3. *Minha esposa e eu sabemos dirigir muito bem.*
4. *Eu sei que preciso estudar mais.*
5. *Os nossos amigos sabem que estamos juntas.*

Exercise: Translate

1. *She loses the keys frequently. Ele perde as chaves freqüentemente.*
2. *Mário always asks for guaraná at the restaurant. Mário sempre pede guaraná no restaurante.*
3. *Sabrina never tells the truth. Sabrina nunca diz a verdade.*
4. *We bring the books to school. Nós trazemos os livros para a escola.*
5. *Mário and Maria put the cups on the table. Mário e Maria poem as xícaras na mesa.*

Exercise: Make a Match

1. *Eu (f) perco as chaves do carro.*
2. *Eu (d) ouço música muito alto.*

3. *Eu (e) trago os livros para a aula.*
4. *Eu (b) digo a verdade à mamãe.*
5. *Eu (c) ponho o lápis na mesa.*
6. *Eu (a) saio de casa muito cedo.*

Chapter 12

Preterite or Imperfect? Exercise A

1. *Quando eu era criança, comia muito chocolate.*
2. *Ontem nós vimos um filme interessante.*
3. *Chovia um pouco quando saímos do cinema.*
4. *Meu pai sempre nos levava para o parque.*
5. *Estava no banho e de repente minha irmã me ligou.*
6. *Em Illinois fazia um frio horrível.*

Preterite or Imperfect? Exercise B

1. *No mês passado eu fui a Aruba.*
2. *Todos as manhãs, minha irmã e eu íamos à praia.*
3. *Na adolescência, nós nos acordávamos muito cedo.*
4. *Anteontem nós nos acordamos tarde.*
5. *Minha esposa cozinhou ontem à noite.*
6. *Minha avó cozinhava todos os dias.*

Future and Conditional Verbs: Exercise A

1. *I'm going to call you tomorrow. Eu vou chamar você amanhã.*
2. *We are going to visit Brazil in the summer. Nós vamos visitar o Brasil no verão.*
3. *You are going to write a book? Você vai escrever um livro?*

Future and Conditional Verbs: Exercise B

1. *O advogado solicitará uma audiência amanhã.*
2. *A prova terá cinco perguntas de ensaio.*
3. *Nós acompanharemos as crianças até o parque.*

Future and Conditional Verbs: Exercise C

1. *Se fosse mais cedo, nós sairíamos para dar uma volta.*
2. *Ele disse à Maria que chegaria tarde.*
3. *As meninas levantariam mais cedo se pudessem.*

Chapter 13

Using Two Verbs Together: Exercise A

1. *A minha irmã quer ir para a Inglaterra no ano que vem. (My sister wants to go to England next year.)*
2. *Eu tenho vontade de comer doce depois das quatro da tarde. (I feel like eating sweets after four in the afternoon.)*
3. *Os meus primos quiseram visitar o Museu de Arte Moderna de São Paulo. (My cousins wanted to visit the Modern Art Museum in São Paulo.)*
4. *A minha amiga Júlia e o marido querem sair para jantar na sexta-feira à noite. (My friend Júlia and her husband want to go out to eat on Friday night.)*
5. *Nós os brasileiros sempre temos vontade de ir à Disneylândia de férias. (We Brazilians always feel like going to Disneyland for vacation.)*

Using Two Verbs Together: Exercise B

1. *Elvis has just left the building. Elvis acabou de sair do prédio.*
2. *May I go now? Posso ir agora?*
3. *Maria can run for a long time. Maria pode correr por muito tempo.*
4. *The teacher has to correct the tests. O professor (or A professora) tem que corrigir as provas.*
5. *We have just finished reading the paper. Nós acabamos de ler o jornal.*
6. *Can you go out tonight? Você pode sair hoje à noite?*
7. *They can come in. Eles podem entrar.*

Exercise: Past Participles

1. *As portas estavam abertas. (The doors were open.)*
2. *O mecânico está muito ocupado. (The mechanic is very busy.)*
3. *O que está escrito ali? (What is written there?)*
4. *A mesa está posta para o jantar. (The table is set for the dinner.)*
5. *Os bancos estão cobertos de neve. (The benches are covered with snow.)*

Exercise: Passive Voice

1. *The two men were seen near here. Os dois homens foram vistos aqui perto.*
2. *The money was spent very fast. O dinheiro foi gasto muito rapidamente.*
3. *What was said yesterday? O que foi dito ontem?*
4. *The food was consumed by the birds. A comida foi consumida pelos pássaros.*

Reflexive and Reciprocal Verbs: Exercise A

1. *Eles (f) se casaram na igreja.*
2. *Nós (c) nos divertimos muito na festa.*
3. *Minha amiga (b) se preocupa com a família.*
4. *Meu irmão (e) se parece com meu pai.*
5. *Os alunos (d) se queixam do livro sempre.*
6. *Eu (a) me deito às 11 da noite.*

Reflexive and Reciprocal Verbs: Exercise B

1. *The professor dedicates herself to teaching. A professora se dedica à educação.*
2. *Our neighbor was surprised with the visit. Nosso vizinho se surpreendeu com a visita.*
3. *The man laughed at the situation. O homem se riu da situação.*
4. *I look like my father. Eu me pareço com o meu pai.*

Chapter 14

Exercise: Practice with Negatives

1. *Eu não me lembro de ninguém da escola primária. (I don't remember anyone from elementary school.)*
2. *A minha amiga Anne nunca se acorda antes das dez da manhã. (My friend Anne never gets up before ten in the morning.)*
3. *Sofia não tem nada contra seus colegas de trabalho. (Sofia has nothing doesn't have anything against her coworkers.)*
4. *Nós não fizemos nenhum exercício hoje. (We did not do any exercises [or: not one exercise] today.)*
5. *Os escritores não completaram nenhuma página nesta semana. (The writers did not complete any pages [or: not one page] this week.)*

Exercise: Positive to Negative

1. *Eu já fui no banco. (I already went to the bank.) > Eu ainda não fui ao banco. (I did not go to the bank yet.)*
2. *Você ainda tem medo de avião. (You are still afraid of planes.) > Você não tem mais medo de avião. (You are not afraid of planes anymore.)*
3. *Tem alguém na sala. (There is someone in the room.) > Não tem ninguém na sala.*
4. *Eles estão fazendo alguma coisa. (They are doing something.) > Eles não estão fazendo nada.*
5. *Elas sempre vão ao supermercado. (They always go to the supermarket.) > Eles nunca vão ao supermercado.*

Exercise: Negative to Positive

1. *Eles não encontraram nada em casa. (They did not find anything at home.) > Eles encontraram alguém em casa. (They found someone at home.)*
2. *Eu não vi ninguém na festa. (I didn't see anybody at the party.) > Eu vi alguém na festa (I saw someone at the party) .*

3. *Nós não o vimos em lugar nenhum. (We did not see him anywhere.) > Nós o vimos em algum lugar. (We saw him somewhere.)*
4. *Você jamais telefona à noite. (You never call at night.) > Você sempre telefona à noite. (You always call at night)*
5. *Eu ainda não terminei o capítulo. (I did not finish the chapter yet.) > Eu já terminei o capítulo. (I did finish the chapter.)*

Chapter 15

Exercise: Interrogative Words

1. *Quando é seu aniversário? (When is your birthday?)*
2. *Quanto custa essa blusa? (How much is this blouse?)*
3. *Aonde você quer ir hoje? (Where do you want to go today?)*
4. *Por que ele foi tão cedo? (Why did he leave so early?)*
5. *Onde você mora? (Where do you live?)*
6. *Como se diz em português? (How do you say it in Portuguese?)*
7. *O que você acha disso? (What do you think of that?)*

Exercise: Asking Questions

1. *Como você se chama?*	*Eu me chamo Daniel.*
2. *Onde você mora?*	*Eu moro no Rio de Janeiro.*
3. *Quantos irmãos você tem?*	*Eu tenho três irmãos.*

Exercise: Translate Exclamations

1. *What a pretty girl she is! Que menina linda (que) ela é!*
2. *What an excellent hotel! Que hotel excelente!*
3. *How badly he drives! Como ele dirige mal!*
4. *What horrible cold weather! Que frio horrível!*
5. *How interesting! Que interessante!*

Chapter 16

The Personal Infinitive: Exercise A

1. *Eu lembro dos nomes dos alunos. (I remember the names of the students.) > É importante eu lembrar os nomes dos alunos. (It's important I remember the names of the students.)*
2. *Vocês dizem a verdade. (You [pl.] tell the truth.) > É essencial vocês dizerem a verdade. (It's essential you [pl.] tell the truth.)*
3. *Elas trazem os livros para a escola. (They bring the books to school.) > É imprescindível elas trazerem os livros para a escola. (It's indispensable that they bring the books to school.)*
4. *Nós visitamos nossos avós. (We visit our grandparents.) > É necessário nós visitarmos nossos avós. (It's necessary that we visit our grandparents.)*
5. *Você e o Roberto põem a mesa. (You and Robert set the table.) > É bom você e o Roberto (vocês) porem a mesa. (It's good that you and Robert set the table.)*
6. *As meninas dormem cedo. (The young girls sleep early.) > É importante as meninas dormirem cedo. (It's important that the girls sleep early.)*

The Personal Infinitive: Exercise B

1. *Antes de eu ligar, eu procurei o número. (Before calling, I looked for the number.)*
2. *Até eles chegarem, nós esperamos. (Until they arrived, we waited.)*
3. *Depois de vocês comerem, podem lavar os pratos. (After eating, you [pl.] can wash the dishes.)*
4. *Para você receber os presentes, é preciso ser um bom menino. (In order for you to receive the presents, you must be a good boy.)*

Exercise: What's the Weather Like?

1. *It's really hot in the Amazon. Faz muito calor na Amazônia.*
2. *It does not snow in Brazil. Não neva no Brasil.*
3. *It's hot in the north of Brazil. Faz muito calor no Norte do Brasil.*

4. *There is some fog on the road. Tem um pouco de neblina na estrada.*
5. *The weather is nice today. O tempo está bonito hoje.*

Exercise: What Would You Wear? (Answers will vary.)

1. *Faz muito sol, a temperatura é de 38 graus Celsius. shortes, camiseta sem manga, sandálias*
2. *Chove muito! impermeável*
3. *Está nevando. botas, casaco de frio, xale, luvas*
4. *Está um pouco frio, a temperatura é de 15 graus Celsius. jaqueta*
5. *Você está em Copacabana! óculos de sol, biquini*

Chapter 17

Subjunctive Forms: Exercise A

1. *Eu preciso que vocês me respondam. (I need you to answer me.)*
2. *Ela deseja que você lhe dê o livro. (She wants you to give her the book.)*
3. *Nós gostaríamos que ele viesse mais cedo. (We wanted him to come earlier.)*
4. *Eles se surpreenderam que ela estivesse/fosse tão magra. (They were surprised that she was so skinny.) [Note: Use estivesse for a recent change of state and fosse for a permanent condition.]*
5. *Se não for muito tarde, vou pegar o ônibus. (If it is not too late, I will take the bus.)*
6. *Enquanto ele precisar de mim, eu vou ajudá-lo. (While he needs me, I will help him.)*

Subjunctive Forms: Exercise B

1. *Se eu me lembrasse de tudo, seria mais fácil. (If I remembered everything, it would be much easier.)*
2. *Elas não se esquecem de nada. (They do not forget anything.)*
3. *Nós gostaríamos que eles trousessem a cerveja. (We would like them to bring the beer.)*
4. *É bom que eles comam tudo. (It's nice that they eat everything.)*

Exercise: Using the Verb *Dar*

1. *I made breakfast but it didn't turn out well.*
   Fiz o café mas não deu certo.
2. *This is just not right!*
   Assim não dá!
3. *I'll call a friend, and we'll find a solution.*
   Eu chamo um amigo e nós damos um jeito. Also: . . . a gente dá um jeito.
4. *The new venture fell through.*
   O negócio novo não deu em nada.

Chapter 18

Exercise: Formal or Informal?

1. *Alô! informal*
2. *Sinto muito, mas a doutora não se encontra. formal*
3. *Gostaria de esperar na linha, senhor? formal*
4. *Oi, posso falar com o Luís? informal*
5. *Gostaria de falar com o Senhor Gomes, por gentileza. formal*

Exercise: Communication Practice

1. *You want to let them know who you are.*
   Alô, meu nome é . . . (Hello my name is . . .)
   OR Alô, eu sou . . . (Hello, I'm . . .)
2. *You would like to speak to Mr. Barros. Por favor, eu gostaria de falar com o senhor Barros. (I would like to speak to Mr. Barros, please.)*
3. *You would like to leave a message. Posso deixar uma mensagem, por gentileza? (Can I leave a message, please?)*
4. *You want to thank the person on the other line. Muito obrigado! (Thank you!) [Use Muito obrigada! if you are a woman.]*

Note: Page numbers in *italics* indicate Answer Key answers.

A, about, 32
Accent marks, 25, 27, 35
Activities, routine, 107–8, *241*
Adjectives. *See also* Comparisons, making about: overview of, 78
  agreement rules, 75
  defined, 78
  descriptive, 81
  gender of, 78–80, *237*
  order of modifiers, 80–82, *237*
  plural, 75–77, *237*
Agreement rules, 75
Alphabet, 25–27
Articles, definite and indefinite, 50–52, *235*. *See also* Contractions
–ar Verbs. *See* Verbs, conjugating
To ask for (*pedir*), 128
Assertions, impersonal, 171
To be. *See Estar* (to be); *Haver* (to be or to exist); *Ser* (to be)
To become (*ficar, tornar-se, fazer-se*), 197–98
Brazilian Portuguese. *See* Portuguese, Brazilian
To bring (*trazer*), 129
C, about, 28
Clothes, 173–76, *250*
Cognates, 20–21, 22–24, 106
Cognates, false, 15, 21, 120
Communication. *See* Conversations
Comparisons, making, 82–85
  equal elements, 84–85, *238*
  superlatives, 85–86, *238*
  unequal elements, 82–84, *238*
Computer, keyboard keys, 35
Conditional tense, 139–41, *244–45*
Conhecer and *saber* (to know), *243*
Contractions, 54–57, *235*
Conversations, 187–200
  communication practice, 199–200, *251*
  exercises, 40, 41, 43, *233–34*
  expressions with *estar com, ter* and, 198–99
  greetings, 36–37
  idiomatic expressions and, 197–98
  by mail, 192–94
  other needed vocabulary, 41–42
  in person, 187–92
  phone calls, 37–38, 194–97
  quick introductions, 38–40
  saying goodbye, 40–41, *233*
Countries and nationalities, 59–61, 79–80, *235, 237*
D, about, 29
Dar (to give), 129, 185–86, *251*
Days of week, 96–97
Demonstratives, 52–54
Diacritics, 25, 27, 35
Diphthongs, 34
Dizer (to say), 129
Double negatives, 154–55
E, about, 32
English to Portuguese glossary, 201–15
–er Verbs. *See* Verbs, conjugating
Estar (to be), 66–77
  conjugating, 66–67, 71, 74, *236*
  describing how you feel, 68–69
  location and, 69–70
  mental states, 68–69
  peculiar uses, 72–73
  physical states, 67–68
  present progressive tense, 70–71
  present tense, 66–67
  ser vs., 71–74, *236*
  states of being, 66–67
  translating sentences, 74, *236*
Estar com (to be [emotion/state]), 198–99
Este/esse considerations, 52–53
European vs. Brazilian Portuguese, 15–17
Exclamations, 163–65, *248*
Exercises
  addressing others (pronouns), 50, *234*
  cardinal numbers, 94, *239*
  communication practice, 199–200, *251*
  comparing equal elements, 85, *238*
  comparing unequal elements, 83–84, *238*
  conjugating *–ar* verbs, 103, 104–5, *240*
  conjugating *–er* and *–ir* verbs, 111–12, 113–14, *241*
  conjugating *ser* and *estar*, 74, *236*
  contractions, 56–57, *235*
  conversation, 40, 41, 43, *233–34*
  definite or indefinite articles, 52, *235*
  exclamations (translating), 165, *248*
  expressions with *dar*, 185–86, *251*
  family relations, 121, *242*

formal or informal, 199–200, *251*
future and conditional verbs, 140–41, *244–45*
gender of nouns, 47, *234*
holidays, 100, *239–40*
indicative or subjunctive, 184–85, *250*
matching verb to sentence, 130, *243–44*
negatives, 156–58, *247–48*
ordinal numbers, 95, *239*
ownership and possession, 87, 89, *238–39*
passive voice, 149, *246*
past participles, 147–48, *246*
personal infinitive, 170–71, *249*
plural forms, 77, *237*
positives and negatives, 157–58, *247–48*
possessives, 86–89, *238–39*
preterite or imperfect, 130, *244*
questions and interrogative words, 162–63, *248*
reflexive and reciprocal verbs, 152, *246*
saying goodbye, 41, *233*
sequence of activities, 108, *241*
ser vs. *estar*, 71–74, *236*
subjunctive constructions, 184–85, *250*
suffixes, 21–24, *233*
superlatives, 85–86, *238*
translation, 74 (*236*), 89 (*239*), 94 (*239*), 130 (*243*)
using *fazer*, 123–25, *242–43*
using *ir* and *vir*, 116, *242*
using *saber* and *conhecer*, 126–28, *243*
using *ter*, 118, *242*
using two verbs together, 143–44, 145, *245*
weather discussions, 172–73, *249–50*
Where can I buy . . .?, 107, *240*
Family relations, 119–21
Fazer (to make or to do), 123–25, *242–43*
Fazer-se (to become), 198
Feelings, describing, 68–69
Ficar (to become), 197
Future subjunctive, 182–83
Future tenses, 137–39, 140–41, 166–67, *244–45*
G, about, 28
Gender
adjectives, 78–80, *237*
demonstratives, 52–54
nouns, 44–48, *234*
To give (*dar*), 129
Glossaries
English to Portuguese, 201–15
Portuguese to English, 216–32
Goodbye, saying, 40–41, *233*
Greetings, 36–37
To have (*ter*), 116–18 (*242*), 199
Haver (to be or to exist), 122–23
To hear (*ouvir*), 128
Hiatus, 35
Holidays, 100, *239–40*
I, about, 33
Idiomatic expressions, 197–98
Immersion program, 20
Imperative constructions, 177–79
Imperfect tense, 134–37, *244*
Impersonal assertions, 171
Indicative or subjunctive, 183–85, *250*
Infinitives
conjugating. *See* Verbs, conjugating
defined, 101
personal, 167–71, *249*
Interrogative words, 160–62, *248*
Introductions, 38–40
Ir (to go) and *vir* (to come), 114–16, *242*
–ir Verbs. *See* Verbs, conjugating
To know (*saber* and *conhecer*), 126–28, *243*
L, about, 30
Learning Portuguese, 17–20
To leave (*sair*), 129
Letters
accent marks over, 25, 27, 35
alphabet, 25–27
combinations of, 27
consonants, 28–31
special, 27
stress pattern, 31
vowels (oral and nasal), 32–35
Location
expressing, 69–70
prepositional phrases and, 70
To lose (*perder*), 129
M, about, 30
Mail, communicating by, 192–94
To make or to do (*fazer*), 123–25, *242–43*
Mental states, 68–69
Modifiers, order of, 80–82, *237*. *See also* Adjectives
Months and seasons, 98–100

N, about, 30
Nationalities and countries, 59–61, 79–80, *235*, *237*
Negative words and constructions, 153–58
  common expressions, 155–57
  double negatives, 154–55
  exercises, 156–58, *247–48*
  positive vs. negative, 157–58, *247–48*
  saying "no," 153–54
Nouns, 44–50
  adjectives and, 75. *See also* Adjectives; Comparisons, making
  agreement rules, 75
  defined, 44
  gender (masculine or feminine), 44–48
  places, 105–7, *240*
  plural, 75–77, *237*
  pronouns and, 48–50, *234*
Numbers. *See also* Time
  0 to 19, 90–91
  20 to 100, 91–92
  200 and up, 92–93
  cardinal, 90–94, *239*
  exercises, 94, 95, *239*
  ordinal, 94–95, *239*
  ser (to be) and, 65
O, about, 33
Occupations, 62–64, *235*
Origin, expressing place of, 59–61
Ouvir (to hear), 128
Ownership and possession, 86–89, *238–39*
Passive voice, 148–49, *246*
Past participles, 146–48, *246*
Pedir (to ask for), 128
Perder (to lose), 129
Personal infinitives, 167–71, *249*
Personal relationships, 64
Phone, talking on, 37–38, 194–97
Physical states, *estar* and, 67–68
Picturing things, 19
Places, 105–7, *240*
Plurals, 75–77, *237*
Pôr (to put, place), 129
Portuguese, Brazilian
  African words and, 17
  European vs. Brazilian, 15–17
  false cognates, 15, 21, 120
  historical perspective, 15–17
  immersion program, 20
  indigenous words and, 16–17
  picturing things, 19
  reasons for learning, 13–14
  similarities to Spanish, 14–15
  studying routine, 19
  suffixes, 21–24, *233*
  tips on learning, 17–20
  typing in, 35
  using what you learn, 18
  Web sites for, 19
  words similar to English (cognates), 20–21, 22–24, 106
Portuguese to English glossary, 216–32
Positive vs. negative, 157–58, *247–48*
Possessives, 86–89, *238–39*
Prepositions
  contractions, 54–57, *235*
  personal infinitive after, 169
  phrases, 70
  reflexive verbs with, 150–51
  verbs with, 104–5, 150–51, *240*
Preterite tense, 132–34, 135–37, 166–67, *244*
Professions, 62–64, *235*
Pronouns, 48–50, *234*
To put, place (*pôr*), 129
Questions
  asking, 159–60, 162–63, *248*
  interrogative words, 160–62, *248*
  question tags and, 163
R, about, 30
Reflexive and reciprocal verbs, 149–52, *246*
Relationships
  family relations, 119–21, *242*
  personal, 64
Routine activities, 107–8, *241*
S, about, 28
Saber and *conhecer* (to know), 126–28
Sair (to leave), 129
To say (*dizer*), 129
Seasons and months, 98–100
Ser (to be), 58–65
  conjugating, 59, 74, *236*
  estar vs., 71–74, *236*
  expressing identity, 58–59
  numbers and, 65
  occupations and, 62–64
  personal relationships and, 64
  place of origin (nationalities) and, 59–61, 79–80, *235*, *237*
  present tense, 59

Sounds
accent marks and, 25, 27, 35
alphabet, 25–27
consonants, 28–31
diphthongs, 34
hiatus, 35
stress pattern, 31
vowels (oral and nasal), 32–35
Spanish, similarities to, 14–15
Stress patterns, 31
Studying routine, 19
Subjunctive constructions
about: overview of, 180–81
future subjunctive, 182–83
imperative constructions and, 177–79
indicative or subjunctive, 183–85, *250*
introduced, 180–81
past subjunctive, 181–82
Suffixes
common, 21–24
exercise, 24, *233*
Superlatives, 85–86, *238*
T, about, 29
Ter (to have), 116–18, 199, *242*
Time
days of week, 96–97
holidays, 100, *239–40*
months and seasons, 98–100
telling, in Portuguese, 97–98
Tornar-se (to become), 197–98
Trazer (to bring), 129
U, about, 33
Verbs
common, ending in *–ar*, 102
passive voice, 148–49, *246*
past participles, 146–48, *246*
personal infinitive, 167–71, *249*
reflexive and reciprocal, 149–52, *246*
using two together, 142–45
Verbs, conjugating
estar (to be), 66–67, 71, 74, *236*
imperative constructions and, 177–79
ir (to go) and *vir* (to come), 114–16, *242*
regular *–ar* verbs, 101–3, *240*
regular *–er* and *–ir* verbs, 109–12, 113–14, *241*
second conjugation explained, 109
ser (to be), 59, 74, *236*
special *–ir* verbs, 112–14, *241*
subjunctive constructions and, 180–85, *250*
ter (to have), 116–18 (*242*), 199
verbs with prepositions, 104–5, *240*
Verbs, important to know, 122–30. *See also Estar* (to be); *Ser* (to be)
dar (to give), 129
dizer (to say), 129
exercises, 130, *243–44*
fazer (to make or to do), 123–25, *242–43*
haver (to be or to exist), 122–23
ouvir (to hear), 128
pedir (to ask for), 128
perder (to lose), 129
pôr (to put, place), 129
saber and *conhecer* (to know), 126–28, *243*
sair (to leave), 129
trazer (to bring), 129
Verb tenses, 131–41
conditional tense, 139–41, *244–45*
future tenses, 137–39, 140–41, 166–67, *244–45*
imperative constructions and, 177–79
imperfect tense, 134–37, *244*
present tense, 131–32. *See also* Verbs, conjugating
present vs. future or preterite, 166–67
preterite tense, 132–34, 166–67
preterite vs. imperfect, 135–37, *244*
subjunctives and, 180–85, *250*
Vir (to come) and *ir* (to go), 114–16, *242*
Vocabulary
clothes, 173–76, *250*
for conversations. *See* Conversations
describing how you feel, 68, 69
expressions with *estar com* and *ter*, 198–99
family relations, 119–21
idiomatic expressions (to become), 197–98
making phone calls, 194–97
places, 105–7, *240*
routine activities, 107–8, *241*
weather, 172–73, *249–50*
Vowels (oral and nasal), 32–35
Weather, discussing, 172–73, *249–50*
Week, days of, 96–97
X, about, 31
Z, about, 29

We Have EVERYTHING® on Anything!

With more than 19 million copies sold, the Everything® series has become one of America's favorite resources for solving problems, learning new skills, and organizing lives. Our brand is not only recognizable—it's also welcomed.

The series is a hand-in-hand partner for people who are ready to tackle new subjects—like you!

For more information on the Everything® series, please visit *www.adamsmedia.com*.

The Everything® list spans a wide range of subjects, with more than 500 titles covering 25 different categories:

Business
Careers
Children's Storybooks
Computers
Cooking
Crafts and Hobbies
Education/Schools
Games and Puzzles
Health
History
Home Improvement
Everything Kids
Languages
Music
New Age
Parenting
Personal Finance
Pets
Reference
Religion
Self-Help
Sports & Fitness
Travel
Wedding
Writing